WIZARDS AND
BRAVEHEARTS

A HISTORY OF THE SCOTTISH
NATIONAL SIDE

WIZARDS AND BRAVEHEARTS

A HISTORY OF THE SCOTTISH NATIONAL SIDE

DAVID POTTER

TEMPUS

THE AUTHOR

David Potter is fifty-six years old. A semi-retired teacher, and lives in Kirkcaldy with his wife, his three children having grown up. He has published nine previous books:
Our Bhoys Have Won The Cup: Celtic in the Scottish Cup
Jock Stein: The Celtic Years
The Encylopaedia of Scottish Cricket
The Mighty Atom: Patsy Gallacher
Wee Troupie: Alec Troup
Celtic in the League Cup
Willie Maley: The Man Who Made Celtic
Walk On – Celtic Since McCann
Bobby Murdoch: Different Class

First published 2004

Tempus Publishing Ltd
The Mill, Brimscombe Port
Stroud, Gloucestershire GL5 2QG
www.tempus-publishing.com

British Library Cataloguing in Publication Data.
A catalogue record for this book is available from the British Library.

ISBN 0 7524 3183 8

Typesetting and origination by Tempus Publishing
Printed and bound in Great Britain

Contents

Acknowledgements

I am indebted to the following: Richard Grant, the other 'learned and scholarly gentleman' mentioned in the introduction; David Taylor of the SFA for his encouragement; my wife and family for their forbearance; the staff at the Wellgate Library in Dundee for their unfailing courtesy and helpfulness in allowing access to old newspapers; many, many members of the Tartan Army (including a few posthumous ones) who have given me their take on various games throughout the ages and finally to Holly Bennion of Tempus for her help.

Introduction

Two learned and scholarly gentlemen (and passionate devotees of Scottish football) were sitting at Hampden one day tucking into the ubiquitous pie that one always finds at Scottish football grounds when one of them said that 'This is the Scottish equivalent of *panem et circenses*'. It was a profound statement. The reference was to the Roman writer Juvenal who claimed that the Roman Emperor, to keep the mob happy, had to give them 'bread and circuses'. The bread was to feed them, and the circuses to entertain them. If he did this, he reckoned, there would be fewer riots and no revolution. Sport was all that was required.

He was of course right. Perhaps the reason why the Scots have not risen against the English in the military sense since 1872 has been that the football field has been the vicarious battlefield. If this is so, it is certainly a welcome change, for in previous centuries the Scots did rebel against their English overlords with predictable, monotonous and bloodthirsty regularity. In recent centuries the two countries have worked together, building Empires, founding colonies and winning wars – all of them with conspicuous success, but it would be a fool who does not notice any underlying rivalry. Fortunately football has provided the safety valve to release these emotions which otherwise could become dangerous and tragic.

*   *   *

It is interesting in this context to compare Scotland with Ireland. In 1872 (and for centuries before and at least a century afterwards) Ireland was the *enfant terrible* of the British Empire with its rebellions, uprisings and general mayhem. It was not until the 1980s that Ireland's football team emerged as a credible threat to that of England. It is hardly coincidental that the success of the Irish teams of Jack Charlton and his successors has also been accompanied by a decline in violence in that previously 'most distressful country'. Ireland had, as it were, grown up and rejected its temper tantrums of previous centuries. It had found football instead.

But to return to Scotland, one is almost afraid to talk about the Scottish national team for fear of immediately becoming drowned in clichés, and the problem of finding something to say about Scotland that has not been said before. The author of this book will make no claims about originality – simply because the fortunes of the Scottish football team have been talked about so often in the years between 1872 and 2004 that absolutely everything will have been said about them by someone or other.

The facts of the matter are that Scotland inspires passion. There have been times and there will continue to be times when Scotland seem as if they could conquer the world; there have been other times (sadly far more frequent ones) when an entire nation has been shrouded in such curtains of despair that it has seemed that no recovery will ever be possible – until, of course, the next match!

*   *   *

The scene was the French town of Lille in October 2003. Scotland were playing Lithuania at Hampden that day in a qualifier for Euro 2004. A party of Scots tourists were distraught at the thought that no-one seemed to know or care how Scotland were doing in this barbaric country of France. France themselves beat Israel on TV and a certain amount of Gallic (and Scottish) gloating was heard when David Beckham missed a penalty for England, but no-one was able to say how Scotland did – until someone remembered that he had a radio with him which was strong enough to pick up BBC Radio Five. Scotland won 1-0 and anxiety and depression lifted from the party, mingled with anger at the French television networks for their arrogant refusal to put the Scotland game on their screen. Auld Alliance indeed!

The author's wife is no football fan, yet cannot but be aware of the atmosphere in the house for days before and after a Scotland game. 1982 saw Scotland exit the World Cup rather unluckily to the USSR. The game was of course on television. Children however had to be put to bed towards the end of the game. There was little point in asking her hysterical husband to do the needful, so the good lady took it upon herself to read the bedtime stories, appealing as she went to the demented man not to shout too loudly… if things turned joyful. She returned half an hour later to find total, all-enveloping silence, the television off, the curtains not yet drawn and husband staring morosely into space and the beautiful crepuscular darkness. 'I take it they lost then?' she said in a masterpiece of meiosis.

*   *   *

It is, of course, easy to fall into the trap of believing that Scotland are the only nation which loses football matches. Other nations too (apart from the lucky one which actually wins the World Cup) will also have their intense navel-gazing, melancholic moments (even England when they famously miss their penalties against the

Germans) but this does not help the Presbyterian Scot one little bit. It is Scotland that is important, Scotland that breaks the heart, Scotland that makes us cringe. The 0-6 thrashing from Holland on 19 November 2003 pierced the heart of every living Scots person.

Foreign visitors to Scotland, particularly those from the Arab world or from Africa, are often amazed that there is such passion in Scotland for its football team when Scotland, as such, is not technically speaking a nation in the political sense of the word. Indeed, South American countries are frequently outspoken in their demands that Scotland should not be allowed to enter its own team in the World Cup, but should be part of Great Britain.

Such demands are usually motivated by hatred of England rather than Scotland, it has to be said, but they show an astonishing ignorance and intolerance of this fascinating symbiotic relationship between Scotland and England which is of course, as we shall see, the very genesis of international football. Those who gathered at Hamilton Crescent in Partick, Glasgow (where West of Scotland Cricket Club now play) on 30 November (St Andrew's Day) 1872 could hardly have realised what they were starting or what they were letting the world in for.

*   *   *

Hitherto the relationship between Scotland and England had been a bloody and a violent one. The Picts of Caledonia did not get on at all well with the Romanised inhabitants of Southern Britain, and although legions of Rome were compelled now and again to give chase and to build walls to keep them out, they could never totally subdue them. Following the departure of the Romans, there came the Dark Ages in which nobody knew what happened, then we had Bannockburn, Falkirk, Stirling Bridge, Flodden, rough wooings, Covenanters, Maids of Norway, Elizabeth I chopping the head off her Scottish counterpart, William of Orange massacring the McDonalds at Glencoe, Jacobites, Johnnie Cope and Culloden... before eventually the penny dropped that a peaceful relationship between the two nations might be no bad thing.

The road to co-existence, however, was far from smooth. The Duke of Cumberland (an excellent role model for Hitler and Stalin) massacred more than a few, some more escaped to Canada and elsewhere, but the Scots that were left, subdued but still smouldering, then worked together with the English to build the largest Empire the world had ever seen. The wild Highlanders joined the British Army with the Army wisely allowing them to stay in their own Scottish regiments and wear kilts. The Scottish Enlightenment of the late eighteenth century gave the world lessons about what peace could do, and gradually other issues like industrialisation and its concomitant poverty became more important than age-old rivalry and hatred between the two nations.

But however much Scotland became part of Great Britain, and however much Queen Victoria loved her Scottish Highlands around Balmoral, as she sulked about her dead German husband, seeking solace (it was rumoured) in the arms of her Scottish ghillie John Brown, Scotland still remained culturally apart from England.

Education, religion and law remained obstinately different. The rivalry and the fight needed to continue as Scotland needed to assert her difference and independence from England. Something needed to happen to stoke up yet again the rivalries that had been artificially doused – and thank heavens it was something peaceful. It was the English game of football.

Rivalry, desire for one-upmanship and hate are all part of the human condition. It is a fine thing to belong to a group. This often tends to mean hating another group. Politics would not exist if this were not so. If hatred is essential, then for goodness' sake, let us hate someone that we do not have to kill. Scotland's bloody history bears eloquent testimony to the folly of violence, as indeed does a trip to the battlefields of the First World War. Scottish football fans are quite happy to admit to a 'hatred' of England and all things English. Such declarations, however, tend to lose their effect somewhat when they ask how Manchester United or Arsenal got on today. It is in fact a paradox of hating someone that we do not really hate.

Although Scotland may frequently try to claim otherwise, the game of football was practised in England before it was in Scotland – at least on an organised basis. Not that it needs matter for Scotland soon followed and football became as important, and very quickly, more important in Scotland. It was cheap, easy and peaceful and an ideal way in which Scotland could assert her identity, living on terms of equality at least, and sometimes even superiority, *vis-à-vis* the Englishmen.

*   *   *

Football had, of course, been played on an unorganised basis in Scotland for many centuries. The six James Stuarts, who ruled Scotland sporadically and badly from the fifteenth century onwards did not like the game at all, and their Parliaments prescribed heavy penalties like 'fiftie schillings' for enthusiasts. In the reign of James IV, who led the country to disaster at Flodden in 1513, authorities fulminated against this game, and James IV himself was reputed to have decreed that 'ye golfe and ye footieball should be utterly cryit doun' throughout the length and breadth of Scotland. James II had said such a thing earlier, and had made it an official pronouncement – but with no great success. Indeed, with the benefit of hindsight and knowing that the 'flooers o' the forest were a' we-ed awa' at Flodden – the Scottish equivalent of the Battle of the Somme – we might well ask the bigoted Stuarts whether football might not have been a better pastime than attempting unsuccessfully to kill Englishmen.

Because all that you require for a game of football is a ball of some description, 'ye footieball' was difficult to stop, no matter what draconian legislation was in force to prevent it. Indeed, even centuries after the Stuarts, the middle classes and the Calvinists would disapprove of football in the same way as they disapproved of sex, drinking and dancing. Yet there was not really very much that they could do to stop the lower orders indulging in any one or all four of such activities on the streets – if not simultaneously, certainly within a short space of time of each other.

But in the early 1870s, when the first international was played, football was definitely a middle-class sport, played by amateurs and gentlemen. It was no accident

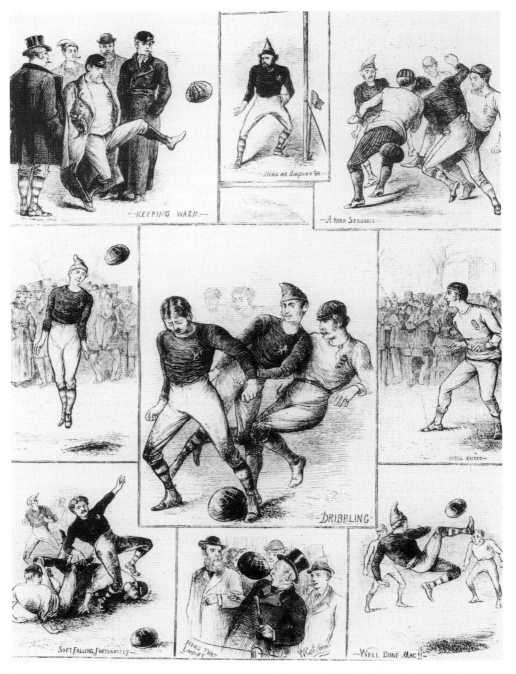

A newspaper drawing of the first international. Observe the shape of the ball, the headgear and the middle-class spectators.
The Graphic.

that the early years of Scotland *v.* England internationals were played on cricket grounds, for the same sort of men who played cricket would also play football. Cricket too was expanding in both England and Scotland (it was of course a far older game than football), but as cricket cannot be played in the rain or in the winter whereas football can, it was no surprise that football overtook cricket in Scotland – where there is sometimes rather too much rain and certainly too much winter. But football in 1872 had not yet reached the working class, at least not officially.

Yet the proletarians would not be long denied their manna. Marx said that religion was the opium of the masses in that it was the drug which made them forget about their exploitation and impoverishment at the hands of the grasping evil capitalists. But religion itself was struggling, all too obviously unable to prevent drunkenness and pregnancies and other things which tended to impair the achievement of a utopian Christian society. In any case, in any dispute, the Church would always, as of course, side with the rich against the poor.

But the new opium was at hand. Saturday afternoons off from the evil factories and mines gave the workers a certain amount of leisure, and as there was a dearth of other entertainment (now that public hangings had been stopped), it was hardly surprising that the masses should look over the wall, as it were, at Queen's Park and others playing football and decide to try it on an official basis. Very soon the game became incredibly popular and very soon the annual encounter between Scotland and England began to take on an undue, but not always unwelcome, significance. Another penny soon dropped that money could be made from this new sport.

*   *   *

That Scotland needed something to assert its identity was obvious. Scotland would never allow itself to become subsumed in England as places like Durham, Yorkshire and even Wales had done centuries previously. Like Ireland, it needed to be a nation. If this could not happen in the political sense, there was no reason why it could not happen in the sporting field. This meant football.

Scotland was in the mid-nineteenth century a cultural desert in some ways. The Edinburgh enlightenment had evaporated, the Glasgow metropolis was growing into a huge obscene slum with dreadful poverty and squalor with large sections of the male and female population in thrall to whisky and ale. Little was around to boast about. Scotland had produced one major literary figure – Robert Burns – a century previously, but the culture of him tended to centre on a figure of a ploughman who talked to mice, drank whisky and impregnated women. He was of course studied in Scottish schools and was much toasted in the comfortable Victorian middle classes of both Edinburgh and Glasgow, but the problem was that education was still the prerogative of too few.

The Scottish masses needed something to identify with, to shout about, to get excited about. For reasons never adequately explained, they never turned to politics to alleviate their woes at a time when conditions would have been fertile for revolutionary talk and conspiratorial agitation. There would be exceptions to this rule, for example the Red Clydeside phenomenon of the First World War years and immediately afterwards, but this was only in response to an evil war. The constant theme of the Scottish working class for well over a century is that they have found their expression in football.

The reason for this, of course, was that Scotland was successful against England more often than not. England beat Scotland only 9 times in the nineteenth century out of 28 games. For Scotland this was success. Even more of a success was the way in which Scotland played. Scotland played the 'passing' game whereas England played the 'dribbling' game. Both these statements are over-simplifications, but until England met Scotland, English teams tended to dribble past opponents or kick the ball upfield while everyone followed the ball in an up-and-under, 'Garryowen', cavalry charge sort of melee that one gets in modern rugby. Scotland on the other hand, as exemplified by the refined gentlemen of Queen's Park, passed the ball to each other in a more sophisticated and thought-out way.

*   *   *

Football remained the standard talk of the Scotsman. The scene is, for example, Germany in December 1918. A Scottish soldier is trying his best to win over the hearts and minds of a defeated German family by offering the children some cake and telling them about Scotland. The embittered mother of the family is not impressed. The Scottish soldier says to her 'Ach never mind, Frau Schultz, aboot the English – we dinnae like them either. It's great when we can hammer them'. The German lady pounces on an opportunity to drive a wedge between the Scots and the hated English. 'Ah, is this your Villiam Vallace, you mean?' Back comes the reply 'Na, Jimmy Quinn!' A long pause ensues until she says 'And was Qvin one of Vallace's followers' 'Na, he wis Scotland's centre forrit in 1910 when we wan 2-0 – and I wis there!'

This is from the play *Our Day Will Come* and it is of course fiction but it represents the idea that football is a far more satisfying way of humiliating the English than killing them. The concomitant of course is that a defeat is correspondingly none too easy to deal with, but it is something that we have had loads of practice with! 1955, 1961 and 1975 are three years that come to mind, and in each of these three years a scapegoat had to be found to prevent any conception of an idea that England might be actually better than Scotland. In each of these three years it was the goalkeeper's fault. Had Scotland had a better goalkeeper than Fred Martin, Frank Haffey or Stewart Kennedy, Scotland would have won, according to the myth.

*   *   *

It is probably true to say that in early twenty-first century Scotland, the Celtic *v.* Rangers struggle is of more significance to more people than the fortunes of the Scottish international side. If this is so, it is to be deplored, for the Old Firm can divide Scotland with nonsense about Catholics, Protestants, Freemasons,

Orangemen, IRA, Ulster, the Pope and the Queen – so much of what is really alien to Scotland – and laughable into the bargain.

Perhaps this was always the case, but two factors have made it worse than it need be. One is the virtual collapse of Scottish teams other than Celtic or Rangers. They will now quite cheerfully discuss whether or not they are going to be third in the Scottish Premier League, for the first and second berths are the subject of a private struggle. The other is the (hopefully temporary) decline of the Scottish national team. Since the appalling events of Argentina in 1978, the Scotland team has been in disrepute for the intervening twenty-five years. Some good things have happened, like the growth of a totally civilized bunch of people who now follow them and although they call themselves the Tartan Army – they are a profoundly peaceful bunch of men and women. But the whole culture of the Scotland team is one of sad underachievement.

For a nation that is so proud of its footballing tradition and so obsessed with the game to the virtual exclusion of all other sports – the Edinburgh bourgeoisie and the Borders farmers prefer rugby, but still keep an eye on the football, Scotland's good snooker players always wonder how their football team is doing, tea intervals at cricket games in May and August feature a rush to the TV in the bar to get the latest football scores – this is sad. Flower of Scotland, as the dreary dirge asks, when will we see your likes again?

ONE

Benign, Middle-Class Amateurs
1872-1890

It was in the best tradition of the British Empire that England's football authorities brought their men up to Hamilton Crescent, Glasgow, Scotland on 30 November 1872 to play what is now regarded as the world's first international football match. There are two ways of looking at the British Empire. One is the traditional right-wing way of regarding it as a philanthropic, benevolent institution whose God-given duty it was to spread Christian civilization among the savages. The other is the cynical, modernist, radical view that the Empire existed for no purpose other than to milk provincials dry.

Both strands were in evidence here. There was indeed a 'missionary' case for bringing Association Football to Scotland in that it would give England someone to play against and as it was a jolly good game into the bargain, the Scots would benefit. It would also answer the hitherto unposed question 'How good were England?' There was also, one suspects, the mercenary motive of making money. People could be prevailed upon to pay money to watch the game. The admission price was set at one shilling, a huge price for 1872 and perhaps about 3,500 (according to some accounts) coughed up to watch the Scotland *v*. England game at Hamilton Crescent on that fateful day. The officials and the crowd little realised what they were beginning.

No evidence exists to suggest that the date (30 November) was a deliberate choice so as to coincide with the day of Scotland's national saint. It was possibly a sheer coincidence because St Andrew's Day in 1872 had as much impact on Scotland's self consciousness as it does in the early years of the twenty-first century – namely very little. In middle-class Glasgow – the target audience of the fixture – there was certainly an awareness of being Scottish, but being British was probably more important. Glasgow was very proud of its name as 'The Second City of the

Empire' and politically, there seems to have been very little support or interest in Home Rule or any other Scottish dimension to the body politic. This is perhaps surprising given the inordinate amount of interest in Irish Home Rule at the time, but Scottish Nationalism seems to have been a non-concept at this time.

Teams representing Scotland had played against England before, but they had not necessarily contained native Scotsmen. They had consisted of a few Scotsmen who were living in England and their number was supplemented by a few guests or 'ringers' provided to make a good game of it. In any case the team was picked by the English authorities! England had tended to win such encounters, which were usually played at cricket grounds like the Oval, but it was now felt that the time had come for Scotland to have a proper team, and for a major game to be played in Scotland.

Scotland did indeed have a proper team, called Queen's Park, and as Queen's Park lacked any real opposition in Scotland, it was hardly surprising that Queen's Park provided every single player for the Scotland team. The impoverished Queen's (who had less than £8 in the bank) took a major financial risk when they hired Hamilton Crescent, the home of West of Scotland Cricket Club, for the game. They were dependent on a large crowd. Fortunately, enough Glaswegians did turn up that day to pay their shilling and convince Queen's Park that this idea of international football did have a future.

It is debatable how long Queen's Park would have lasted without this fixture. Their basic problem was that they had no one else to play against and thus were compelled to play games against each other within their club: e.g. Smokers *v.* Non-Smokers, Married Men *v.* Bachelors. The Scotland *v.* England idea was a totally new concept.

*   *   *

England's men were from both Oxford and Cambridge Universities, a few Army teams, Notts County and Sheffield Wednesday. Perhaps the Englishmen got a surprise when the Scotsmen put up a brave fight on a very heavy pitch on a dreich archetypal Scottish November day to earn a 0-0 draw. No indication appears that the crowd were unhappy with this 'nae goals, nae fitba' game and indeed most Scottish newspapers mention the game in the context of Scotland doing themselves proud.

The North British *Daily Mail* gives us some sort of account of the game. It confirms that England played in white and Scotland in blue with white 'knickers' and blue-and-white stockings as well as, bizarrely, 'red cowls as a headgear'. Both teams had eleven men, but England had a goalkeeper, a back, a half-back and eight forwards whereas Scotland deployed six forwards, two half-backs, two full-backs and a goalkeeper. There would also have been the cultural clash of the English dribblers against the Scottish passers. There is no indication of a referee, but two umpires, Mr Alcock of England and Mr Smith of Scotland, one for each half of the field, officiated. The closest to a score came just on the stroke of half-time when Bob Leckie of Scotland had a 'good kick' and it caused 'tremendous cheering from all parts of the ground'. Although the majority thought it was a goal, it was 'given no goal, the ball having passed hardly an inch over the tape'.

Although England had a broader base of players from which to chose, Scotland had a slight advantage in that all their players were from Queen's Park, which meant that they all knew each other. This was particularly important in that Scotland played the passing game, whereas the English game was different. The reporter of the North British *Daily Mail* tells us that 'England, especially forward, astonished the spectators by some pretty dribbling, an art then novel and curious'.

There also seems to have been a distinct lack of any bad tackles, injuries, booing, crowd disturbances or any of the less pleasant side of football. At the end of the game, Scotland's captain, Robert Gardner, who was also the goalkeeper, ran out from his goal into the centre of the field to call for three cheers for the English team. The Englishmen reciprocated, everybody shook hands and then went off to the Carrick's Royal Hotel for a dinner, and then a Victorian soiree in which every-one was invited to perform their own party piece of singing, recitation or even a piece of juggling or fire-eating.

The game does seem to have been played according to Association rules (i.e. no handling) and would have at least been recognisable as a football match. The ball, however, according to the newspaper drawings, seems to have been more like a rugby ball as it was slightly elliptical in shape. The goalkeeper would wear the same gear as everyone else, and seems to have been allowed to handle the ball in his own half, although there was no clear definition of what actually was his 'own half'. The pitch would have had no lines whatsoever apart from the 'boundaries'. Such frip-peries as centre spots, penalty boxes, etc., would come later.

The spectators were middle class, as indeed were the players. At least one spec-tator, however, did not pay his shilling. This was Wattie Arnott, who would play for Queen's Park and Scotland a decade later. Wattie and some friends had arrived to see the game but were distressed to discover that the admission charge was so high. Even privileged middle-class boys did not have that sort of money in 1872, but the resourceful lads were able (improbably) to persuade the driver of a hansom cab to allow then to stand on the top of the cab to watch the game. Wattie does not tell us whether the cab driver charged a reduced fee for this privilege. Perhaps the cabby was simply a football fan himself and joined the boys on their precarious vantage point!

*   *   *

In 1872, Gladstone was the Prime Minister. Queen Victoria was on the throne and now at last beginning to give a few signs of realisation that other women also had husbands who died. It had been put to her that her prolonged sulk over her much lamented Prince Albert was not really working to the advantage of the monarchy in this country. 1872 was also the year in which Gladstone's government had passed the Education Act in Scotland (a couple of years behind that of England). This meant that every child 'even those of the working classes' had to receive an educa-tion, and it would have long-term consequences for Great Britain and not least for the development of football.

That progress was being made in the Victorian era was further indicated by the fact that the English team would travel home by train, as more and more people were beginning to use that new method of transport. The 'gridiron' had been around for more than forty years now, but was still looked upon with a certain amount of suspicion by large sections of the population because of its noise, dirt and speed. It meant that the Englishmen would be back in London by Monday evening at the latest – far quicker than the stage coach (which took at least a week) or the boat (which was possibly slightly quicker than the stage coach but dependent on tides and winds).

1872 was of course long before the saturation coverage of football, and indeed not every newspaper gives the impression of knowing much about the game, although they do insist that the game was played on 'the Association system', meaning the laws codified by the English authorities in 1863. They result of 0-0 would not again be repeated between the two nations until 1970, almost 100 years later and in totally different circumstances and conditions.

Before the Englishmen returned home, a return match was arranged. Happily, the game had seen a surplus of £33 and 8 shillings, and this would go towards Scotland's travelling expenses to England for the following year! The game would be played on 8 March 1873 at another cricket ground, this time Kennington Oval in London, now the home of Surrey CCC.

*   *   *

In 1873 the Scotland team did not entirely consist of Queen's Park players. There was William Gibb of Clydesdale, and three Anglo-Scots (i.e. Scotsmen currently playing for English teams) in Arthur Kinnaird of The Wanderers, and John Blackburn and Henry Renny-Tailyour of the Royal Engineers. Neither Kinnaird nor Renny-Tailyour were born in Scotland, but chose to play for the country because of their Scottish connections.

It was said that the Scottish Football Association were unhappy about having to pay the exorbitant expenses of railway fares and hotel bills for eleven players and insisted that eight was the maximum they would take. The other three would therefore *have* to be Anglos. If this was true, it would not be the last time that Scotland's authorities scrimped and saved to the detriment of the team and the game. In 1954, in the first venture on the World Cup, Scotland could have taken twenty-two players, but decided on the grounds of economy that thirteen would suffice! Stories like these make it difficult for Scots to shake off their reputation for being avaricious.

The crowd at the Oval in 1873 was 3,000 and the entrance fee was again one shilling. If any founder members of the Tartan Army were there, they would have been disappointed with Scotland's showing for they lost 4-2. England scored twice early on, but then Scotland rallied, and to Renny-Tailyour belongs the distinction of scoring Scotland's first ever goal. Gibb then scored another, but England eventually – with 'superior dribbling' – scored two late goals.

A grim-faced looking Queen's Park team who have just won the Scottish Cup in 1874. In 1872, they provided all the Scottish team and were still the mainstay in 1874.

As we have discovered, in the early days England were reputedly the masters of dribbling whereas with Scotland it was passing. How true this was we do not know, but we must smile at an entry in the *Dundee Courier & Argus* of Monday 10 March 1873 which claims that the Scots actually drew with the English the previous Monday in Glasgow. 'Our correspondent claims that the play consisted of mauls and scrimmages fought on neutral territory, the only indication of superiority in either side being that the Scotch were forced to touch down behind once'. Clearly, this game played in Glasgow was certainly 'football', but perhaps not the genre of the game we are talking about!

There was of course at this stage no clear delineation of the several codes of the game (at least in the eyes of the Press) and players like Arthur Kinnaird, for example, played both what we now call football, and also what we call rugby. It was clear however that the 'association' variety was gaining ground about this time, for several other clubs were being formed to give competition to Queen's Park, notably 'The Rangers' in Glasgow, and two famous teams in Dumbartonshire, namely Dumbarton and the Vale of Leven. A Scottish Cup was to be contested from 1874 onwards.

*　　　*　　　*

But the working classes were still not involved, deterred presumably by high admission prices for watching the games and by the snooty atmosphere of most football teams. Yet football was played on the streets, on beaches in summer, kirk yards (hence presumably the Scottish phrase 'makin enough noise to wauken the deid') and in the few public parks that existed in Scottish towns. Letters appeared in newspapers frequently denouncing this game as being 'noisy' and 'exciting' and 'inciting rabbles' and 'encouraging conduct which would shame any self-respecting Christian'. Other, more tolerant members of the letter-writing fraternity pointed out that if athletic young men were playing football, they were less likely to be visiting 'ale houses or ladies of dubious reputation' with whom they could do something that 'they would regret for the rest of their days'.

Perhaps the rise of the game was all due to Henry (Harry) McNeil. The Queen's Park man masterminded Scotland's first ever victory when Scotland beat England 2-1 at Hamilton Crescent on 7 March 1874. Some accounts say he scored the equalizing goal, others say that he was merely the 'administrator of the movements' which led to the goals being scored by Anderson and McKinnon, but it was certainly McNeil who became Scotland's first real hero since Bonnie Prince Charlie of 130 years previously. Some of McNeil's passing was superb, and McNeil had the honour of being carried into the pavilion by eager and enthusiastic crowds.

McNeil (with his brother Moses) was very much involved in the foundation and early days of Rangers, but it was Queen's Park for whom he played. Unlike many Scottish heroes, there did not seem to be any great flaw in his character which led to or contributed to his downfall, for he continued as a Secretary for Queen's Park for many years after his playing days were over before he eventually died in 1924, some fifty years after his first great moment for Scotland.

But there were more such moments to come for McNeil. The fixture was now established as an annual one and played on the first Saturday in March. Scotland, with McNeil as an inspiration, dominated it for the next few years. A 2-2 draw at the Oval in 1875 was followed by a fine Scottish victory in 1876 at Hamilton Crescent. A phenomenal crowd of 15,000 – the size of assembly which would normally make Victorian politicians twitchy about dangers to public order (note, not public *safety*) – saw Scotland triumph 3-0, goals coming from three Queen's Park men: William MacKinnon, Thomas Highet and the hero of the hour Henry McNeil.

It was possibly this game of 1876 which confirmed that football was to be Scotland's obsession for the next 130 years (at least). The match, in fact, was in danger of being called off, for the ground was partly flooded. The crowd was enthusiastic, even those who had paid half a crown to get in and the cries of 'Good Old Scotland' resounded round the douce suburb of Partick for many hours afterwards.

Significantly the Press, which had not previously been all that interested in the game, now chortled in its leader columns 'It would seem as if the Scots were as superior at football to the English as the latter are superior at cricket'. It was clear that the football game was now beginning to get a hold of quite a few Scotsmen, for teams were springing up all over the country, especially in Edinburgh and even as far away as Dundee and Aberdeen – and in all areas, the poorer sections of the populace were becoming more and more interested.

Three weeks after the triumph over the English in 1876, Scotland felt sufficiently confident to invite Wales to play them at Hamilton Crescent. This time the crowd rose to 17,000, the better weather and slightly lower prices perhaps explaining the larger crowd, and Scotland beat the Welsh 4-0, McNeil once again being among the scorers. His brother Moses McNeil also played that day. Moses had been one of the founding members of Rangers in 1873 and on that day became the first Ranger to earn a cap for Scotland.

In 1877, Scotland went on tour of the British Isles. The railway system, which was now very efficient, fast and reliable, allowed the Scotland team to travel to The Oval on Saturday 3 March and then to call in, as it were, to Wrexham to play Wales two days later on the way home. This would be the first international game in the Principality, for England did not play there until 1879. The crowds who saw Scotland off at Glasgow Station on Friday 2 March, re-assembled to see them home on Tuesday 6 March, the indisputable champions of Great Britain, with the morning editions of the newspapers trumpeting that fact. England had been dispatched 3-1 and Wales 2-0. Interestingly, the crowds at the Oval and Wrexham had been 2,000 and 4,000 respectively – a good bit below what one would have expected in Scotland.

Thus had the picture changed in five years. In 1872, England had patronisingly brought the game to Scotland. Very quickly, the roles had been reversed and Scotland were now the kingpins of the sport. A similar phenomenon was happening more or less at the same time in cricket. A matter of days after their defeat by Scotland at football in 1877, England lost what became known as the First Test Match to Australia in Melbourne. Were these the first signs of the crumbling of the British Empire?

1878 saw further success for Scotland. England came on their fourth visit to Scotland, this time not to Hamilton Crescent (which had outlived its usefulness for football but would continue to be a venue for Scotland at cricket well into the twenty-first century), but to the First Hampden Park on the south side of the city. This time, although McNeil played and scored his almost obligatory goal, the real hero of the hour was Vale of Leven's John McDougall, who scored a hat-trick in the emphatic 7-2 defeat of the Englishmen. The game was played in quintessentially Scottish conditions – loads of mud, a slippery ball and a slippery pitch. Clearly Scotland would have the advantage in such circumstances. Some reports give an attendance of 20,000, others merely 10,000 – but it was certainly a tremendous occasion.

The Scottish team contained three players from the Dumbartonshire village side Vale of Leven. The Vale were in their moment of glory for they lifted the Scottish Cup in 1877, 1878 and 1879 and at long last there was at club level a real rival to Queen's Park. This was indeed the heyday of Scottish village football. In time and with the coming of professionalism, village football would have to yield to the big city, but for the time being, the countryside was as good as the metropolis.

Scotland felt sufficiently confident in their abilities to beat Wales, who appeared at First Hampden on 23 March 1878, that they chose a totally different team from those who had beaten the English. Their confidence was hardly misplaced for the

Scottish reserve side routed the disorientated Welsh 9-0. The Scottish Press, while full of praise for the all-round competence of the Scots, admitted that it was a 'hollow affair', for Scotland 'scored at will'. Two goals were disallowed, and there was a certain suspicion that they were valid goals but that the referee Mr Gardner of Glasgow, clearly a compassionate man who felt that the Welsh had been sufficiently humiliated, 'erred on the side of strictness' towards the Scots.

A temporary spoke was put in the wheel of the all-conquering Scots in 1879 when, at Kennington Oval, England emerged victorious 5-4. This game was played in early April and here the weather problem was one of high winds rather than wet and dampness. With the wind at their backs, Scotland survived the loss of an early goal to go in at half-time winning 4-1. It was however a different story in the second half as the Englishmen, 'refreshed and restored' with the wind behind them, broke down the stubborn Scottish defence to level the game at 4-4. Then John Smith of Mauchline (the town in Ayrshire where 100 years previously Robbie Burns had enjoyed his poetry, drink and women) got the ball between the sticks but 'the English appealed for offside and the umpires sustained their appeal'. Scotland's cup of woe was complete when Bambridge of Swifts scored the winner.

A certain amount of frustration was relieved however a couple of days later when Scotland beat Wales 3-0 at the Racecourse in Wrexham with the same mighty Smith of Mauchline (who was a student at Edinburgh University, taking several degrees before qualifying as a doctor) scoring twice.

*   *   *

Thus ended the first decade of international football with Scotland unquestionably deserving the title of 'World Champions of the 1870s'. They had beaten England four times, lost twice and drawn twice, and had comfortably dispatched Wales in each of the four times that they had faced them. This success at international level was now clearly reflected throughout the country. Every town now had at least one and possibly more football teams, and although it would be some time before the game was properly organized at a national level (with the laudable exception of the Scottish Cup), it was clear from the increasing amount of space being dedicated to the game in newspaper coverage that interest was intensifying.

The Scottish Cup was growing year by year. It had started off, more or less, as a Glasgow and District tournament in 1873/74, but by the end of the decade teams from Edinburgh, Dundee and Arbroath were competing for the 'Scottish'. Prestige and pride was very much involved, but for the moment the tournament was dominated by only two teams, namely Vale of Leven and Queen's Park. In this respect perhaps, the wheel has come full circle in that domestic trophies in the early twenty-first century are once again dominated by two teams – albeit a different two and in grossly different circumstances!

If Scotland lost the 1879 game 4-5, they managed to reverse the score the following year at Hampden. In point of fact, the game was nothing like as close as the scoreline would suggest, for Scotland were a comfortable 5-2 up until Charlie Campbell of Queen's Park, the centre half and 'strongest header of a ball in the land' was injured and had to go off. Scotland had to deploy their forwards in a defensive position. This was not a success as Scotland lost two late goals and had to defend desperately at the end.

To the Scottish supporters however, this was a great victory, and much celebrated following last year's uncharacteristic lapse. Wales came to Scotland two weeks later, and once again Scotland showed their strength in depth by playing a reserve side and still beating the bewildered Welshmen 5-1. The Welsh could hardly complain about being insulted by all this. What would the real Scottish team have done to them?

Scotland's next three games were spectacular thrashings of England (twice) and Wales in 1881 and 1882. Recent research has come up with what some might consider to be an astounding fact that the captain, one Andrew Watson, was black. The fact that he appears (from photographs at least) to be black with a tawny complexion and curly hair is remarkable for two reasons. One is that there were very few black people in those days in Scotland, and the other was that the newspapers did not think fit to mention Watson's ethnic origin in their accounts of his performances.

Yet the latter factor need not surprise us too much. For one thing, the newspapers were too busy singing the praises of his performances, and it may be that Victorian society was not really as obsessed with race as we are today! The real delineation of course was social class, and in this respect, Watson was very definitely on the right side, as it were. In fact he belonged to a 'class' which was fairly numerous.

In May 1857, a black plantation worker called Rose Watson in British Guyana gave birth to a son. The father was the owner of the plantation, a Scotsman by the name of Peter Miller. Slavery had by now, technically at least, been abolished in the British Empire, but there was a fine difference between slavery and so called 'free labour'. It was not unknown for ardent masters of plantations to seek solace in the arms of their poverty-stricken female workers. This seems to be what happened here, but the lecherous Mr Miller at least seems to have done the decent thing by his son. He brought him to the United Kingdom and provided money for an education. Following an education at Halifax Grammar and Harrow, Andrew found himself at Glasgow University studying physics in the mid-1870s. There he started to play the Scottish game of football with a team called Parkgrove, before being good enough to move to Queen's Park and then to play for Scotland. His father, after all, was a Scotsman.

That his race (and illegitimacy) was no disadvantage to him was proved by the fact that he was also Secretary of Queen's Park and took part in English football as well. He married a Scottish girl, and nobody ever seems to have raised an eyebrow about the colour of his skin. He remains one of the most successful Scottish players of all time in that he played in three games – which were won 6-1, 5-1 and 5-1. It is also highly unlikely that he ever suffered any racial abuse or discrimination.

Clearly these spectacular victories had a galvanising effect on the game in Scotland, for here was something that Scotland could do and do well. Interest grew, and even more football teams began to be founded. In 1883 Dumbarton at last broke the stranglehold of Queen's Park and Vale of Leven on the Scottish Cup by winning it after a replay in the final. That the game was still fundamentally honest and noble, however, was proved in the semi-final. Dumbarton beat Pollokshields Athletic 1-0, but the Glasgow team complained that the goal was not a goal in that the ball had actually gone past the post. Goal nets had not yet been thought of, and Dumbarton were honest enough to admit that the protest was justified and agreed to a replay. It is hard to imagine that happening in today's cut-throat professional world!

*   *   *

1883 also saw Scotland continue their winning ways, beating both British teams. Wales were beaten 2-0 on the way home from Bramall Lane, Sheffield where Scotland had won by the narrowest of margins. It was 10 March, and spring had not yet reached Sheffield, for Bramall Lane was under several inches of snow. Hundreds of volunteers (including the players) with the help of the sun and the wind, managed to clear the pitch of snow and they were rewarded with a good game. Dr John Smith was still with Scotland, although now playing for Queen's Park, and he twice put Scotland ahead before half-time only to see the fighting Englishmen equalize, both times with fine goals. The second half saw both teams come close, but it was Scotland who got the winner. Accounts vary as to whether it was John Kay or Malcolm Fraser (both men played for Queen's Park which might perhaps explain the uncertainty) but it was a high drooping ball towards England's goalkeeper H.A. Swepstone of the Pilgrims. The goalkeeper had the sun in his eyes and stepped back too far, possibly slipping on the still-wet turf, and crossed the line. Scotland claimed a goal, and although the Englishmen protested 'in favour of the distraught Swepstone', the goal was upheld by the Irish referee Mr Sinclair. This meant that Scotland had now beaten England four years in a row. The Thistle was indeed very prickly for the English Rose.

The following year, it became five in a row. But by this time a new factor had entered the international equation when Ireland joined what was beginning to be called the British International Championship. There were problems with Ireland: in the 1880s it was a troubled unsettled land with murders and bombings as Prime Minister Gladstone tried his level best to settle things with Charles Stuart Parnell and calm down the agitators of the Irish Land League. In such circumstances, British sides were reluctant to go there. This phenomenon would of course be replicated in the 1960s. To a certain extent, the fears for security in the 1880s were addressed by the reassuring thought that the game was generally played in the north of Ireland, in Belfast – the industrial and Protestant part of the country where Parnell and the Fenians had less influence.

There was another, footballing, objection to Irish participation in the British Championship. The Irish were simply not good enough. Their first international against England in 1882 had been a 13-0 thrashing, and even the Welsh beat them 7-1 in that same year. But a creditable result on St Patrick's Day 1883, when the Irish held the Welsh to a 1-1 draw in Belfast, persuaded the Irish authorities to make another attempt to invite the mighty Scottish team to play the next year in Belfast.

Scotland, after some initial dallying, decided that if they were to call themselves the Champions of Britain or even the world, they would have to beat Ireland as well. Thus it was that on Friday 25 January 1884, they sailed to Belfast. It being Burns Day, pipes were there to wish them well as they departed the Broomielaw in Glasgow and captain Wattie Arnott, a well read and urbane gentleman of Queen's Park, no doubt organized a Burns Supper on board ship that night.

The following day in typical Irish rain, Scotland took the field at Ballynafeigh Park, Belfast before 2,000 spectators and beat the Irish 5-0. The Irish, although down-hearted at their defeat, were splendid hosts and made sure that they asked Scotland for 'advice and encouragement' before their return to Glasgow.

*　　　*　　　*

Old Cathkin Park, Govanhill was the venue for the English game of 1884. Once again, over 10,000 watched the Scotland *v*. England tussle and many more listened outside to the roar of the crowd. It was a fine day, although the pitch was slippery after some overnight rain. John Smith yet again was Scotland's hero with an early goal (the only goal of the game as it turned out), but captain Arnott deserved praise for his holding together of the Scottish defence when England pressed in the second half.

Scotland were now cock-a-hoop, and if there were the slightest doubt that Scotland were the best team in Britain, it was comprehensively dispelled a fortnight later when the Welsh came to Old Cathkin Park and were defeated 4-1 by a Scottish team which contained only four men of the eleven who had started against England. Such was the sustained power and versatility of Scottish football in the mid-1880s, even though the players considered good enough to play for Scotland were still confined to the Glasgow and the Dumbartonshire area – and were all still undeniably middle class.

The following year, 1885, saw Ireland's first ever visit to Scotland. On 14 March, they lined up at First Hampden Park against a Scottish team which could probably be considered the second eleven, as it contained only a handful of men who would make it for the 'tour' to England and Wales later on in the month. On a pleasant but blustery day, the Irish were given loads of encouragement by the magnanimous Scottish crowd of 'about 4,000', but were soon outclassed. In the 8-2 rout, Scotland actually scored twice while the Irish defender George Hewison was off the field 'due to a mishap to his garments' and the necessity of sparing the blushes of the genteel Glasgow ladies present. 8-0 up in the last few minutes of the game, Scotland eased off, and Ireland scored their first two goals against Scotland 'to the delight of the crowd who clapped them vigorously'.

Scotland did not have it so easy against England, even though they had their full team on the pitch. The game ended in a draw, but as Wales had also drawn with England, Scotland's 1-1 was enough to give them the Championship when they beat Wales 8-1 at Wrexham on the way home. The England game at The Oval was one of the best that the writer of the *Dundee Advertiser* had seen, but perhaps his judgement was swayed by the fact that the Press were well looked after and suitably 'refreshed'. A scrambled goal by Dumbarton's Joe Lindsay was counteracted by one scored by Andy Amos of Old Carthusians when Dumbarton goalkeeper McAulay, distracted by the setting sun over the pavilion, could only parry a shot.

The Welsh game at Wrexham is dismissed in *The Scotsman* as being little more than a 'rout', although Paton, Lindsay, Hamilton and Allan are singled out for praise – two men from each of Scotland's best two teams – Queen's Park and Dumbarton.

*   *   *

The year 1886 saw the first threat to the International Championship. In 1885, England had bowed to the inevitable and legalised professionalism. This was merely officially sanctioning what had been going on for a long time with 'under the counter' payments or money placed in the shoes of players, so that when they came off the field and took off their boots to put on their normal footwear, they would feel a few coins in their shoes and would know to say nothing as they limped out of the ground! But there was a particularly unhappy side effect of all this for Scotland, in that Scottish players could now be officially enticed away over the border to earn money – and now they could *legally* earn money for playing the game.

The Scottish authorities, still dominated by Queen's Park, set their faces strongly against this professionalism, being horrified at the thought of anyone earning a living from sport. Professionalism would not become legal until 1893 in Scotland, but everyone knew that the paying of players was common practice for many years before then. How else, for example, would Celtic on their founding in 1888 be able to lure James Kelly from Renton?

The whole issue of professionalism and amateurism still rumbles on in various sports. Cricket was the sport that was most affected, for as late as 1963 there was a distinction between Gentlemen (amateurs) and Players (professionals), and there was the famous Lord Hawke who, as late as 1925, prayed to God that no professional would ever captain England! Fortunately in football, the dispute was less enduring, although no less bitter. Queen's Park remain to this day opposed to profes-sionalism and are proud of their Latin motto *'ludere causa ludendi'* – 'to play for the sake of playing' – but they are a quaint and loveable anachronism of a bygone age.

In 1886, however, it was deadly serious. The Scottish Football Association was unhappy about Scottish amateurs playing English professionals in the annual inter-national. They made a few silly demands that England should select only amateurs, and when these demands were (not unreasonably) thrown out by the Englishmen, threatened the cancel the fixture. However, wiser counsel prevailed. It appeared that, however much the Scottish authorities deplored players making money out of the game, they had no objection to making some profit themselves, and reckoned that the loss of an 11,000 gate would be a tremendous financial blow. The Scottish authorities reluctantly backed down – and the game went ahead. It was the gentle art of hypocrisy at work here!

The weather on 27 March 1886 at First Hampden was 'unpropitious' with wind and rain, but even so, 'long before the hour of starting, small knots of people were to be seen outside the gates eagerly discussing the chances of their favourites'. In addition, the *Dundee Advertiser* states that the enthusiasm of the 'dribbling game' fans had not abated. Presumably, this means England fans, as England were still the 'dribbling game' exponents, and Scotland the 'passing game' experts.

The game was a good one, although most of the Scottish Press conceded that England were the better team. England led 1-0 for most of the match, but Scotland worked hard and their late equalizer scored by George Somerville of Queen's Park was greeted by the 'tossing of newspapers in the air'. The newspapers had of course been used to shelter unprotected heads from the torrential rain, but the rain had now ceased and the soaked newspapers were now redundant – other than for expressing joy at Scotland levelling the score! The game finished 1-1, and thus Scotland shared the Championship, for in the 'subsidiary fixtures' (as they were patronisingly called) Scotland beat Ireland 7-2 and Wales 4-1.

*   *   *

In 1887 the *Weekly News* reports condescendingly on Irish football in its report on the game of 19 February at Hampden Park. Around 3,000 had gathered to see the Irishmen 'all from Belfast and its immediate neighbourhood, but it is clear that the Association game has made a great deal of progress in recent times'. Scotland were expected to win and did so quite comfortably. It was by no means Scotland's strongest team who took the field, but within five minutes of the start James Lowe of St Bernard's (Edinburgh) had centred for Willie Watt of Queen's Park to head beautifully into the net.

Scotland, however, did not press home their advantage and just before 'half-time was called', Ireland managed to score in a scrimmage when Browne stabbed the ball past Ned Doig of Arbroath in the Scottish goal. This goal caused a sensation 'among the Irishmen on [*sic*] the stand and at [*sic*] the pavilion', but 'in less time than it takes to write it' Jenkinson of Hearts scored again for Scotland.

The second half was dull as Scotland had no real wish to humiliate their guests although they did score two further goals through Johnstone of Third Lanark and Lowe of St Bernard's. By the end of the game, the 'field was almost void of spectators' as Scotland were so far ahead.

Leamington Road, Blackburn was the venue for the all important England *v.* Scotland game on 19 March 1887. Football in Blackburn was in its heyday, and the Rovers had won the English Cup for the past three years, having beaten Queen's Park (who in those days competed in the English Cup as well as the Scottish Cup) in the final on two of the three occasions. On this occasion 12,000 people saw a keen contest on a difficult pitch, which the referee, Mr Sinclair of Ireland, deemed only just playable. Jimmy McCall of Renton opened the scoring, but an Englishman with the rhyming name of Tinsley Lindley equalized before half-time.

The second half was all action and three more goals came in the space of two minutes in the middle. Leitch Keir of Dumbarton and Jimmy Allan of Queen's Park scored for Scotland while Dewhurst scored for England in between the two Scottish goals. But the Man of the Match for Scotland was Dumbarton's James McAulay in the goal who performed wonders in the last ten minutes 'to say nay' to the eager England forwards, as Scotland won 3-2.

Two days later, after celebrating on the Saturday night but observing, one hopes, the Sabbath with due decorum, Scotland moved on to Wrexham to defeat Wales 2-0 and thus win the International Championship again, having defeated all three British nations for the second time. 1887 was a great year for Scotland, although the row about professionalism rolled on and on, albeit with diminishing intensity as everyone realised that it was only a matter of time before Scotland would follow England's lead and legalise the paying of players.

*   *   *

In 1888, on 10 March, the international scene moved on for the first time to Edinburgh, to Easter Road, the home of Hibernian, a team avowedly and unashamedly for Roman Catholics of Irish descent who had settled in Scotland. Scotland beat Wales 5-1, the Hibs crowd being delighted by the goal scored by 'Darling Willie' Groves, the hero of the Edinburgh Irish. Over 8,000 were there that day – a creditable crowd given that Scotland were playing Ireland at rugby that day at Raeburn Place, little more than half a mile away.

A week later at First Hampden, England arrived. There had been snow in the morning and the ground was still hard, but that does not excuse Scotland's performance, for they appalled the 15,000 crowd by going down 0-5. Tinsley Lindley opened the scoring on the half-hour mark, but it had been one-way traffic long before that. The Scottish Press could do little other than hold up their hands and say that Scotland were 'slow and ponderous' whereas the 1888 English team was probably their best ever, as well as being hungry and motivated. It was indeed the first time they had won in Scotland. Some slight consolation was forthcoming when Scotland went to Belfast and won 10-2 with a reserve team full of those with a point to prove, namely that they should have been playing last week against England.

Revenge was forthcoming however the following year 1889 at Kennington Oval. Having already thrashed Ireland 7-0 at Ibrox in March, Scotland travelled to London to play on 13 April in front of a large (10,000) but genteel crowd who clapped politely but did not show the fervour that Scottish crowds already showed. Scotland kicked off playing towards the gas tower – which is still a feature of the ground and could until recently be seen at Test Matches. Scotland also had the disadvantage of the wind and were 0-2 down at half-time. Yet they felt aggrieved for they scored seconds *after* 'time was sounded' (the half-time whistle), and the goal was disallowed by referee Sinclair of Ireland.

But with the strengthening wind behind them, it was a different Scottish team in the second half. Neil Munro of Abercorn (Paisley) scored with a long high shot, then Jimmy Oswald of Third Lanark equalized after good work by Willie Berry of Queen's Park. The England defence worked wonders to keep out the Scottish attackers until the final minute when Scotland's Man of the Match, Jimmy McLaren of Celtic, sent a long ball through to Dave McPherson of Kilmarnock to nudge home.

It was a famous victory, replicating that of 1887 and doing a great deal to erase from the memory the shocking performance of 1888. On the way home on the Monday the reserves played a 0-0 draw with Wales at Wrexham in a game that was as dull, apparently, as it sounds. The game is barely mentioned in most newspapers and omitted entirely from others.

*　　　*　　　*

1890 saw Scotland break new ground in their venues. The Welsh game was played at Underwood Park, Paisley, the home of Abercorn. Scotland won 5-0 in an 'extremely uninteresting game', the Welshmen being indebted to James Trainor of Wrexham in the goal for keeping the score down. A similarly easy time was had by a totally different Scottish team when they beat Ireland 4-1 at Ballynafeigh Park, Belfast. Although the score was 1-1 at half-time, Scotland, with the benefit of the breeze in the second half, romped home.

But Scotland had a harder game when England came to a new Hampden Park (now known as Second Hampden) on 5 April 1890. The new ground admitted 30,000 spectators – a record attendance who paid the enormous sum of £1,400 to get in. The writer in *The Scotsman* is impressed by the presence of ladies, who in the lovely spring sunshine 'gave the place a look of brightness seldom seen at our winter game'. Indeed it was a huge crowd with a large contingent from Edinburgh who took advantage of the offers of the Caledonian Railway: 2s/6 would take third-class passengers from Princes Street Station to Gusketfaulds Station which was only a few minutes walk from the ground. First-class passengers, however, would have to play 5s/6 to be conveyed to the ground.

There was a break-in when a crush barrier collapsed, but it was soon brought under control and it was not as bad as at 'some rugby matches in Edinburgh' according to the scribe of *The Scotsman*. He is also impressed by Queen's Park's general efficiency in installing the latest telegraph equipment, a Wheatsone and Duplex apparatus staffed by ten operators, so that the fans in the English cities of London and Birmingham (not to mention the Scottish hordes in Edinburgh, Dundee and Aberdeen) would not have long to wait for information about the game. The large crowd was entertained before the match and at half-time by the music of the Dumfries Industrial School.

Scotland should have won this game, which ended in a 1-1 draw. England's star man rejoiced in the unlikely name of Harold Daft (and the Press could not resist making a meal of 'Daft's deft touches') but it was another Harold, Wood of Wolves, who opened the scoring. Scotland equalized through 'Kitey' McPherson of Cowlairs.

This man earned his nickname by his ability to float balls in the air, and this goal was a splendid example of his prowess, as 'Kitey' calmly placed the ball into the roof of the net.

Scotland pressed all through the second half, and the moment of injustice came when Henry Allen of Wolves quite clearly fisted the ball off the line. In those days, the attacking team had to appeal for a penalty before it could be awarded, but Mr Reid of Ireland, clearly unsighted, turned down the claim and the game finished 1-1. Scotland, for whom James Kelly of Celtic had been absolutely outstanding, were not so outraged, however, that they could not appear at the post-match banquet at the Alexandra Hotel to propose the health of the English Association and the referee!

TWO

Professionalism and the National Obsession 1891-1914

By 1891 big changes were happening in the game. Lines began to be introduced onto the field of play with a penalty line some twelve yards from the goal, in case a penalty was awarded. There had to be an appeal however, as in modern day cricket, but whether the claimant would say 'How's that' is not recorded! The goalkeeper also had his 'box', except that it was a curious thing in the shape of a woman's bosom, and would not be replaced by the modern rectangular box until after the turn of the century.

There were bigger and more important changes happening on the political side of the game. The most important as far as Scotland was concerned was the founding of the Scottish League, the first games being played in August 1890. This development did not meet with the approval of the Scottish Football Association, who saw (quite correctly) that it was the precursor for the introduction of professionalism and the result for the Scottish teams of 1891 was that anyone suspected of receiving any kind of reward was not selected for Scotland. This affected men like 'Kitey' McPherson of Rangers and James Kelly of Celtic, as the SFA, remote from the general feelings of football people, cut off their nose to spite their face.

Both Wales and Ireland were defeated narrowly, 4-3 and 2-1 respectively. Wales in particular at Wrexham on 21 March felt ill done by, for they lost their star man Charles Parry to injury early on and even the Scottish Press agreed that they were worth a draw in the strong crosswind. The weather was also bad when Ireland came to Old Celtic Park a week later but against Scotland's weakened side, the Irish provided a fast, interesting game and really deserved what would have been their first draw against Scotland.

The folly of the internecine argument about professionalism within the game in Scotland was seen in the England game at Ewood Park, Blackburn on 4 April 1891.

Two sets of people organized boycotts – Blackburn supporters because there were no Blackburn players in the English team and Scottish supporters because of the perceived folly of the SFA and in particular the Queen's Park establishment – who had too much influence over Scottish team selection, it was felt. In spite of these factors and the dreadful weather, 31,000 turned up at Ewood Park and there were 'excursionists from all parts of the kingdom' present.

Scotland had hard luck with refereeing decisions in the 1-2 defeat, only their fourth in twenty years of playing the game. But while praising the efforts of the Scottish players, the *Dundee Courier* avers 'no mistaking that the flower of Scotland [*sic*] was not in the team and if the Association had been amenable to reason in their matter of difference with the League and less disposed to stand on their dignity, Scotland today would not be mourning a defeat'. No mincing of words there! The use of the world 'mourning' is by no means inappropriate, for large crowds gathered outside newspaper offices in Glasgow and Edinburgh. When they were told the half-time score of England 2 Scotland 0 'groans and execrations' were heard, and genuine fears expressed for a 'Flodden-type hammering' but Kilbirnie's Frank Watt pulled one back near the end, and the crowds, 'though saddened, were not distraught' when they heard the full-time score and slunk off to lick the wounds of the nation.

*   *   *

Fortunately the dispute was resolved by 1892, a year which brought several notable happenings. On the 19 March Scotland were in Ireland at a ground with the quaint name of Solitude, the stadium of Cliftonville in Belfast. It was hardly Scotland's first team, containing as it did men like George Bowman of Montrose and Jimmy Ellis of Mossend Swifts, but they seemed to be good enough to beat Ireland. Irish football had improved in recent years, however, and this year Ireland had drawn with Wales and lost only narrowly to England. A large and excitable crowd of 10,000 were there to see Scotland.

Scotland were holding a 2-1 lead when the moment of controversy happened. It concerned Dave McPherson of Kilmarnock who 'got on the leather and shooting straight, it seemed to go over the bar and burst through the net' (according to the writer of *The Scotsman*), i.e. the ball entered the net from above! The referee Mr Taylor of Wrexham gave the goal when Scotland claimed it but the Irish crowd issued 'a perfect storm of angry execrations'. Scotland were thus 3-1 up but Gaffikin of Ireland pulled one back, and the last few minutes were frantic as Ireland strove to earn what would have been their first ever draw against Scotland.

The Scotsman's reporter then graphically describes the crowd scene at the end of the game. 'As the referee who subsequently admitted in the presence of both teams that he had made a mistake in awarding the third goal to Scotland, was leaving the field, the spectators broke in and but for the fact that both teams got round him and escorted him to the pavilion, he would have had a pretty rough time of it. One man was arrested but subsequently released for threatening the referee.' It is clear from this passage that football hooliganism is far from being a new phenomenon.

A totally different Scottish team then took the field for the Wales game, as the selectors continued their policy of using the Wales/Ireland games as trials for the big one. This game, the first international ever to be played at Tynecastle Park, Edinburgh, was an absolute travesty. Scotland won 6-1 but the game was played from start to finish in a snowstorm. It being March, the snow did not lie, although the ball did from time to time pick up a coating of snow, but it was hard to play football or even see the players in such blinding conditions.

The snow came on about midday, and had it not been for the fact that travel problems would have made it difficult to re-arrange a game with the Welsh, it would surely have been called off. The big disappointment was the crowd, which *The Scotsman* writer places optimistically at about 1,200. The scribe cannot resist laughing at the mounted police there in large numbers in case of crowd disorder and almost outnumbering the spectators who spent all game sheltering against the enclosure wall which offered some protection from the blizzard. A few cries of 'Good Old Scotland' were heard as Scotland, with three Hearts men on board in an attempt to get a crowd, ran riot. The SFA were highly displeased when the total takings amounted to only £25.

*   *   *

The game against England in 1892 saw the Press so disgusted with Scotland's dismal capitulation (to the tune of 1-4) that it says very little about the game other than grudgingly admitting that England were 'good'. More attention is paid to the ground itself at Ibrox. Three weeks previously there had been crowd trouble at the Celtic *v*. Queen's Park Scottish Cup final as Ibrox struggled to contain the massive crowd and the game had to be declared a friendly. This time the Rangers management had worked hard, decking their stand in crimson and orange and organising entertainment with the pipes and drums of the Dumfries Industrial School, and having a Highland Fling demonstration at half-time. It was as well that the pipers and dancers did a good job, for there was precious little to cheer about on the park as Scotland were 0-4 down at half-time and many of the 20,000 crowd did not even stay for the second half, so disgusted were they by Scotland's performance. Scotland did rally a little after the break and Jack Bell of Dumbarton pulled a goal back, but the game was played out in a 'dismal silence'.

If Wales had come close to beating Scotland in Wales in 1891, that cannot be said to be true of 1893 as Scotland, with a strong team this time, travelled to Wrexham on 18 March to lash them 8-0 with Wales never really in it. Johnnie Madden of Celtic scored four goals and Johnnie Barker of Rangers notched three. The team was then much changed for the arrival of Ireland on 25 March, but once again Scotland were triumphant, by 6 goals to 1.

This was the first international to be played at what was then Scotland's finest stadium, New Celtic Park. This ground had been open now for a year and was quite clearly the best stadium in the country with a strong claim for future internationals against England. Old Celtic Park had of course been used for the Ireland international in 1891, and for a long time Celtic Park would seem the logical place for a game when Ireland were the visitors. Shamrocks indeed grew on the turf, having been planted there by the Irish patriot Michael Davitt in 1892. On this occasion, Scotland employed four Celtic men in the interests of attracting a large crowd. In the event 12,000 appeared.

Most of the team which beat Ireland retained their place for the visit to England on 1 April. This game was to be played on the Richmond Athletic Ground in London and would be graced with royalty. The Duke and Duchess of Teck would be present with their daughter, Mary, who would of course in time become Queen Mary. She in fact lived at nearby Richmond Palace and had already been engaged to one son of the Prince of Wales called Victor Albert. When this unfortunate man died in 1891, she hung around, and nothing abashed, found herself engaged to the future George V (the brother of her late fiancé) a month after this particular game. Later in the summer on 6 July 1893 they married and in due course reigned happily over the British Empire from 1910 until 1936.

It was perhaps a sign of the growing popularity of football and its acceptance by the establishment that she was presented, not to the teams (who after all might contain a few professionals of working class-origin!), but only to the captains. So it was that James Kelly of Celtic (ironically an avowed professional and Roman Catholic into the bargain) was called across to be presented to the Princess Mary or May, as she was sometimes called. Some of the rest of the team resented the fact that they were not allowed to shake her hand, but protocol was protocol. Willie Maley, later manager of Celtic and a devotee of royalty, was one of those upset about this, but in some of his writings manages to imply that he actually did shake hands with his future Queen!

It was a fine but windy day on the classic sward of Richmond. Scotland in fact played well and soon after half-time were 2-1 up with two goals coming from Queen's Park's Willie Sellar, but then England came more and more into the game and ran out 5-2 winners, a scoreline that flattered the Englishmen, who had now nevertheless won three games in a row against Scotland.

*   *   *

New ground was broken in 1894 when Ayrshire was chosen for the Scotland v. Wales international on 24 March. It was a beautiful spring day and special trains were hired from Glasgow and Edinburgh as 10,000 descended on Rugby Park, Kilmarnock. Such was the pressure on the railway that the Scottish team themselves, who had met in Glasgow, were thirty minutes late. The Ayrshire crowd had a good day, for they saw Scotland win 5-2 with 'Dyke' Berry of Queen's Park leading the way. The crowd were impartial and 'cheered the good play of both sides' according to one Welsh source. 'Many Welshmen will be thinking of returning to Ayrshire for a holiday following this pleasant experience.'

A week later, Scotland beat Ireland at Solitude – which seems to have been at the base of a hill for Ireland were described as defending 'the mountain goal' in the first half. Ireland had already drawn with England and came close to obtaining their first elusive draw with Scotland, after Scotland became complacent with a 2-0 lead and Ireland pulled one back.

The England game was played on 7 April at New Celtic Park with a massive (record) crowd of 45,000 inside, some of whom spilled onto the cycling track, but not onto the pitch. Scotland's team was made up of men from Celtic, Rangers and Queen's Park, apart from Isaac Begbie of Hearts. Scotland should have won this game comfortably but Celtic's Sandy McMahon was profligate of chances which would have put Scotland comfortably ahead even before half-time. In the event, it was 1-1 but England now had the strong wind. The spectators were 'too engrossed in discussing Scotland's chances against the wind to pay much attention to the musical strains' of the pipers of Dr Guthrie's Institute at half-time.

In fact Scotland did score against the run of play in the second half through 'Kitey' McPherson of Rangers, an occasion which saw 'hats, sticks and handker-chiefs frantically waved' by the excited Scottish crowd, but Scotland were not able to hold out against the tremendous English pressure and the strong east wind. Only five minutes remained when John Reynolds of Aston Villa aimed a thirty-yard shot with the wind which evaded everybody including the unsighted goalkeeper David Haddow. England thus earned a point, but Scotland won the Home International Championship because England had failed to beat Northern Ireland.

*   *   *

If 1894 was a success, the same cannot be said of the following year where Scotland drew disappointingly with Wales at Wrexham, then beat Ireland at Celtic Park 3-1 in a victory that was described as 'good, but not all that good' before collapsing 0-3 to a rampant England side at Goodison Park. This was a particular disappointment for the Scottish fans in the vast crowd, some of whom had sailed down from Glasgow the night before. This small band might have been called the 'Tartan Navy', perhaps! The crowd was given as 42,000, possibly slightly more than the previous year at Celtic Park, but they saw a one-sided contest in which England really should have scored more goals. It now meant that Scotland's last three trips to the 'Land of the Saxon' as the *Glasgow Herald* put it, had been fruitless.

21 March 1896 saw the good city of Dundee in a ferment of excitement. In accordance with the SFA's policy of playing internationals throughout Scotland, a game had been awarded north of the Forth for the first time, and it had been given to Carolina Port, home of Dundee FC. Local interest was to be encouraged for Alec Keillor and William Thomson of Dundee were to be Scotland's wingers, and Scotland's linesman was to be Mr Crichton of Arbroath.

Trains came to Dundee from all over Scotland, but particularly from the Angus and Fife hinterlands. The ground was well prepared for the 4 p.m. kick off, and the gates were opened as early as 1 p.m. The capacity of 22,000 was not quite reached but the ground was comfortably filled, as Scotland came out in blue to be photographed. Previously Wales had appeared (in white) to the strains of *Men of Harlech*, obligingly rendered by the local band.

Neil of Hibernian scored twice (one 'a shot which never left the ground'), local man Keiller scored with a 'slanting shot' and Paton of St Bernards had a lucky one which went in off the post, in what was a one-sided 4-0 rout. The festivities were rounded off with a meal at a local hotel and both teams departed in the direction of Glasgow at 9 p.m that night.

A week later what was more or less a different Scotland team took on Ireland in Belfast. Here, in a thrilling 3-3 draw, Ireland recorded their best-ever result over Scotland. It would have been an Irish victory but for a late goal scored by James Blessington of Celtic after 'a new ball had been called for', such had been the damage inflicted on the previous one in the ferocious wind and rain which limited the crowd at Solitude to 8,000.

The Irishmen were delighted with this, but it was Scotland who won the Home International Championship the following week on 4 April 1896 at Celtic Park, Glasgow. A world record crowd of 56,000 attended this game against England for 'latterly nothing but the result of this tussle was talked about' in Scotland the previous week. When the gates opened many people 'who had been in the vicinity since the early morning' flooded in and the 'pay boxes were busy places'. Scottish supporters were constantly reminded that 'there had not been a victory for the Thistle since 1889' – and clearly had decided to see Scotland put an end to all this.

The game was cursed by crowd trouble, mainly during the period preceding the game. Such was the pressure on the 'embankment' (the eastern end of the ground) that the crowd encroached at several points. The 500 police were unable to deal with this situation and the presence of Gordon Highlanders from the Maryhill Barracks was required to assist the maintenance of law and order, especially when some stoning of the police took place as well.

It is interesting in passing to see the way that such late Victorian hooliganism is reported. It is mentioned in passing and words like 'boisterous high spirits' are used from time to time, but the very presence of the Gordon Highlanders and their deployment does seem to be rather a blow to those who argue that Victorian Britain was a peaceful place and that law and order was effectively maintained by the police force (the 'Bobbies' or the 'Peelers' whom Robert Peel had founded more than half a century earlier).

For this game, Scotland made the policy decision that they would now field 'Anglo-Scots' or 'Anglos' (players born in Scotland but who now played for English clubs). It was not a decision reached without some serious heart searching, and indeed protests from 'Home Scots' players who would now find it so much more difficult to get into the Scottish team, but the decisive factor was presumably the 3-0 tanking the previous year at Goodison. Such a thing could never be allowed to happen again. There would from now on, however, be a battle for the release of Anglos from their English employers.

Scotland fielded six Anglos, and five Home Scots, one of whom was an amateur, Willie Lambie of Queen's Park. Lambie it was who scored the first goal, a rebound from the goalkeeper and he was instrumental, along with Hyslop and Blessington, in the lead up to Jack Bell's goal. Scotland went in at half-time two goals to the good, and survived English pressure in the second half until the eightieth minute when Bassett, who had been 'called offside' on several previous occasions, breached Ned Doig's 'citadel'. But Scotland held out, and there were many reports of singing and dancing in the London Road and Gallowgate districts of Glasgow that night with Neil Gibson of Rangers being declared the 'greatest football player alive' by the exultant fans for his fine half-back play. Receipts for this game were an unbelievable £3,744.

*   *   *

The 1897 campaign opened with a good game, which resulted in a 2-2 draw at Wrexham. Scotland's team was not a particularly strong one as it contained no Anglos (who would probably not have been released by their clubs) and only one Ranger, James Oswald. The other Rangers players were involved in the Scottish Cup final on that day. The very fact that the Scottish Cup final was on the same day as the trip to Wales indicates perhaps that the Welsh game was still not being taken seriously enough by the authorities – in spite of the 2-2 draw there a couple of years earlier which should have indicated that the Welsh really now ought to have been given more respect.

The following week Scotland duly beat Ireland 5-1 at Ibrox, again with all home Scots but this time with four Rangers. It was a dreadful day of sleet and wind, and the authorities were disappointed with the 10,000 crowd, but the game itself was only a precursor to what was to follow. The England game would be played at the Crystal Palace the following week and the 'Selecting Seven', followed by an eager crowd of Press men and fans all 'repaired to the Bath Hotel' where after a 'sederunt of one hour and a half', they announced the team – and it contained Anglos. The telegraphs were duly dispatched to inform the players of their selection. The Press (which even in these days believed that it could pick the team) were delighted that their forecasts had come true.

But an incident arose concerning goalkeeper Ned Doig, generally agreed to be the best in the world. Sunderland refused to release him, for they were playing a League game that day. Illogically, however, they allowed Hugh Wilson to play in midfield. Therefore it was John Patrick of St Mirren who was in the goal at Crystal Palace on Saturday 3 April 1897. Scottish fans united with their Press to protest against this, but Sunderland, not for the last time, were adamant.

The team departed at 1.25 p.m. on Friday from St Enoch's Station Glasgow amid scenes of 'incredible bustle where at one point it seemed that the players and officials might not get onto the platform, as there were thousands of men and boys' there to see the team off. John Patrick, the replacement goalkeeper, was given a special pat on the back and he was gracious enough to admit that he wasn't as good as Doig.

Those who vilified Sunderland for their 'poor excuse' need not have worried, for Scotland won 2-1 anyway and Patrick had a good game. Steve Bloomer scored first for England but then Tommy Hyslop of Rangers equalized before half-time. The second half was a tough battle, but it was Jimmy Millar of Rangers who scored the winner with a fierce drive seven minutes from time.

The *Dundee Courier* paints an informative verbal picture of all the grounds in Scotland where football was being played that day. The games were finished, but everyone stayed where they were waiting for a tannoy announcement or a sandwich board man to walk round the ground once the telegram arrived to tell the 'news of battle'. A boy on a bicycle usually arrived from the local post office with a telegram for 'The Secretary', but he was, on occasions like this, hijacked and made to divulge his glad tidings, so that everyone knew before the lad even reached the ground.

The *Courier* now wallows in romantic hyperbole telling everyone that 'more fully than ever Scotland is the home of football' thanks to the performances of the 'cream of our sons'. The players themselves had a night out in London to celebrate, then were given all Sunday to recover or go to church (which was usually *de rigeur* in Victorian Britain) before travelling back home on the 10.45 p.m. train. Such was the delight of the SFA, that the players were even given breakfast in a Glasgow hotel on the Monday morning as a grand 'wind-up' to the proceedings (it would now of course be called a 'wind down').

*　　　*　　　*

Scotland's first game in the 1898 campaign was a comfortable 5-2 beating of Wales at Fir Park, Motherwell. The conditions were good but Wales were poor as Jimmy McKie of East Stirling (winning his first and only cap) scored at least two goals and possibly a third if some reports are to be believed. The *Glasgow Herald* was not pleased with the behaviour of either team. At the end there was not much handshaking and 'more cuffs than compliments' were exchanged.

The following week, on 26 March 1898, the Scottish team were off to Belfast with a different bunch of players in Scotland's undeclared policy of spreading honours around as they were likely to beat Ireland anyway. Indeed they did, 3-0 this time, with R.S. McColl of Queen's Park getting himself on the scoresheet. No Rangers players were picked for they were busy winning the Scottish Cup that day, beating Kilmarnock 2-0 in the final. A man ran on to attack the referee, Mr Lewis of England, for no rational reason but 'sadly symptomatic of that most distressful country' that Ireland was, according to the *Dundee Advertiser*.

The name 'Sunderland' was once again none too popular with Scottish fans on 2 April 1898, for the Wearsiders had refused yet again to release goalkeeper Ned Doig. This time midfielder Hugh Wilson was also retained by Sunderland on the grounds that they were hoping to win the League and were playing Sheffield United that day – but Sheffield United had released Ernie Needham to play for England! Sunderland got what they deserved when Sheffield United won the English League, but that was of no consolation to the Scottish fans whose team went down 1-3 to England in a performance that was 'a disappointment' according to the *Glasgow Herald*.

Following the crowd problems in 1896, Celtic Park had been expanded and the gates were opened in the morning at 11 a.m. to allow the fans in for the 3.30 p.m kick off. It was not necessary to close the gates before the start, but 70,000 were inside the ground to see England get the better of Scotland with Ned Doig's replacement, Kenny Anderson, an amateur from Queen's Park, sadly out of his depth and responsible for the first goal. Yet Scotland fought when two down and pulled one back through Jimmy Miller of Rangers and might have equalized had the great Dan Doyle of Celtic not made a 'bloomer' to allow Steve Bloomer to score a third.

The reporter of the *Dundee Advertiser* hints at something when he says that the crowd was in excess of 70,000 but the takings were only £1,829, 'as if the crowd were 36,580'. What is he trying to say here? Embezzlement? Surely not! Trying to evade tax? Perhaps. He clearly thinks that there is something amiss, and it is noticeable that other reports give the crowd as 40,000 – something that might explain the lowish takings. The Dundee man, however, is slightly more cynical than the others!

*   *   *

1899 saw Scotland thrash the lesser two countries but revert to the less-than-happy experiences in England which had been the norm for some time, apart from 1897. A stronger than normal side went to Wales to put the home side to the sword, the famous R.S. McColl scoring a hat-trick in the 6-0 rout. The following week Ireland came to Celtic Park for a game that was a mismatch. Ireland were having one of their interminable internal disputes and a contretemps meant that six men refused selection at the first attempt, and three of their replacements also refused to come to Scotland. The Scottish press is sympathetic with the Irish selectors who were at their 'wits' end' until they managed to scrape together eleven men.

In fact the game was under threat, for bad weather hit Scotland on the day of 25 March 1899. Most games were off and Celtic Park was covered in four inches of snow, but under the energetic guidance of Celtic manager Willie Maley, a squad of volunteers were offered free admission to the game if they helped out. Over 200 took up Maley's offer and the game proceeded under Arctic conditions. 12,000 people paid £343 to see this travesty which Scotland won 9-1, Ireland's solitary goal being greeted with the loudest cheer of the day.

Two weeks later, on 8 April, bad weather was still in evidence as 3,000 Scots took advantage of much-reduced railway fares to travel to Aston Grounds, Birmingham (now known as Villa Park, home of Aston Villa). But the snow and the wind reduced the crowd to 25,590 when more might have been expected. They saw a good game which England edged 2-1. England scored twice in the first half, but Scotland with the advantage of the biting wind in the second half scored through Bob Hamilton of Rangers. England's defence, under the guidance of a chap with the strange name of Henry Thickett, was under severe pressure for the rest of the game, but 'try as Scotland might, the equalizer came not' says the writer of the *Dundee Advertiser*.

A draw would have been deserved but the forwards were 'a miserable lot' and could not avail themselves of their opportunities.

*   *   *

Scotland's first international of the twentieth century was played at Pittodrie Park, Aberdeen on 3 February 1900. It seemed a strange choice for the ground had only been opened for less than a year, and the team that played there, Aberdeen Football Club, were not the team that we would later know by that name. They would be added to by a team called Orion and another called Victoria United in 1903 – the year now acknowledged as their foundation. Moreover, 'Aberdeen' were not yet in the Scottish League, preferring for the moment to play in a local league.

It was thus a missionary venture. The Scottish authorities were laudably keen to spread the game to all parts of Scotland, and as Pittodrie could reputedly contain about 15,000 spectators, it would make sense to give the game to the Granite City. After all, Aberdeen was as big as Dundee and that city had already staged the Wales international in 1896, and Motherwell had done likewise in 1898. Edinburgh, Kilmarnock and Paisley had also staged international matches.

Thus Aberdeen was swamped by football fans that cold February day with Aberdeen's usual biting wind off the North Sea, but apart from local interest in what was virtually Scotland's reserve team (no Anglos were chosen, for their clubs would have refused) there was little general interest. Wales were still not considered top opposition. In any case, events at Spion Kop and Ladysmith in South Africa were engaging everyone's attention, as Britain (including Aberdeen's Gordon Highlanders) was heavily involved in the Boer War.

Scotland won quite easily 5-2, and a month later, another Scottish team went to Belfast to beat the Irish 3-0. All this was in preparation for the big international, which was this time to be a special occasion. It would become known as the 'Rosebery International' for it concerned the famous Lord Rosebery, also known as the Earl of Rosebery.

Lord Archibald Philip Primrose Rosebery was a football fan, something that was (and still is) rare among the aristocracy. He was born in London in 1847 but as one of his country houses was at Dalmeny near the Forth Bridge, he considered himself Scottish. He was a famous owner of horses and one time Honorary President of the SFA. He was a Liberal in politics and had been Prime Minister of Great Britain for a brief and unhappy spell between 1894 and 1895. He was more interested in sport than in politics, however, and in the two years that he had been Prime Minister, his horses had won the Derby – something that did not go down well with the religious wing of the Liberal Party. There had also been one or two mutterings about 'fixing'.

In the same way that HRH Princess Anne supports the Scottish rugby team now, Rosebery supported the Scottish football team then. He 'sponsored' the Scotland team for this international, donating a new set of strips to the team in his racing colours of yellow and purple, and insisting that the Celtic Park pavilion was similarly decked out in his colours. Scotland had previously worn his colours in 1881 and

Lord Rosebery, who sponsored Scotland many times at the start of the twentieth century.

1882 against England and would do so again in 1905, 1906, 1907, 1908 and 1909 (although dark blue was more common) but in view of the massive involvement on this occasion and his own personal appearance at the ground, this game is known as the 'Rosebery International'.

It was a triumphant Lord Rosebery who addressed the multitudes at the end. Scotland, in front of 65,000 who paid about £4,000, had comprehensively beaten England 4-1. R.S. McColl had scored a great hat-trick and Jack Bell the other for Scotland while England's solitary counter came from Steve Bloomer. Lord Rosebery was gracious, expressing concern for William Oakley of England who had been injured but hoping that 'no worse civil war will ever occur between us'. Rosebery would continue to give upper-class support, albeit sporadic and desultory, to Scotland until his death in 1929.

It was a great time for Scotland, none more so than for R.S. McColl (otherwise known as 'Toffee Bob') and of course the founder of the R.S. McColl chain of shops that still exists today. He was a fine player and in particular had the two great assets of a centre forward – namely the ability not to be barged off the ball and a cannon-ball shot. His second goal was graphically described in the *Dundee Advertiser*: '…McColl romped between Crabtree and Oakley, disdaining contact, to propel the sphere past Robinson'.

*　　　*　　　*

The first international in 1901 was an embarrassing one, in that Scotland beat a poor Irish team 11-0, only two goals short of equalling England's record score against the same opposition some nineteen years earlier. Scotland simply went berserk that day with Sandy McMahon of Celtic and Bobby Hamilton of Rangers scoring four each. A peculiarity of this game was that Scotland fielded two John Campbells, one who played for Celtic and the other who played for Rangers.

The trip to Wales in early March was a tough one, and Scotland did well to come home with a point. A point was all they got in the England game that year as well. It was a hard fought game at the Crystal Palace on a gluepot of a pitch, but the draw meant that England won the Championship, for they had hammered the Welsh whereas the Scots had only drawn.

*   *   *

And so we come to 1902, the year of the first of several Ibrox disasters. Scotland had waltzed past both Ireland and Wales that year, the Welsh game being played at Cappielow Park , the home of Greenock Morton. It was the venue of the England game, however, which was to have far reaching and tragic consequences.

In these days, venues were decided by a vote at the SFA. There was always keen competition to host the England international. A new Hampden Park was now being built, and this would clearly be a good place in future years, but in the meantime Celtic Park seemed to be reasonably adequate for the fixture, as indeed had been proved in the 1890s and certainly in 1900 for the Rosebery International.

However, much to the chagrin of Celtic, Ibrox won the vote because Rangers had spent some money to upgrade their ground just for this occasion. It was also the first time that both teams were all-professional (i.e. Queen's Park and Corinthians supplied no players) and Celtic's unhappiness with the authorities was hardly eased when no Celtic players were picked for the Scottish team – not even their two stars McMahon and Campbell.

A crowd of 80,000 flocked to Ibrox the afternoon of Saturday 5 April 1902, in spite of the heavy rain which often seemed to attend the Scotland v. England game. The crowd were naturally excited and contained a great deal of Scottish soldiers home on leave from their triumphant campaigns (as the newspapers depicted them) in South Africa. Much alcohol was consumed, as normal, but the crowd, although rowdy and boisterous, were basically good humoured and there was no hint of violence or any crowd trouble.

Ibrox had been revamped in 1899 and at what is now the Broomloan Road end of the ground there stood an impressive-looking wooden stand. People climbed up stairways to reach the top of the high terracing which was made of wood, but was built at such an angle that a reasonably good view was guaranteed. Such was the rush of latecomers, however, that rather too many spectators had gathered at one particular point. The terracing, of course, was uncovered and the heavy rain had soaked the timbers. A few creaks were heard at the start of the game, but everyone joked about it being the England goalkeeper's bones creaking.

The game had gone ten minutes when the terracing gave way. The incident concerned the quixotic and flamboyant Bobby Templeton of Aston Villa. Bobby, in later years, would star on the left wing for Celtic, but on this occasion he was on the right wing. A long diagonal ball from Rangers' John Drummond found Templeton. The crowd, enthusiastic as always, followed the ball swaying from left to right. This movement, plus the undeniable fact that the wooden floorboards had been weakened by continual rain, determined the fate of so many people.

A loud crack was heard even above the normal roar of the crowd, and suddenly several members of the crowd disappeared and fell thirty or forty feet into a yawning gap. Screams and yells punctuated the air and the referee brought the game to a halt. After some preliminary examination of the confusion in which it was not particularly easy to discern what actually had happened or how great the damage was, it was decided to play on, for the police thought (quite correctly) that it was better to keep the rest of the crowd inside the stadium than have them thronging the streets outside to see what exactly had happened. The game continued and both teams scored just before half-time. Concentration, however, must have been difficult given the steady flow of stretcher bearers carrying the injured round the track into the pavilion.

Some of the players, apparently, were quite shocked to discover at half-time that stretcher cases of the injured were lying in the corridors leading towards the dressing rooms or in the treatment room. Several had obviously died, for their heads were covered. Some mounted policemen and boys on bicycles had been dispatched to find any kind of transport to convey the injured to hospital. A loudspeaker announcement asked for anyone with medical experience 'whether military or civil' to report to help.

Yet even when the teams reappeared for the second half the rest of the crowd were not aware of the total catastrophe. One or two people perhaps would be injured, but in the meantime the game was more important. The players were more aware of what had happened, and it is hardly surprising that the game fizzled out lethargically in a 1-1 draw, enough, as it turned out, to give Scotland the Championship – or so it appeared.

Glasgow seethed with rumours that night with talks of bombs planted by Fenians, Anarchists or South African extremists as the death toll rose inexorably. It was not until the following morning that the rest of Scotland learned about the first major tragedy of Edwardian Scotland: 26 people had died and 587 had been seriously injured with many more incurring minor injuries. The game itself was declared null and void and rescheduled, illogically, for Villa Park, Birmingham because it was thought that Glasgow would still be a city in grief.

The Villa Park game played on 3 May was a 2-2 draw. The standard of football eventually brightened up, but had started very low key after all the tributes being paid to the dead. It was obvious that it would have been a better idea not to play this game at all, and allow the Ibrox result to stand, but at least a percentage of the gate was given to the Ibrox Disaster Fund.

Many competitions and exhibition matches were now arranged for the fund. Rangers' good name was blackened and Ibrox was never again used for a Scotland *v*. England fixture. Rangers' playing performances on the field now went into a severe decline and although they won the Scottish Cup in 1903, they did not do so again until 1928. One of the more bizarre explanations of this phenomenon was that it was a curse laid upon them by the dead of the Ibrox disaster!

*   *   *

The 1903 international campaign began on Monday 9 March at the Cardiff Arms Park when Scotland beat Wales 1-0. Thus began the tradition of playing the Wales *v.* Scotland game on a Monday afternoon in early March. It was a good idea, for it was a holiday in Wales in honour of St David, and it allowed the Scots to play for their clubs the Saturday before or indeed in the annual Scottish League *v.* English League game which tended to be played on that date. The goal in 1903 came when Finlay Speedie pounced on a mistake made by the impressively named Morgan Morgan-Owen to beat the goalkeeper in the heavy rain. It was a good win and it would be a long time before such success on Welsh soil was repeated.

This was followed by Ireland's first ever win over Scotland. It came at Celtic Park on 21 March 1903. As we have discovered, Scotland in those days often used the Welsh and the Irish games as trials for the important game against England, and the team was far from Scotland's strongest. For one thing they were all Home Scots (possibly to save expenses) and for another several were played out of position. Ireland, on the other hand, had all 'Anglo-Irish'. The weather was 'boisterous' but this does not explain how Scotland played so badly. Connor of Brentford scored with a header early on, then late in the game Kirwan of Tottenham Hotspur dribbled round the Scottish defence to score. The Scottish crowd were so disgusted by their team's lack of effort that they cheered on the Irishmen. Indeed many of the crowd would have been Glasgow-Irishmen in any case, who might have enjoyed this spectacle. With or without such 'Trojan horse' support, Ireland thoroughly deserved their win.

All was forgiven, however, when Scotland beat England at Bramall Lane Sheffield on 4 April. This time the goalkeeper and two backs – Doig, McCombie and Watson – were all Sunderland players and in spite of an early goal, the Scots stuck at their task. Bobby Templeton, now of Newcastle, was outstanding as was Bobby Walker of Hearts and it was Walker who scored the second goal a minute after Finlay Speedie had notched the first. All the 'Scotch excursionists' were delighted with their team and the 2-1 victory, although one journalist who clearly does not like Rangers says 'all the Rangers men Robertson, Hamilton, Speedie and Smith were not so good as the others' and Smith in particular was 'a passenger in a third-class compartment'. Alec Smith would nevertheless go on to win 20 caps and countless League medals. Some passenger! Some compartment!

*   *   *

1904 was not such a good year for Scotland. Dens Park, Dundee saw a dismal 1-1 draw. Scotland should have done better in view of the unavailability of Wales' great Billy Meredith but Scotland had local players Sharp and MacFarlane drafted in to ensure a big crowd and their star man, Bobby Walker of Hearts, had to leave the field before half-time suffering from an unspecified 'illness' (not an injury). It was the other Walker, John of Rangers, who scored Scotland's goal in the early stages but it was cancelled out by Robert Atherton. Wales then pressed for a winner, aware that they had never beaten Scotland, but it never came.

A 1-1 draw was also the score in Dublin at Dalymount Park. 7,000 were there to see a team which contained only two Anglo-Irish, the rest being Home Irish against a team of Home Scots. Harold O'Reilly of a team called the Freebooters played well but it was Sheridan of Everton who equalized for Ireland. Bob Hamilton of Rangers had scored for Scotland.

Celtic Park was the venue for the England game yet again on 9 April 1904. Ibrox was still out of commission following the horrendous events of two years previously, and the new Hampden Park lost the vote for it was felt that it might not be quite ready for the Scotland v. England international. In fact it was ready, having been opened on 31 October the previous year and would stage its first big event, the Scottish Cup final, the week after the England game. But rather than take the risk, Celtic Park was used again. It was a dreadful day with 'hail, sleet and hurricanes in evidence all morning' in Glasgow with the Celtic groundstaff (and even their players) clearing the saturated turf. They dared not take the risk of having to call the game off at such a late stage given the crowd problems that had existed on previous occasions, particularly in 1896, but they need not have worried.

At about 3 p.m., half an hour before the scheduled 3.30 p.m. kick-off, the sun appeared and out came the Govan Police Pipers to play 'songs, sentimental and otherwise'. The crowd was much reduced thanks to the foul weather and possibly because there were no Celtic players in the Scottish team, but this did mean that the crowd (of about 45,000) could see the game in comfort.

The *Glasgow Herald* says that the Scottish team ran on 'to a huge cheer', but then on came the English to a cheer 'almost as hearty'. This comparative lack of partisanship in the crowd need not surprise us too much. Obviously, a Scottish crowd wanted a Scottish team to win, but they were basically there to watch the football and the Englishmen deserved some support as well. A hundred years on, such an attitude is indeed rare!

Scotland played well against the wind in the first half, but seemed to have exhausted themselves in so doing, for England took charge in the second half and it was no surprise when Steve Bloomer scored the only goal of the game. The *Glasgow Herald* is very critical of the Scottish forwards, but does say that Mr Nunnerley of Wales could well have granted them a penalty. It was not to be, however, and Scotland thus completed a miserable season of two draws and a defeat.

*   *   *

1905 saw Wales at long last beat Scotland. The game continued the tradition of being played on a Monday – in this case 6 March – the Welsh holiday. 6,000 were there at Wrexham on a windy but pleasant day to see Scotland well beaten to the

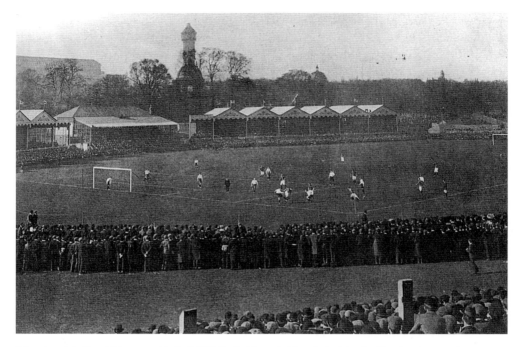

A fine view of the Crystal Palace ground in April 1905. Scotland lost unluckily to England that day. Note there is no penalty arc.

tune of 1-3. Scotland had no excuse: their goal came from a Robertson speculative shot long after they were three goals down and the game merely proved what had been apparent for a long time, namely that Wales, with their star man Billy Meredith, were catching up with both England and Scotland.

The Scottish team wasn't entirely a reserve side either, and the Press were not slow to criticise their team for such a poor performance 'while taking nothing away from the Leek of St David'. Partial honour was restored when Scotland thrashed Ireland 4-0 on 18 March. It was a different Scottish team, all Home Scots and with five Celtic players in it, presumably with the intention of persuading a large crowd (35,000) to come to Celtic Park. But the Irish supporters (both the ones who had come from Ireland and the Glasgow-Irish) must have been amazed to see Ireland take the field in light blue, and on the day after St Patrick's day at that!

On 1 April, Scotland went in glorious sunshine to the Crystal Palace. The 'glass house at Sydenham' as it was otherwise referred to, was a beautiful venue for this encounter. The play, however, was scrappy and *The Scotsman* was none too impressed by the lack of enthusiasm of the fans. 'The English enthusiast has not yet taken to this international so thoroughly as we do in Scotland', although according some accounts the attendance was 60,000. Others are more conservative (and plausible) at 32,000.

Scotland were marginally the better team with Peter Somers of Celtic particularly impressive, and indeed Bobby Walker of Hearts scored – only to have it disallowed because Alec Young of Everton was in an offside position. Then England scored a goal which was either brilliant or a fluke, depending on one's nationality. Joe Bache of Aston Villa 'swung a boot at the ball and it flew into the net' according to *The Scotsman*, whereas the English Press rave about a brilliant goal from thirty yards. *The Scotsman*, redolent of sour grapes and proving that there is no such thing as neutrality in Scotland *v.* England games, sums up the game thus: 'I trust you have gained the impression that England's victory was hardly deserved. On play it certainly was not.'

*   *   *

1906 saw a new era in British politics. In January, the Liberals of Henry Campbell-Bannerman, one of the very few Scotsmen to become Prime Minister, had defeated the Conservatives by a landslide, and seemed determined to force through some much needed reforms (before they themselves were engulfed by the rising tide of Socialism, as expressed in the large vote for the Labour Party). There was therefore a certain euphoria in the air as it seemed that life for the working man might be taking a turn for the better.

Scotland's miserable form seemed to be continuing in 1906, however, with the second defeat in a row by the Welshmen. This one was all the worse for being on Scottish soil, at Tynecastle, Edinburgh. Edinburgh had lagged behind Glasgow as a football city, but there was a tremendous crowd at Princess Street Station at 6 p.m on Friday 2 March 1906 to see the mighty Welshmen, in particular the three Jones forwards who had names like 'Lot' and 'Love' as well as the more mundane 'Richard' to differentiate them. The Welshmen were taken in their carriages to their hotel – the Old Ship Hotel in East Register Street – before going on to be entertained at the Empire Music Hall.

It was the Welsh who did the entertaining the following day at Tynecastle. *The Scotsman* was worried about the large crowd that was assembling. In fact there was a break-in at the northern or railway end of the ground, although the game was not affected, and everything began promptly at 3.30 p.m. 'after the usual tedious photographic operations'.

Scotland, without their star man Bobby Walker, played badly and the few chances that came the way of centre forward Jimmy Quinn were not taken, whereas for Wales 'Lot' and 'Love' Jones did what was necessary. 'Lot' scored in fifty minutes 'after a burst along the touch line, [he] flashed the ball in on goal and Raeside ought certainly to have cleared but somehow or other he managed to let the ball out of his hands and into the net past the foot of the post'. A huge groan apparently arose after this blunder by Third Lanark's Jimmy Raeside, but Scotland never lifted their game, and when 'Love' scored from the edge of the box midway through the half, most of the Edinburgh supporters realised that 'the game was up' and went home.

The very few Welshmen at the game were delighted at this first victory on Scottish soil. They shook hands with everyone they met in the environs of the ground and *The Scotsman* was forced to declare that 'the Welshmen are indeed a force to be reckoned with in international football'. Only Donny McLeod of Celtic had a good game for Scotland, and it was hardly surprising that wholesale changes were made for the visit to Dublin.

In the Edwardian era, a trip to Dublin would be the one most prized and cherished by a Scottish footballer, involving as it did a pleasant sea voyage to the Emerald Isle. This year it was actually on St Patrick's Day, 17 March 1906 and 8,000 (a good crowd for Dublin, which had never been a hotbed of football like Glasgow or Liverpool) were there in high spirits for the game. The weather was good, and the crowd were entertained by the band of the Cameron Highlanders who played Scottish and Irish music. It was not just the band of the Camerons who were there that day, however – the squaddies were there in strength as well, for on days like St Patrick's Day it was often an idea to have a low-key troop presence in case of political disturbances.

But the crowd were well behaved and thoroughly appreciated the play of the Scotsmen. Bobby Walker was back, but it was Tommy Fitchie of Woolwich Arsenal who got the only goal of the game. Fitchie was an interesting character. Normally he would not have been released by Arsenal for this game, as English teams tended to refuse such requests, but Fitchie was an amateur, had no contract and could therefore please himself. A patriotic Scotsman who had been born in Edinburgh but was brought up in London, he wanted to play for Scotland, told Arsenal so, and went.

Tommy did not retain his place for the England game. There was an added interest this year, for it would be the first to be staged at the new Hampden Park, built by Queen's Park for just such occasions. An amazing 102,741 turned up to see the game, and the gates were closed before kick-off time, to the disappointment of thousands. The writer of *The Scotsman* is lyrical about the crowd. He compares it (improbably) with Mount Vesuvius (which was experiencing one of its periodic seismic disturbances at the time) and goes on to say 'In the bright sunshine which prevailed, the spectacle, especially for those occupying a comfortable seat in the Press Box or reserved stands was a brilliant and imposing one… the roads and streets outside were literally black with thousands upon thousands eagerly hurrying towards the turnstiles'. £4,300 was raised that day.

Considering that the East Terracing hardly existed, and that the stand was a funny construction of two wide towers and nothing between, it stretches our credulity to believe that the crowd was so vast, but football fans in 1906 did not mind a little discomfort. Mercifully, no-one was seriously hurt and *The Scotsman* is very impressed by the police, the layout of the ground and the ample crush barriers.

The game was a good one, and Scotland won 2-1. England suffered an early blow when Harry Makepeace of Everton, himself a late replacement for Houlker, was carried off after a collision with Andy Aitken of Newcastle United and took no further part in the game. Makepeace was an interesting character, for as late as 1921 he also played for England at cricket, making him one of the very few to do so at both sports. Clearly England missed the Evertonian, but Scotland played superbly that day, both goals being scored by Jimmy Howie of Newcastle United. The first one seemed to have been saved by goalkeeper Ashcroft, but he was adjudged to be over the line by referee Nunnerley. England's goal came too late to make any difference.

* * *

1907 was Wales' year. They deservedly won the Championship, but their win against Scotland on Monday 4 March at Wrexham was a narrow one, a late goal from Grenville Morris from a rebound being all that separated the teams. 'Great cheering naturally followed this unexpected success and the Welshmen set themselves to defend their citadel with grim determination' says *The Scotsman*, and when 'hostilities ceased' it was still 1-0.

A team of Home Scots were then sufficient to dispose of Ireland at Celtic Park on 16 March, the same hotel serving as base for both teams and also for a party afterwards, for it was the eve of St Patrick's Day. Played in front of 26,000, Scotland won this one-sided game 3-0 and it could have been more, but the referee, Mr Lewis of England, blew for time five minutes early. Perhaps he was being kind.

6 April saw the first example of a Tartan Army being mobilised to go to a football match, rather than the odd bunch of eccentrics, as had been the case previously. Railway companies, realising that the game was in Newcastle, ran 'Football Specials' or 'Caledonian Excursions' from Edinburgh, and *The Scotsman* reckoned that about 8,000 Scotland supporters were there 'wearing kilts, glengarries and brandishing thistles' (imitation thistles, one presumes) from very early in the morning.

Yet the crowd was a disappointment. It was expected that St James Park would reach its capacity, but after 2 p.m. Newcastle United printed a few posters, rushed to the town centre and pasted them on billboards to the effect that there was plenty of room, and that anyone could come along. 35,829 saw a tame affair with the Scottish team of nine Anglos and two Home Scots (Charlie Thomson and Bobby Walker of Hearts) unable to force the victory that their vociferous travelling support demanded. 'The Southrons were as mediocre as the Northerns' said the frustrated *Glasgow Herald*. The game ended 1-1.

* * *

Football talk was dominated in 1908 by the great Celtic team and their famous centre forward Jimmy Quinn. Jimmy could get himself into trouble, but he was a prodigious goalscorer. Yet it was not he who was the talk of Dens Park Dundee when Wales came there on 7 March, for Quinn was not playing that day. The man who scored Scotland's late winner was Willie Lennie of Aberdeen, 'the marvellous midget', who ran from midfield between two defenders to score a wonderful solo goal and send 18,000 Dundonians home happy. This made the score 2-1, for Scotland had equalized when Bobby Walker of Hearts was brought down in the penalty box but instead of claiming a penalty, merely passed the ball (as he lay on the ground) to Alec Bennett to score. The referee, Mr Mason of England, played the advantage rule and allowed the goal. Considering Scotland's recent poor form against Wales, this was a good result.

Scotland then went to Dalymount Park, Dublin, and defeated the home team 5-0 with the mighty Quinn scoring four goals. It was a wonderful performance by the man from Croy, and he could not now be left out for the England game. The *Dundee Advertiser* thought that 'Old Sol must have been a lover of Scotland and Quinn, for it had rained incessantly up to kick-off, but it ceased miraculously whenever the referee blew his whistle so that the sun and stars could admire Jimmy's goals.'

Quinn's success posed a selection problem for the England game at Hampden on 4 April, for Anglos were available and Andy Wilson of Sheffield Wednesday had enjoyed a good season. Yet Quinn could not be ignored. In the end it was poor Willie Lennie who missed out as Quinn was given what had been his original berth for Celtic on the left wing. This seemed to be a good idea in the twenty-seventh minute when Quinn made a great run to the corner flag before firing across a great ball for Wilson to score.

England's equalizer was a debatable one. Windridge of Chelsea lashed a shot which beat goalkeeper McBride, then hit the bar (or, it was claimed, the net) then bounced down on or over the line – depending on one's viewpoint or nationality. Mr Mason, the English referee, gave a goal and Charlie Thomson, the Scottish captain agreed after the game that he thought the goal was a good one. This seems to have been the forerunner of the Geoff Hurst incident in the World Cup final of 1966 in that it was argued about for weeks afterwards, and Scotland felt hard done by. Most people in the crowd thought that if Quinn had been in the centre it might have been a different story, but other talking points were the record crowd of 121,452, the closing of the gates long before the start and the break-in by people who forced their way on to the running track, to be pelted by the stones and missiles of those at the back whose view was thus impaired. Fortunately nobody was hurt.

The previous day, the Prime Minister Henry Campbell-Bannerman, a fine Scotsman, had resigned on the grounds of ill health (he would die three weeks later) and Asquith was summoned to Biarritz where King Edward VII was on holiday to be asked to form a Government. Even that could not upstage the national obsession of football – in spite of those who did not like the game. According to the *Dundee Advertiser* '… so much is spoken against it by the clergy in the pulpit at Presbytery meetings and by those narrow-minded critics who cannot see anything better than their particular hobby'. Clearly, religion was now beginning to lose out to football – a trend that would continue for the next 100 years.

*   *   *

1909 was a poor Scottish year. For the fourth time in five seasons they lost to Wales, this time on St David's Day in Wrexham. Jimmy Quinn was a late withdrawal and had to be replaced by 'Sailor' Hunter of Dundee, but Scotland were 3-0 down at half-time, only coming into the game in the second half to pull two back through Bobby Walker of Hearts and Harold Paul of Queen's Park.

In a departure from precedent, Ireland came to Scotland to Ibrox on a Monday exactly two weeks after the Wales game. It was no departure from precedent, however, to see a great Scottish victory, this time 5-0, and the Man of the Match was Celtic's Jimmy 'Napoleon' McMenemy, who had the Ibrox stand 'rising time and time again to salute his brilliance'.

Napoleon was dropped in favour of Bobby Walker for the England game at Crystal Palace on 3 April. The weather was good (as on the previous occasion at the Crystal Palace) and the captains of the team were presented to the Prince of Wales who, in little more than a year's time, would assume the throne as King George V. But that was the end of the good news for Scotland, for George Wall of Manchester United scored two fine early goals and Scotland never got back into the game, even with Jimmy Quinn in the side and even with Jimmy Stark missing a penalty in the second half. Spotted in the crowd that day were two great cricketers – W.G. Grace, the legendary doctor of Gloucestershire and Archie McLaren of Lancashire, holder of the record number of runs for an innings – 424 against Somerset. They would have been delighted at how well England played.

*   *   *

1910 saw happier days return for Scotland – at least over England. Previous form had been inconsistent. They beat Wales 1-0 but lost to Ireland by the same margin. A poor game against Wales at Kilmarnock on 5 March had been brightened up only by a goal from Falkirk's Andrew Devine. Devine, playing his one and only international, got the ball 'well outside the penalty line [sic] and let drive without hesitation. The ball rose as it sped and hit the underside of the crossbar with awful force, glancing thereafter into the net. There never has been a shot like it on Rugby Park', says the scribe of the *Glasgow Herald* (with a touch of hyperbole, one feels). Scotland won by this solitary strike.

McMenemy was injured and Bennett was off form, but that does not entirely excuse the defeat in Belfast on 19 March. Defender George Law of Rangers should have stopped Ireland's only goal of the game, and Jimmy Quinn of Celtic had an off-day, clearly missing the service from his friend Jimmy McMenemy.

As a result, the writer of the *Dundee Courier* has a gloomy prognostication about the England game on 2 April 1910. 'While I would be pleased and surprised to see the Thistle emerge victors, it is a forlorn hope and the only result which can be looked forward to with any confidence is the downfall of Scotland'. This is strong, not to say treasonous stuff, but the writer goes on to say that playing Jimmy Hay at left-back is 'nothing short of an absurdity' and that Scotland's half-back line of Aitken, Thomson and McWilliam will never cope with the 'thrusts' of the Englishmen.

106,205 (a little short of the 121,000 of two years previously) turned up at Hampden Park to see it much changed, for it had been the scene of a riot in 1909 at the Scottish Cup final. A new telegraph station would be in operation to feed the eager English Press, desperate for news of the game, and much of the stand had been rebuilt as indeed had the surrounding wall. 284 police would be on duty, and thirty were detailed to escort the English charabanc from their headquarters at St Enoch's Hotel.

The game saw Scotland well on top throughout, and the two goals featured Jimmy Quinn. Templeton set up Quinn who charged through the full-backs and, when Hardy came out of his goal, Quinn's shot hit him but rebounded to Quinn's Celtic colleague Jimmy McMenemy, who made no mistake. Ten minutes later, Quinn once again avoided being sandwiched between the full-backs by charging through them at full speed and this time he scored himself.

The description of the crowd's reaction is illuminating. 'Flags and handkerchiefs could be seen waving, whistles were shrilling and bells were ringing' as the Scottish crowd erupted at such brilliance:

> *Didn't know Quinn?*
> *Pride of the Celtic?*
> *Look here, Saxon*
> *Where you bin?*
> *Not to know Quinn?*
> *Quinn of the Celtic?*

The Englishmen would certainly know all about him now, for he distributed the ball with genius. McMenemy was 'pure art' and Templeton did loads of back-heeling and generally played to the gallery. The much maligned half-back line of Aitken, Thomson and McWilliam was splendid, with McWilliam of Newcastle in particular singled out as 'Peter the Great'. In a few weeks time, he would go on to win an English Cup medal to add to the League medals that he already had. Scotland's reverse in Ireland did not matter too much in any case, for Wales beat Ireland and thus Scotland became the British Champions again.

*   *   *

1911 saw Scotland's international season open at Ninian Park, Cardiff on Monday 6 March. The crowd was only 14,000, but play was stopped when a barrier collapsed. It was a fine game, with Wales seeming to have won it when Morris took advantage of the absence through injury of Scotland's captain Peter McWilliam to score, but in the very last minute Bobby Hamilton of Dundee equalized. Wind and rain dominated proceedings at Celtic Park on 18 March when Ireland came, but Scotland, brilliantly served by outstanding inside forwards Jimmy McMenemy of Celtic and Sandy Higgins of Newcastle United, won comfortably.

The big game was, as always, the England one, this year played at Goodison Park, Liverpool – close enough to Scotland for ten special trains to leave St Enoch's Station Glasgow in the wake of the 'team' train, which was suitably decorated with a horseshoe and tartan ribbons. The horseshoe had been solemnly presented to Jimmy McMenemy at the station. The Scottish team was in the capable hands of Willie Struth, then trainer of Clyde but who would after the First World War become the legendary manager of Rangers. He made sure that there was no nonsense when they arrived at their hotel in Southport on the Friday night, for they were immediately taken to the music hall for innocent entertainment.

Instead of the expected 70,000, there were only 38,000 spectators – and most of them seemed to be Scots, as games outside of London involving England tended to struggle for attendances. The Scottish contingent had cause for complaint, for after England had scored against the run of play, just before half-time, Alec Bennett of Rangers put over a lovely cross which Newcastle's Sandy Higgins did not quite meet cleanly enough. Both he and the ball collided with the post, and the ball trickled over the line (according to the Scottish contingent) before it was cleared.

Scotland, convinced that they had been 'done' piled on the pressure in the second half. Jimmy McMenemy was outstanding, as was the player known as 'Swindon' Walker. John Walker played for Swindon – an unlikely provenance for a Scottish internationalist – hence his nickname to distinguish him from Bobby Walker of Hearts. The deserved equalizer did not come until two minutes from time, when the much-maligned Alex Smith of Rangers took a corner kick and this time Higgins met the ball cleanly and powered home a great header. A draw, however, was scant reward for a Scotland team who had played by far the better football. The 'goal that wasn't given' by Mr Nunnerley of Wales was much dissected and talked about for years afterwards, often in the context of the goal that was given for England at Hampden in 1908.

*   *   *

1912 might have seen another Scottish clean sweep. 1-0 over Wales at Tynecastle, 4-1 over Ireland in Belfast and then a draw with England at Hampden. Quinn scored Scotland's only goal at Tynecastle late in the game, then a poorish Scottish team easily beat Ireland who were themselves weakened by internal disputes (not for the first time) about how the game should be run, causing quite a few boycotts and refusals to play. Then Scotland lost their chance to beat England by a strange team selection.

127,307, a new record, were there at Hampden on 23 March, in spite of a countrywide railway strike which one would have thought would have affected the gate, given that rail was virtually the only way of travelling long distances at this time. But Scotsmen will find a way to get to see their team. Indeed, in the environs of the stadium some of the respectable residents were unhappy about 'the concourse of charabancs and other vehicular traffic' in the douce South side of the 'Empire's Second City'

The fans would have been surprised to see the mighty Jimmy Quinn on the left wing. Left wing had been Quinn's original position with Celtic, but he much preferred the centre. It would be recalled that Quinn played on the left wing in 1908 to accommodate Andy Wilson of Sheffield Wednesday. Quinn had made a goal that day four years ago, but 1908 paled into insignificance in comparison with his epic performance in 1910 where he virtually beat England on his own. Quinn was given the left-wing position in 1912 because Scotland were felt to be rich in centre forwards and another Sheffield Wednesday man, David McLean (who ironically left Celtic Park in 1909 because he could not get displace Quinn), was given a run in the centre, with Andy Wilson brought in at inside left.

Sadly, the ploy did not work this time. Quinn was 'like a square peg in a round hole' and Scotland had to be content with a 1-1 draw, the goal coming from Andy Wilson. The man of the match was Bobby Walker of Hearts, but he could not eke out a victory and this year's honours were shared, basically because Scotland were playing with three centre forwards and lacked sufficient midfield creativity.

*   *   *

1913 saw Scotland cock-a-hoop as they travelled to Wrexham to play Wales on Monday 3 March, for the Scottish League team had comprehensively defeated their English counterparts on the Saturday. Scotland might have done well, however, to play more of the Scottish League players against Wales – in the event only four played in both games – for the game at Wrexham, played in pouring rain, was a disappointing 0-0 draw. The crowd was only 5,000 – a bitter disappointment for the Welsh authorities who had spent a great deal of money to put in extra seats.

For some reason, the Irish game this year was played not in Scotland, but in Ireland at Dalymount Park, Dublin – thereby breaking the sequence of Scotland one year and Ireland the next. Ireland had already beaten England, but Scotland's weakened team was good enough to win 2-1. *The Scotsman* singles out Aberdeen's Donald Colman, the captain, for praise but correctly predicts that he will not be picked for the England game at Stamford Bridge, home of Chelsea. 'Had he been a Ranger or a Celt' it would have been a different matter, the reporter adds cynically.

To the chagrin of the Scottish Press, the Anglos outnumbered the Home Scots and thus at St Enoch's Station, Glasgow, on the day before the game, only five players boarded the train to the shouts of 'bon voyage' and 'play up'. They were Jimmy Brownlie (the Third Lanark goalkeeper), Bobby Walker of Hearts, the Rangers duo of Willie Reid and Jimmy Gordon and Celt Alec McNair, who as the press had correctly predicted got the nod over Donald Colman.

The game, played in front of 52,000 spectators, hinged on what we would now call a foul. It was a shoulder charge on goalkeeper Brownlie by 'Villain' (because he played for Aston Villa) Joe Hampton. Brownlie had the ball in his hands but 'the human hurricane from Birmingham was too quick for Brownlie who was bundled over the line with the ball in his possession'. To modern eyes this is a foul, but it was then considered perfectly legal, as long as the goalkeeper's feet were on the ground, and it was the shoulder, not the elbow which did the charging. Amazingly this piece of legal thuggery was allowed, and even approved of, until the early 1960s, when under Continental influence, it died out. The 1958 English Cup final had seen a particularly nasty example of this phenomenon.

The Scottish Press in 1913 does not complain about this goal, the only one in the game. Indeed, the referee was Scottish, a Mr Jackson. 'Looker-on' in the *Dundee*

London 1913. A private method of transport for the Tartan Army.

Advertiser says 'Tis a mad world, my masters' but does not refer to the dubious goal in this context. Rather, he attacks the Anglos who were not nearly co-ordinated enough. This was hardly surprising, for they possibly had never played together before and certainly did not know each other. Yet Scotland might yet have won with a bit of luck. Joe Hodkinson of Blackburn Rovers was sneered at. 'He got the notion that he could beat McNair by football... which showed he has much to learn', but this does sound like sour grapes. It was England who won the game.

*   *   *

Never had the *Glasgow Herald* been so enthusiastic about a football game as it was on Monday 6 April 1914. Three pages contained news about Scotland's marvellous 3-1 victory over England, driving off the pages any concern about the Orangemen in

Ireland threatening Civil War, Suffragetes starving themselves to death, the instability in the Balkan region or any possible war between the USA and Mexico, who were both spoiling for one. The ecstasy was divided equally between the quality of the performance (making up for dismal draws with Ireland and Wales earlier in the season) and the sheer size of the crowd. It was 115,000 – still some short of previous years – but over 40,000 had been shut out some thirty minutes before the kick off as the crowd was already of dangerous proportions. People from 'Stornoway to Sheffield' had been among the excluded and the writer was particularly sorry for the English 'trippers' who had been touring and shopping in the city and had left it too late.

Some of the unlucky ones saw some of the game. They climbed the hillock on the north side of the ground (the North Stand had yet to be built) and by dint of standing on each other's shoulders were able to give some sort of primitive running commentary to each other. The roar of the lucky ones inside the stadium would in any case have given them some sort of a clue about the outcome of the match.

Around 300 trams had left the city centre from noon onwards, and trains had left for Mount Florida 'every few minutes'. The crowd was 'spectacularly congested', particularly at the tops of the terracing where people refused to move down to where they could have more room. The crowd contained loads of England supporters with white rosettes and favours and also in attendance, as a guest of Glasgow's Lord Provost Stevenson, was the French consul and his wife.

'The result was a triumph of styles' chortles the *Glasgow Herald*'s leading journalist, 'the slow, calculated moves of the home forwards, the covering up and placing of the half-backs had no counterpart on the other side where all was flurry and confusion.' Charlie Thomson of Sunderland scored for Scotland in the second minute with a thirty-yard pile driver after a corner kick, then after England levelled undeservedly before half-time, Jimmy McMenemy simply took charge, spraying passes and dominating proceedings. It was McMenemy who put Scotland back in the lead with a rising shot, then, when he tried something similar ten minutes later, the ball hit the bar but rebounded for Rangers' Willie Reid to do the needful.

The game finished to the accompaniment of loud cheering for every kick of the ball that Scotland took, and Glasgow had seldom seen such celebrations as it did that night. It was a pity that an era had now come to an end, although no-one knew it at the time. The assassin's bullet was being prepared in Serbia and none suspected that of the six-figure crowd there at Hampden that day, an astonishing percentage would never see another International match.

THREE

From Victory International to Victory International

The years between the world wars of the early twentieth century were Scotland's best. Excluding Victory Internationals (for they are not considered official), Scotland, between seasons 1919/20 and 1938/39, played 60 internationals against the other British countries and won 34 of them with 10 draws, thus making Scotland clearly the best British team of the era. Against non-British opposition, Scotland played 15 games and won 10 of them. Over the period of twenty years, it would be hard to dispute the claim that Scotland were the world champions of football.

Yet with characteristic Scottish obstinacy, they refused to give themselves the chance to prove it officially. The World Cup started in 1930 and was played in 1934 and 1938 – but no British team took part. In 1930, the tournament was held in faraway Uruguay and attracted little interest in the British Isles. It is less easy to justify the attitude of the British authorities to the World Cup in 1934 and 1938, when the tournament was held in Europe and was won by Italy on both occasions. Scotland had actually lost to Italy on a tour in 1931, but in mitigation it must be said that it was by no means the full-strength Scotland team. It would have been interesting to see how a strong Scotland team would have fared in the World Cup of that era. Rather well, one suspects.

The years between the wars are studded with fine Scottish performances and great Scottish heroes. Pride of place must, of course, go to the Wembley Wizards of 1928 who beat England 5-1, impressing no doubt the watching Duke of York (later to become King George VI) who was entertaining the King of Afghanistan. But there were also magnificent trebles in 1921, 1925, 1926 and 1929 over the three home nations and the famous goal of 1933, which is credited for being the birth of the Hampden Roar.

Heroes abounded. There was Andrew Wilson in the immediate post-war years. Hughie Gallagher of Airdrie, Newcastle and Chelsea was an archetypal Scottish self-destruct character if there ever was one, a brilliant footballer but flawed personality. There was the dribbling wizard called Alec James, the great Rangers left-winger Alan Morton, dubbed the 'Wee Blue De'il' by an English journalist, the famous Bob McPhail ('Greetin Boab') and Celtic's legendary Jimmy McGrory.

Attendances were huge. The record is 1937 when 149,407 according to some accounts (and there were almost certainly more when one allows for the amount of boys who were lifted over the turnstile, and the amount of daredevils who scaled the walls) watched the Scotland *v.* England international, but wherever the game was played, there was always massive interest. Labour problems, General Strikes, world depression, unemployment, the Spanish Civil War and the rise of Hitler played very much second fiddle to the all-important questions of 'What will be Scotland's team against England this year?' and 'Will we win?'

Great Britain, in the months and years immediately after the First World War, was a curious mix of contrasts. Nominally the winners of the conflict (although the amount of widows, orphans and disabled ex-soldiers made one wonder what it would have been like to lose), the country obstinately and cynically refused to deal with her social problems, and as a result lawlessness and labour problems abounded among the many disturbed young men that the war had thrown up. Yet there was also a desire among those who survived to live and to enjoy life to the full before any other cataclysm visited itself upon mankind. To the Scottish working class, enjoyment meant an awful lot of football.

*　　　*　　　*

Scotland played two Victory Internationals in 1919 against England, drawing one and losing the other, but the first official international did not take place until Thursday 26 February 1920 at Ninian Park, Cardiff when Wales and Scotland drew 1-1. Wales were in fact the better side according to most sources, and Scotland were indebted to Tommy Cairns of Rangers for a late equalizer. A better result was forthcoming a fortnight later at Celtic Park, Glasgow when Scotland outclassed Ireland 3-0. A feature of this game was that Liverpool supplied both goalkeepers – Elisha Scott for Ireland and Kenneth Campbell for Scotland. Scott was the busier 'keeper and is to be credited for keeping the score down.

The England *v.* Scotland clash on 10 April 1920 was one of the best of them all. Hillsborough, Sheffield was the venue, the pitch was wet and muddy, a large contingent of 'tartans' (as they were described by the English Press) had made their way down and they saw a great game with Scotland just losing out. Kenneth Campbell was still in the goal for Scotland, but he had changed club since the Irish game, having joined Partick Thistle just a few days previously. Scotland, with Liverpool inside right Tommy Miller inspirational, were 4-2 up at half-time, but found the strong running Englishmen just a little too strong for them in the second half. England won 5-4, but Dundee's Alec Troup had the chagrin to see, in the last minute, his shot hit the upright and rebound to an England defender.

Scotland in fact deserved a draw, but their fans were none too despondent, many of them taking the chance to visit some of their old Army friends in the North of England.

* * *

1921 saw Scotland in the ascendancy when they beat all three British countries. A narrow but satisfactory win against Wales at Pittodrie (Aberdeen's second international) was followed by a 2-0 win in war-torn Belfast in a game played before a 30,000 crowd and a heavy presence of British soldiers. The war for Irish independence was of course in full spate in the South. The situation in the North, on the other hand, was far more complicated, and Belfast in particular existed in a state of anarchy as Protestants resisted the Catholic demand for independence.

But Scotland's greatest moment since the end of the war came on 9 April 1921 when they played brilliantly to beat England 3-0. The crowd was given as slightly less than 100,000, which was still outstanding considering the problems of transport brought about by rail strikes – a recurring theme of early twentieth-century Britain, for the same had happened in 1912. A feature of the game was the large number of England fans who had adopted a Great War song, in token presumably of their white shirts.

Scotland *v.* Wales, Pittodrie 1921. From left to right, back row: McMullan, Harris, Pringle, Cunningham, McStay, Marshall. Front row: Archibald, Wilson, Campbell, Cassidy, Troup.

Whiter than the whitewash on the wall
We'll wash you in the water
Where you wash your dirty daughter
And all will be whiter than the whitewash on the wall

Not for the first nor the last time was the performance of a goalkeeper a crucial one. This time it was the unfortunate Harold Gough of Sheffield United in the England goal who should have done better to prevent the second and third goals scored by Alan Morton and Andy Cunningham respectively. The first had been scored by Dunfermline's Andy Wilson in a scramble. (This man was Andrew Nesbit Wilson, not to be confused with the other Andy Wilson who played for Scotland before the war.) But, in spite of the goals being fortuitous ones, Scotland thoroughly deserved their win, and Glasgow went berserk that night. Scotland were the undisputed Champions of the British Isles!

Just at the start of that game, something remarkable had occurred. The National Anthem had been played, the teams were in position and the referee Mr Ward was just about to start when there appeared in front of the stand a line of men in Indian file, each with his hand upon the shoulders of the man in front of them. They wore either bandages on their eyes or dark glasses. They were the war-blinded being ushered in to their special enclosure in front of the main stand, where a few volunteers would give them a commentary and information on the game.

Some limped as well, some wore Glengarry hats with their ribbons fluttering in the breeze, a few had medals pinned to them. Others wore 'hospital blue' uniform, and the tail of this procession was brought up by a few men in wheelchairs or bath chairs. One of the English players went over to the referee and asked him to delay the start of the game until the wounded managed to get into their benches. Another English player began to clap, an action immediately copied by all the other players, English and Scots alike, and England left-winger Jimmy Dimmock of Tottenham Hotspur was seen to go across and shake hands with one of them, as the crowd joined in the clapping. Scotland would win that day, and all their players would be feted, but it was the war wounded and disabled who were still the real heroes.

*   *   *

The following season, 1921/22, saw a reverse at Wrexham in early February on the sensible day of Saturday – but there were extenuating circumstances. The game was played in a snowstorm which abated only intermittently, and there is a certain suggestion in some reports that the referee Mr Ward (who himself was seen out helping the groundstaff with a broom to sweep the snow off the pitch) only allowed play under severe pressure from both authorities who wanted play to proceed. They became even more insistent when a train full of wild-looking Scotsmen, who had themselves been delayed, arrived demanding action. The game was played with a ball which 'looked like a Christmas pudding' and Wales clearly adapted better to the conditions than Scotland did, leading 2-0 at half-time.

At half-time, with the snow intensifying, Mr Ward must have considered an abandonment, but again resisted his conscience. Indeed, shortly after the game restarted the snow stopped and a watery sun appeared. Scotland now struck back and Sandy Archibald scored halfway through the half, but Wales – through two men called Evans (they also had two called Davies and two called Jones that day) in the centre of their defence – managed to keep the great Andy Wilson from scoring.

Excuses about farcical conditions cut little ice in the eyes of the Scottish public and the selectors were compelled to make sweeping changes for the next game. Scotland had not now won in Wales for almost twenty years and this was considered a great slight on the nation's pride. One has to be sorry for Will Collier of Raith Rovers and Michael Gilhooley of Hull City whose only international this was, but the changes did produce a rich reward in that Scotland won the other two internationals.

The tradition of playing games against Ireland at Celtic Park was continued and Scotland won a poor game 2-1. Wilson got the goals after Ireland had gone ahead just before half-time, and a feature of this otherwise unremarkable encounter was that the ball got itself impaled on a spike of the railings that Celtic had been compelled to erect after crowd trouble at a game in 1920.

Villa Park, Birmingham was the venue for the England *v.* Scotland match in 1922. It was a close-fought encounter and Scotland were perhaps fortunate to edge it. Their goal inevitably came from Andy Wilson halfway through the second half, but it was a lucky one as the ubiquitous Wilson happened to get in the way of a goal-keeper's clearance. Campbell was in inspired form in the Scottish goal as Scotland registered their first win on England soil since 1903.

*   *   *

1923 saw Andy Wilson score in every one of the three internationals as Scotland won the Championship again. They drew with England but England's shortcomings against the other two countries meant that the 2-2 draw at Hampden Park was enough to win the title for Scotland. It was a fine game with both teams having enough chances to win, but Scotland's best performance of the campaign was at Love Street, Paisley, the home of St Mirren on 17 March when they beat Wales 2-0, Wilson scoring twice.

A lesson had been learned by the authorities following the snow in Wrexham the previous year. No internationals were scheduled for February, but the campaign opened in Belfast in early March. Such common sense was rewarded with a fine dry day and a good even game, with the teams only separated by an Andy Wilson goal halfway through the second half.

Wilson was clearly regarded as a hero in Scotland, even though he now played for Middlesbrough rather than Dunfermline. He was called 'King Andrew I' and 'Andrew King of Scots' but injuries were beginning to catch up with him. He played in spite of the handicap of a badly damaged arm, the result of a wound in the last year of the First World War, and he was quite clearly the hero of a nation who badly needed such a person. He had made his debut in the unofficial Victory International of 1919 under odd circumstances. He was still a patient in Stobhill Hospital but was allowed to go to see the match. Such were the vagaries of transport in these days that Scotland were a man short. Wilson volunteered his services and played!

He was clearly a remarkable man and it would take someone special to replace him as centre forward of Scotland. Fortunately, just such a person was waiting in the wings. A small but tough centre forward had appeared for Airdrie. This was Hughie Gallacher, without doubt one of the truly great exponents of Scottish football. Like many another true football genius, his private life was flawed and his pugnacity and determination on the field often led to unnecessary aggression against opponents and trouble with referees, but for speed, eye for goal and a superb shot, there were few finer than Hughie Gallacher.

It was Joe Cassidy of Celtic who held the centre forward spot in the first international game of the 1923/24 season. This was at Cardiff on 16 February 1924 and Scotland played distinctly badly to go down 0-2. Defeats by Wales were always hard to take, because the feeling persisted that, given Scotland's greater size and the sheer amount of professional football played by Scotsmen, Scotland should beat Wales. They hadn't for some time, however, particularly on Welsh soil (since 1903, in fact) and newspapers made fun of all the 'wails' that one heard when Scotland played Wales. It was fast developing into a national complex.

Changes were made for the Ireland game with only goalkeeper Bill Harper of Hibs and Alan Morton on the left wing retaining their place, such was the intensity of the emotion at losing yet again in Wales. Hughie Gallacher was now at centre

Hughie Gallacher, arguably Scotland's best player of all time. He won 20 caps between 1924 and 1935.

forward, but the team did not play well against Ireland at Celtic Park. The pitch was dry, the wind was blustery, the football was uninspiring. Scotland won 2-0, but the goals were late in coming and Gallacher, hard though he tried, could not get through the tough Irish defence of Sam Irving, Michael O'Brien and Billy McCandless. It was Andy Cunningham of Rangers who notched the first counter and Dave Morris, the commanding centre half of Raith Rovers, who headed the late decisive goal.

Gallacher did not get the nod for Scotland's first ever trip to the magnificent new Wembley Stadium, which had been built only a year previously. Wembley was without doubt the finest stadium in the world, built subliminally at least, if not consciously, with the idea that Britain, having won the First World War, deserved the greatest stadium. Indeed it was called the Empire Stadium. Sadly, there was little pay-off for winning a war in other aspects of life for the vast majority of the population.

Gallacher's Wembley moment was yet to come, but for the meantime it was Neil Harris of Newcastle United who had the centre forward berth and who was much involved in Scotland's only goal, which went in off the post and the goalkeeper's back! That was in the first half, but Scotland could not maintain their lead. England's centre forward was Charlie Buchan (who would later found a magazine called the *Football Monthly*) and his industrious work gave the ball to Walker of Aston Villa who equalized. For the rest of the game, England pressed but Buchan could not get the better of Morris and the game finished without further scoring, although England were prodigal of a few chances.

It was a fine experience for the Scots to play at this stadium. Indeed, comparatively few Scottish players would ever enjoy this privilege. Following the chaos at its opening the previous year in the English Cup final, the attendance was much restricted to 37,500 and there were wide empty spaces. Such draconian measures were unnecessary and in subsequent years, England *v*. Scotland games were much closer to the recognised capacity. It would be the attraction of going to Wembley that would encourage so many Scottish fans to save their money for the biennial trip in one of the greatest football traditions of them all.

*　　　*　　　*

There are those who argue, with some justification, that Scotland's team of 1924/25 was the best ever. Well captained by David Morris of Raith Rovers and bolstered in defence by the Old Firm pair of Willie McStay of Celtic and Davie Meiklejohn of Rangers, Scotland carried all before them. The left-wing Rangers pairing of Tommy Cairns and Alan Morton was particularly devastating, and up front of course was the new hero, Hughie Gallacher.

On a gluepot of a pitch at Tynecastle, Edinburgh on 14 February, Gallacher scored twice in a competent 3-1 victory over Wales. His first goal was good enough, a fine dummy then a shot from the edge of the box, but the second goal which effectively killed off the Welsh involved Gallacher beating five men including the goalkeeper, who dived at his feet as Hughie merely shifted his weight to the other foot and lobbed homewards. The 25,000 crowd were ecstatic and even his Welsh opponents clapped and shook his hand!

Before the Irish game in Belfast (which Scotland won competently 3-0), there was a bizarre attempt by an Irish newspaper reporter to claim that Hughie Gallacher was not Scottish, but Irish. This was presumably a confusion with Celtic's Patsy Gallacher, who was indeed Irish and equally talented, but a birth certificate proved the point to the red-faced Irish journalist. The Irish FA had refused to have anything to do with this mad behaviour, but they must have wished that Hughie was an Irishman!

It was the English, however, who would suffer most at the hands of the great wee Bellshill man. 92,000 were at Hampden on 4 April 1925 to see Scotland win decisively over the English, by 2 goals to 0 – and both were inevitably scored by Hughie Gallacher. The first was another of these goals that cause us to curse video recorders for having been too slow in being invented, for we must really take the word of journalists and supporters who claim that it was a fine shot from the edge of the box which screamed high into the corner of the goal. That was in the first half, and then his second came late in the game as England were threatening to equalize. It was a typical centre forward's goal he was simply on the right spot at the right time, but it clinched another hat-trick of Scottish victories over the three British countries.

* * *

1925 may or may not have been Scotland's best ever year, but it would be impossible to underestimate the effect that these victories had on the Scottish nation. Scotland had suffered dreadfully since the First World War as Lloyd George and his successors had spectacularly failed to make this country 'a land fit for heroes to live in'. Health and housing were appalling, industrial troubles were commonplace and there was the all-embracing, all-encompassing phenomenon of poverty, which even the short-lived Labour Government of 1924 had been unable to do anything about. Those who had jobs suffered dreadful conditions for unsatisfactory wages, and those who had no jobs suffered the indignity of rejection, joining the queues of those who ten years previously had been told that they were the life blood of the British Empire, but who now lacked limbs, suffered debilitating illnesses or simply could not face the world thanks to shellshock. Great Britain, they said, had *won* the war! It was indeed hard to disagree with the socialist claim that the Great War had been fought 'to make the world a safer place for Henry Ford and Pierpont Morgan', the two most famous capitalists of the day.

There were possibly two things which could alleviate the lot of the Scottish working man. One was alcohol – with its horrendous consequences – and the other was of course football with its heroes and stars. It is little wonder, given the malnutrition of the general population, that small footballers abounded and became heroes in the same way that Charlie Chaplin in the cinema was the small man hero who stood up against the big bully. Hughie Gallacher, Patsy Gallacher, Alec James, Alec

Troup, Alan Morton were all small men, and much loved by their fans in a form of subliminal identification.

But 1925 saw Scotland at its height, and what a pity it was that there was no World Cup in those days. Scotland would surely have won it, given the fact that the rest of the world lagged way behind Great Britain in football terms. Things were changing there as well, but it would be a few years before the Scottish Football Association would deign to play anyone in a full international apart from the other three British nations.

The 1925 team that beat England was made up entirely of Home Scots, i.e. players who played for Scottish teams – including, to one's surprise, Partick Thistle, Airdrie, Ayr United and Raith Rovers (who provided captain Davie Morris). Jimmy Nelson of Cardiff City had played against Wales and Ireland, but he was the only Anglo. There were two reasons for this dependence on Home Scots. One was that there were often problems (not for the first nor the last time in history) in getting Anglos released from their none-too-sympathetic clubs, but the other was the significant factor that the Scottish League was good enough.

This state of affairs was not destined to last for very much longer. The days of the great Airdrie and Raith Rovers teams were coming to an end, as they could not resist the temptations of a large transfer fee from English clubs. Davie Morris, for example, would soon go to Preston North End and Hughie Gallacher to Newcastle United. It was a sad fact of Scottish life that 'we are bought and sold for English gold'. It meant that careers took new and more lucrative turns – but the players concerned did not necessarily become any better.

*   *   *

The Scottish international team continued its triumph, repeating in 1925/26 what it had achieved the previous year. A notable success was achieved in Cardiff on Hallowe'en when Scotland beat Wales 3-0, the first triumph on Welsh soil since 1903. Central Station Glasgow saw a good send off on the Friday and a tumultuous return on the Sunday for the seven Home Scots in the team. Hyperbolic Press reports compared the much-awaited defeat of the Welsh on their home 'leek-growing' soil to the relief of Mafeking in the Boer War. It was as if a national scandal had been purged from the memory.

It was indeed a fine victory, made all the more significant by the changes of personnel from the previous season – Willie Robb of Rangers took over in goal, Adam McLean of Celtic replaced the injured Alan Morton, and two new inside forwards earned caps, both ex-Raith Rovers players – John 'Tokey' Duncan of Leicester City and Alex James of Preston North End (of the famous baggy pants). Surprisingly, Davie Morris, the captain and hero of the hour in April was dropped in favour of Tom Townsley of Falkirk.

Scotland now had the look of invincibility about them and for once in their history did not destroy themselves, but lived up to their awesome potential. The success was repeated at Ibrox in February 1926 when Ireland were put to the sword four times, with Hughie Gallacher, now a Newcastle United player, scoring an impressive hat-trick. He had visited Ireland with the Scottish League the previous November and had been the victim of a death threat! 'Someone must have found out that I am a Protestant', joked Gallacher. The threat may just have been a hoax, but in Ireland of the 1920s such things were always taken seriously. Not too seriously though, for Gallacher assured everyone that he could shoot better than the gentlemen of the IRA! On both the occasion of the Scottish League match and in the full international of the following February he proved his point.

The England game this year was held, not at Wembley, but at Old Trafford, Manchester on 17 April 1926. This was the first of the really big post-war invasions of what is now called the Tartan Army. Manchester was comparatively close to Scotland and trains were now frequent and reliable. In addition, the nation definitely had something to be proud about on the football field, whatever else was going wrong on the industrial and economic front where a General Strike was imminent. 'Shoals' of trains left Glasgow on Friday night to arrive very early in the morning in Manchester.

Thus it was that Mancunians awoke to people singing about Loch Lomond and the Wells O' Wearie. A more fitting song would have been 'Hey Johnnie Cope are ye waukin yet', but this was a peaceful occasion with friendship the order of the day. One thing was traditional, though, and that was the Manchester weather. It was raining heavily, but that did not dampen the Scottish spirits.

The mill girls from Lancashire were impressed by the kilted Scotsmen, some of whom would offer to show what, if anything, they were wearing underneath the traditional garment. The Germans in the First World War had called the Scottish regiments 'The Ladies From Hell' – a term much enjoyed by the Scots. Some would serenade the young girls (and even the older ones) with songs about Mary

Scotland v. England at Old Trafford 1926. From left to right, back row: Gibson, McMullan, Dougray (referee), Summers, Harper, Cunningham. Front row: Jackson, Gallacher, McStay, Hutton, Thomson, Troup.

Morrison and Banks and Braes, and were sometimes invited in for breakfast. One Manchester matron was quoted as saying that the Scots race was 'absolutely barmy', and another said that they all looked like Robbie Burns.

On paper, Scotland were far better than England, who had experienced a very poor season hitherto. But a major doubt was raised about the game itself, for the wind and the rain intensified throughout the morning. What saved the match was the wind because it prevented puddles of water gathering at any one spot. By afternoon, the rain had eased somewhat, but the pitch was very heavy.

The conditions did not suit Hughie Gallacher, and he was in any case well policed by his direct opponent, John Hill of Burnley. But he was involved in the only goal of the game with a fine pass for Alec Jackson of Huddersfield Town (previously of Aberdeen), who scored late in the first half. The second half was fast and furious with England battering the hard-pressed Scottish defence. Scotland relied heavily on massive boots up the park by Jock Hutton of Aberdeen and Willie McStay of Celtic for breakaways by the likes of Everton's Alec Troup. England came close twice near the end, but it was Scotland's day once again.

The Scots had now won back-to-back Grand Slams, and the feeling of invincibility persisted. Quality English newspapers, often far more interested in the exploits of Jack Hobbs and Maurice Tait on the cricket field, had to admit that the 'Jocks' and the 'Tam O'Shanters' were the kings of the football field. The big, wealthy English clubs seemed to share that opinion for the draining of talent from Scotland to England intensified.

*   *   *

However, trouble was brewing in that spring of 1926 for Great Britain as civil strife intensified. This time it was not Scotland *v*. England as it had been many times in the past – whether on the battlefield or nowadays (thankfully) on the football field. This was a deeper confrontation between rich and poor, boss and worker, capitalist and trade unionist. It was the General Strike which began in early May. Had it lasted more than a fortnight, the consequences would have been impossible to tell. As it was, the Trade Unions supinely caved in.

Contrary to what was said at the time and has been said since, this was far from a 'gentleman's disagreement' and a 'typically English way of settling differences'. The atmosphere of intimidation and vindictiveness was not forgotten, and if anything the grinding poverty became worse in the defeated coalfields of Lanarkshire and Fife. It would of course need another war and a new sense of political direction to solve that problem, but in the meantime the misery continued.

More and more, the working man in Scotland realised that football was all that he had and all that he was likely to have for recreation. Possibly boxing, greyhound, horse or pigeon racing challenged intermittently the all-embracing passion for football, but the only real mass sporting entertainment was the beautiful game. Furthermore, for a Scotsman, it was something that Scotland could very obviously do and do successfully. It would be a long time before Scotland would be able to accept that other nations could be as successful as they were. The tradition of Scottish supremacy died hard.

When Scotland did lose to England at Hampden on 2 April 1927, the nation was plunged into mourning. It was the first time that Scotland had lost at home since Wales beat them at Tynecastle in 1906, over twenty-one years previously, and the first time that Scotland had lost at Hampden since its opening in 1903. This particular result came as a shock as Scotland had comfortably disposed of Wales and Ireland, and indeed for large parts of the game against England at Hampden looked comfortably in charge. Morton was particularly in form on the left side of the field and his rival for the left-wing position, Adam McLean of Celtic, had been switched to the right and was also doing well. The redeployment of McLean had seemed like a trick to keep the Celtic supporters sweet, but it was working and indeed Scotland's goal had come from a cross ball from McLean to Morton. England were a hard working but none-too-inspired outfit, singularly failing for a large part of the game to get the ball to their great centre forward William Ralph Dean, commonly known as 'Dixie'.

But there are times when fortune is cruel to someone, and in this case it was Bob Thomson of Falkirk playing his first (and only) international. First Dean got the better of him to equalize when a more determined tackle might have won the ball, and then the luckless Thomson was woefully short with a backpass to allow Dean to score a late and ill-deserved winner for England.

For a while Hampden was stunned, almost unable to believe that England could actually beat Scotland. Then the heartless element turned on Thomson and booed him as he left the field, causing apparently a tremendous amount of distress to his family watching in the stand. But worse was to come. Captain Willie McStay, (the great uncle of Paul McStay of the 1980s and '90s) caught on the hop after the game, saw fit to criticize Bob in a singularly tactless fashion as he was looking for a scapegoat. McStay of course should never have done so, but it showed what it meant for a captain of Scotland to lose to England.

*   *   *

For a while it looked as if Scotland were in decline next season. They managed to throw away a two-goal lead in Wrexham to scrape home with a draw in October. Then Ireland managed a rare victory (only their third since 1884) at Firhill in late February. This was the international debut of Celtic's great Jimmy McGrory but Jimmy had a poor game, and Gallacher was back for the England game.

The team selection for Wembley on 31 March 1928 attracted a great deal of criticism, for it was full of little-known Anglos and contained only three Home Scots in Jack Harkness, the goalkeeper of Queen's Park, Jimmy Dunn of Hibs and Alan Morton of Rangers. There was a cartoon of the three of them on the train saying that if there were only one more, they could have had a game of bridge! But by the end of the game, there was good reason to believe that Harkness, Nelson, Law, Gibson, Bradshaw, McMullan, Jackson, Dunn, Gallacher, James and Morton would live for ever. They would be dubbed the Wembley Wizards.

The score was 5-1, but it was the manner of the victory that was significant. Frankly, England were overwhelmed. Alec Jackson scored a hat-trick (two of them were headers) and Alec James another two before England got a consolation goal. It was a wet miserable day, but the Scottish supporters went berserk with joy. There were probably not as many of them there as would appear in later years, but those who did attend would talk about this game until their dying day. Not until Celtic won the European Cup in 1967 would Scotland have a finer football day.

* * *

The following year was another famous Scottish victory, although it was perhaps more for its unusual nature than the quality of the football on view that it became well known. 13 April 1929 was a gusty, windy day at Hampden Park, and already the 'Hampden swirl' was a known factor in games there. It seemed that as the terracing was high, the wind was sucked into the ground to create all sorts of problems for the players. The game was poor with England, who were, if anything, marginally the better team. Scotland suffered a grievous blow when Alec Jackson of Huddersfield Town was taken off with what looked like a broken elbow. It was not as serious as that, but Jackson tells the story of how he was lying in the Victoria Hospital, aware that the game must now be nearly over, when he heard a huge roar.

What had happened was that in the last minute Scotland had forced a corner on the right at the Mount Florida end of the ground. Alex Cheyne of Aberdeen tried an inswinger, hoping perhaps to find the head of Hughie Gallacher or centre half Davie Meiklejohn of Rangers who had gone up for the corner. The ball was caught in the swirl, goalkeeper John Hacking of Oldham Athletic jumped too early and the ball sailed past everyone into the net. There was a moment's pause before referee Mr Josephs (notorious for his long dramatic pauses before making a signal) turned and pointed upfield. Not everyone knew that it was legal for a goal to be scored direct from a corner kick, and there was a certain confusion before the roar which Jackson heard.

This completed another domestic treble for Scotland, for they had already comfortably disposed of Wales and Ireland, Hughie Gallacher having scored a hat-trick against Wales at Ibrox and five goals against the Irish in the 7-3 rout in Belfast. As Champions of Britain, Scotland now broke new ground by going on a continental tour of Norway, Germany and Holland. It was not a first-choice Scottish team because some were unavailable – Gallacher for example was on a tour of Italy with his team Newcastle United – and it was a light-hearted, almost patronising experience as Scotland showed the Continentals their game.

* * *

Eyebrows had been raised at the visit to Berlin, for forgiveness about the First World War had not been entirely achieved throughout Scotland. Germany still suffered a certain amount of international isolation and opprobrium, not being welcome at the League of Nations, for example, until many years after the conflict. But other

Scottish teams, notably Celtic, had played in Germany since 1918 and had been impressed by the reception. In fact Germany put up a fine show and would have beaten Scotland had it not been for a late equalizer from St Johnstone's Willie Imrie. Norway and Holland were competently dealt with, however, and Scotland would have been justified in calling themselves the Champions of Europe.

At this time there were moves afoot to begin a World Championship, the Jules Rimet Cup – the first one to be held in Uruguay in 1930. Scotland and England refused to go. British football did not need to prove itself on such exotic pastures as South America. Season 1929/30 saw Scotland off to a comfortable start by defeating Wales 4-2 in Cardiff and Ireland 3-1 at Celtic Park, but Scotland received a severe blow to their pride at Wembley in April when revenge was extracted for the Wembley Wizards of two years previously.

This time it was England who were the Wembley Wizards as Scotland went down 2-5. The defeat cannot entirely be blamed on the absence of Hughie Gallacher, who chose to play for Newcastle against Arsenal that day. Newcastle were battling against relegation and insisted that Gallacher should play for them. Gallacher, who had hitherto been anything but a dedicated team man for the Geordies, on this occasion toed the line – to the immense distress of the Scottish nation. It was of course hardly the first or the last of a 'club *v*. country' tug of love – something that causes intense angst to the average Scots fan. What was less easy to explain, however, was why Jimmy McGrory of Celtic was not chosen as the replacement, the honour going instead to James Fleming of Rangers, a competent centre forward but not as good as McGrory, who was now reaching his peak. It was probably the repeated refusal to pick McGrory for a game at Wembley that alienated (at least temporarily) the Celtic support from the Scotland squad. Being representatives of an ethnic and religious minority (albeit a large one) Celtic and their fans were often prickly about Scotland – feelings not helped when Rangers fans often sang Scottish songs like the Wells o' Wearie and Loch Lomond in their repertoire. It was often claimed (and not entirely without cause) that Celtic fans were not interested in Scotland. At certain points in history, it would have to be conceded that this was the case.

It was, however, not the absence of McGrory that was the cause of the defeat. It was the defence in 1930 that let Scotland down, for England were four goals up within the first half-hour! Buchanan and Meiklejohn of Rangers (who sometimes, it was believed, got things too easily in Scotland) were all at sea against Crooks, Jack and Watson and for a while double figures looked possible. The Scots, however, rallied and achieved the comparatively respectable score of 5-2.

The selectors clearly blamed goalkeeper Jack Harkness for some of the carnage, and when Scotland sailed to France to play in Paris in the middle of May, they had with them the young John Thomson of Celtic, who had impressed everyone at club level and with several good performances for the Scottish League. Hughie Gallacher was back on board as well and scored Scotland's two goals in their comprehensive 2-0 victory. Later that summer the first World Cup was held in Uruguay, but it was an event virtually unnoticed in the British Isles.

*   *   *

The 1930/31 season saw two depressing draws against Wales and Ireland, but a fine victory at Hampden over England. The game against England had at least one distinguished Scottish supporter. It was none other than the first ever Labour Prime Minister, J. Ramsay MacDonald, now at the head of his second Government. The illegitimate boy from Lossiemouth had done well to reach so far, but his supporters were becoming more and more disillusioned with his inability to solve the unemployment problem, let alone introduce the paradise on earth which they had heard so much about. In a few months time, he would welsh on his Labour credentials and form a National Government with the Tories! Nobody knew that, however, as he was introduced to all the players, earning a huge cheer from the Scottish support. His demeanour in the Hampden stand throughout the game made it plain that he was an unashamed Scotland supporter.

This was a season in which only Home Scots were deployed. At long last, Jimmy McGrory was given a game against England and he thanked the selectors with a goal shortly after George Stevenson of Motherwell had scored a somewhat fortuitous one. That the Scottish victory was never in doubt was due to Meiklejohn's stranglehold over Dixie Dean. Scotland then went on another tour of Europe with a weakened side containing, for example, no player from either Celtic or Rangers, who were on tours of their own. A stern lesson that Continental teams had to be taken seriously from now on was handed out by two thrashings: 5-0 from Austria and 3-0 from Italy. Scotland rallied however and beat Switzerland 3-2 on the last match of the tour.

*   *   *

The first Home International of the new season was a very difficult one for all concerned. It took place at Ibrox on 19 September 1931, exactly two weeks since Celtic and Scotland's John Thomson had met his death in tragic and accidental circumstances at the same ground. The man accidentally responsible for the death was called Sam English and he might have been chosen for Ireland. It was perhaps as well that he wasn't. McGrory of Celtic and the three Rangers – Meiklejohn, Brown and McPhail – had all played in the game in which Thomson had died and it cannot have been easy for them, nor for Bob Hepburn of Ayr United who took over in goal. Scotland beat a poor Irish side 3-0.

Another win was registered at Wrexham in October 1931, although it was a tighter affair and Scotland had to work hard to get their 3-2 victory. Disaster followed at Wembley in April 1932. Once again the selectors did not go for Anglos because of problems of availability, and chose all Home Scots. This was understandable, but less logically, Jimmy McGrory of Celtic and Bob McPhail of Rangers were not playing in favour of Neil Dewar of Third Lanark and Charlie Napier of Celtic. Napier was not in his best position, and Dewar was adequate, but hardly in the McGrory or Gallacher category. Scotland played very badly and lost 3-0, although they did manage to regain a modicum of respectability with a win over France in Paris a month later – and Dewar scored a hat-trick.

1933 is, however, one of the more famous years of Scotland's history against England. A thrashing by Wales in October 1932 at Tynecastle meant that McGrory and McPhail simply had to get their places back, and they were joined by Aberdonian Douglas 'Dally' Duncan of Derby County on the left wing. All three had teamed up for Scotland's first goal, but then England equalized and as the game wore on, it looked as if a draw would have to suffice.

But then the 'Hampden Roar' was born, first in the level of encouragement, then in acclaim for a great winning goal. 'Doc' Marshall found McPhail, who released McGrory with an inch-perfect pass. McGrory then rounded the full-back and as goalkeeper Harry Hibbs came out to narrow the angle, fired a superb shot into the far corner of the net. The 134,000 crowd went berserk, and the roar was apparently heard all over Glasgow. It was, of course, more than just the cheer of a football crowd in appreciation of a great goal. It was a nation's cry as the pent-up frustration of all the depression years (and the genuine fear of what was beginning to happen in Germany and elsewhere in Europe) was for once released. It was a thoroughly cathartic experience. Scotland had beaten England (and a talented English side it was) and that was all that mattered for the moment. It also meant that, for a spell, the Old Firm rivalry was put to the back burner for the two main participants of the goal and the victory had been Bob McPhail – 'Greetin Boab' – of Rangers and Jimmy McGrory, Celtic's greatest ever goalscorer. Catholic and Protestant did not matter quite so much when Scotland beat England!

*   *   *

But the wheel of fortune turned immediately and 1933/34 saw Scotland in the unusual position of taking the wooden spoon, losing to all three British nations, the 0-3 defeat at Wembley in 1934 being particularly hard to bear, as it was the third defeat at Wembley in a row. England were indeed taking revenge for the Wembley Wizards of 1928. It was difficult to rationalise why the Scottish side had collapsed so swiftly, but certainly a factor was the inconsistent, erratic and quixotic team selection. The legitimate question was posed, yet again, by both sets of Old Firm fans as to why McPhail and McGrory, the successful partnership of last year, were not included this time. Neither of them in fact ever graced the Wembley turf. It was just as well perhaps that Scotland showed no interest in the 1934 World Cup. It might have been a forerunner of things to come.

Things took a turn for the better the following year. Although Ireland snatched a late winner to triumph in Belfast in October 1934, Scotland beat Wales at Pittodrie a month later, and then in front of a massive crowd, which included the Duke of York (the future King George VI who genuinely liked football) in April 1935, Scotland recorded their fourth successive Hampden victory over England. Both goals came from corner kicks taken by Charlie Napier of Celtic and scored by Dally Duncan of Derby County. This game was watched by 129,000 and it would have been more if the authorities had not panicked and closed the gates with thousands still outside. The police, however, were unable (and in some cases unwilling) to stop the hundreds who scaled the wall.

The next year, 1935/36, saw Scotland draw with Wales, beat Ireland and then in a classic encounter on a windy day at Wembley gain one of their most famous draws. England had gone ahead but Scotland were pressing furiously and towards the end of the game gained a penalty when Johnnie Crum was brought down in the box. The job of taking the penalty fell to young Tommy Walker of Hearts. Wembley was hushed as he placed the ball. He walked back to take the kick... but the wind had blown the ball off the spot. Calmly, he replaced it. Then the same thing happened again. The crowd were now in a frenzy of impatience but Tommy, showing a very cool temperament, slotted the ball home.

Scotland deserved a win, but had to be satisfied with a draw and it was enough to win them the International Championship, for which they were awarded a new trophy. It was called the King George Jubilee Cup in honour of the twenty-five years that King George V and Queen Mary had been on the throne. Sadly, the old king did not live to see this game, for he had died in the January of that year. But his wife, who had been introduced to both the Scottish and the English teams as long ago as 1893, was still alive – and indeed would survive for almost another couple of decades.

*　　　*　　　*

Scotland's next two Home Internationals were played against the backdrop of politics. Germany came to Scotland in October 1936 to play at Ibrox Park, and their country's flag, quite rightly, had to be flown from the flagpost. This was the hated and offensive swastika, already the scourge of large parts of Europe as Hitler had already taken over the Saar Valley, was persecuting his Jewish population, involving himself in a civil war in Spain, making an unhealthy alliance with Mussolini and casting covetous eyes on Austria and Czechoslovakia. He might well have been jealous of Scotland as well, for Jimmy Delaney scored both goals in Scotland's 2-0 victory.

It was domestic politics which dominated the pre-match talk on Wednesday 2 December 1936 at Dens Park, Dundee. Wales were the opposition and they had a massive support with them, singing *Land of My Fathers* and other songs which are now more identified with Welsh rugby crowds. But Great Britain was in the throes of an unprecedented crisis in which it seemed that the King, Edward VIII, would have to resign or abdicate because of his twice-divorced American lady friend Mrs Wallis Simpson. Edward did in fact abdicate a few days after Wales had beaten Scotland 2-1, continuing their good run of success against Scotland at this time.

17 April 1937 saw at least 149,547 people inside Hampden Park for the world-record crowd. Walking past posters inviting everyone to join the International Brigades in the fight for Spain, the crowd took the advice to arrive early, but even so the gates had again to be locked as even Hampden could not swallow the amount of people wanting to see football at that time. A week later a similarly huge crowd would turn up to see the Scottish Cup final between Celtic and Aberdeen: such was the insatiable appetite for football in Scotland in the 1930s.

England, with a very impressive team containing Stanley Matthews and Raich Carter, were on top for most of the first half but only had one goal to show for their efforts. They had cause to regret this, for Scotland were a transformed team in the second half and won 3-1 thanks to a goal from Frank O'Donnell and two from old 'Greetin Boab' McPhail. Scotland then went on tour of Europe – to the now tense Austria and Czechoslovakia (who were both imminently expecting the Nazi jackboot). Scotland drew with Austria and beat Czechoslovakia 3-1, and left for home having agreed a return match in December at Hampden.

Scotland would win that game in December 1937 5-0, some recompense for a miserable autumn which had seen a defeat in Wales and an uninspiring draw against Ireland at Pittodrie. But the game which really mattered to the Scotsman, as always, was the one against England at Wembley in April 1938. This time Scotland won to give them their first Wembley victory for ten years. The same Tommy Walker who had scored the penalty in 1936 gave Scotland an early lead, and from then on rugged defending by Bill Shankly, Andy Anderson and Tommy Smith kept out the star-studded England forward line, in which the young Stanley Matthews was already being dubbed 'The Wizard of the Dribble'. A curiosity of this game was that Scotland fielded four players from Preston North End.

* * *

The 1938/39 season was played under the shadow of impending and inevitable war. Hitler had been bought off in the autumn of 1938 when he was given part of Czechoslovakia, and Scotland 'celebrated' by completing the comparatively unusual feat of beating both Ireland and Wales, something that had not been achieved for almost a decade. Hungary then came to Ibrox in December to lose 3-1, with rumours abounding that some of the Hungarian team intended to apply for political asylum and to stay in Scotland rather than return and face a future which was not so much uncertain as definitely pessimistic.

Scotland's last international before the Second World War was a weak 1-2 defeat to England at Hampden Park. England's winning goal came late, but they were well worth their victory. A feature of this game was the impassioned singing of the National Anthem. Scottish fans booing during the National Anthem is a comparatively new phenomenon dating only from the 1960s. It was usually treated with respect, and on this occasion both England and Scotland supporters sung fervently. War seemed only days away following Hitler's seizure, by sheer brute force and without any pretence at diplomacy of the rest of Czechoslovakia.

War was declared in September of that year. Internationals between Scotland and England continued to be played, albeit on an unofficial basis. The reason for this, of course, was propaganda. For Scotland it was almost always bad news, in that weakened Scottish teams whose players were overseas or otherwise unavailable, almost inevitably lost to England, conceding six goals on three occasions and infamously eight on 16 October 1943.

Yet these games were always well attended, frequently by royalty, Prime Minister Winston Churchill or Field Marshal Bernard Montgomery, showing that love of football was not to be killed off by Hitler. The BBC World Service would broadcast these

Field Marshal Montgomery is presented to Matt Busby before a wartime international at Hampden.

Prime Minister Winston Churchill is presented to the Scottish team before a wartime international at Wembley.

games to the African Desert, Italy, Burma and the High Seas and they were much appreciated by the troops, even though the laugh was often on the 'Jocks' for their team's poor performances.

*   *   *

The Scots would have the last laugh, however, on 13 April 1946 in the Victory International. Most of the troops were home. Hitler had been dead for almost a year, and the hunting out of Nazi criminals was in full progress throughout war-devastated Europe. The widows and orphans were learning how to face life. In Britain, the Labour Government was beginning its gargantuan task of creating a Welfare State so that there would be no more poverty and no more want.

Hampden Park was full to its 140,000 capacity as one would expect. The only difference was in the amount of soldiers in the crowd, including quite a few curious Americans. In homes throughout Scotland, the old battered radio on which messages such as 'fight them on the beaches' in 1940 and 'the morning has come' in 1944 were broadcast to the nation was now being used for a more peaceful purpose of the Scotland v. England Victory International.

How the war-weary Scottish nation with the limbless ex-Servicemen, the shell-shocked veterans of Dunkirk and D-Day, the heroes, the Home Front, the conscientious objectors and even the war profiteers rose of one accord that bright April day to acclaim the only goal of the game, Jimmy Delaney's late winner! Now the war was indeed over. Scotland and England had been an unbeatable combination against Hitler, but now more peaceful times beckoned and this meant that, on the football field at least, England became the enemy once again – albeit one with whom you shook hands at the end of ninety minutes!

FOUR

Welfare State and World Cups
1946-1960

It is very easy to become nostalgic about this era. In life in general, there was an improvement in almost everything, as Britain, under the vigorous leadership of Labour's Clement Attlee followed by benign Conservatives like Winston Churchill and Harold McMillan, at long last began to learn the secret of producing healthy babies and, to a large extent, to solve the appalling problems of poverty, bad housing, shocking education and general neglect of health services which had been a feature of life since the Industrial Revolution.

Full employment now became the norm. Not only that, there was usually loads of overtime as the nation suffered from the opposite of unemployment. Foreign workers were brought in to do the jobs that the native Britons scorned – a phenomenon that would lead to a certain amount of social unrest, albeit in England rather more than Scotland. Wars seemed to be over, although there was Korea and the tiresome necessity of National Service. This was the obligation on healthy young men to serve in the forces for two years. It was mercifully abolished in 1961, although it played havoc with careers and love affairs, not least those of professional football players.

By 1960, foreign holidays were a possibility for the working family. Cars, televisions and telephones began to change lifestyles and the quality of life improved. Milk was pumped into babies with relentless ferocity, and needles stuck in their arms by grim-faced white-coated nurses to eradicate most of the dreadful diseases of the 1930s. On the football field, there appeared floodlights and a white ball. Goalkeepers no longer wore thick polo-necked yellow jerseys, and referees didn't always wear black.

*　　*　　*

Times were indeed 'a-changing' as the song said, but one thing that did not alter was the Scotsman's deep and passionate (and to a large extent unrequited) love for his international football team. In particular, the new age meant that the World Cups of 1954 and 1958 could be watched on television, and that the general prosperity meant that the biennial trip to Wembley to see the England *v.* Scotland game was no longer determined by whether one could afford it, but rather whether one could obtain a ticket. There was, sadly, a flourishing black market for Wembley briefs, as well as a quasi-masonic secrecy about how they could be got.

It was an era in which Scotland produced many good players but failed to produce a good team. Rather too frequently did Wales and Northern Ireland beat Scotland. The returns from England games at either Hampden or Wembley tended to resemble funerals – in stark contrast to the exultant and euphoric departures. Scotland did well at Wembley in 1949 and 1951, respectably in 1947 and 1953 but the games in 1955, 1957 and 1959 were miserable disappointments. Scotland never beat England at Hampden between 1937 and 1962 and, apart from one particular last-minute heartbreak in 1956, never really looked like doing so.

On the world stage, Scotland had their moments, beating teams like Spain and Portugal now and again, but made the fatal and to us, half a century later, incredible mistake of not taking the World Cup seriously enough. Incredibly, Scotland might have gone to Brazil in 1950, but insisted that they would only go if they were the British Champions! In 1954 and 1958, the lackadaisical approach of the authorities – in stark contrast to the enthusiasm of the Press and the public – meant that the tournament was grossly under-prepared for. It was a shame, for there were in Scotland enough good players at that time to make some sort of an impact if they had been properly led, but as a German general said of the British Army in the First World War, it was a case of 'lions led by donkeys'.

*   *   *

The euphoria engendered by Jimmy Delaney's late goal in the Victory International of April 1946 can never be underestimated. The boost that it was to a war-weary nation would last for a good few years – indeed it would have to, for Scotland were a long time in getting back into any sort of form. The first post-war international was at Wrexham on 19 October 1946 where 29,568 (most of them Scots using up their 'demob' money on release from the Services) saw a poor Scottish team go down 3-1 to Wales, even though Willie Waddell of Rangers had given Scotland the lead with a penalty.

In spite of this reverse, some 98,776 fans turned up at Hampden to see Scotland *v.* Ireland in the first post-war home international match on 27 November 1946. This would be an astonishing attendance in any circumstances, but when one considers that this was a Wednesday afternoon on a dreich stereotypical Scottish November day, the figure is almost incredible. But such was the love of the Scottish football team. What a shame that the crowd were rewarded, (or perhaps punished) by a 0-0 draw!

The first visit to Wembley in April 1947 (after the worst Scottish winter of all time) was also a draw, this time 1-1, but historians tend to agree that this was one of the better England *v*. Scotland games. Prime Minister Clement Attlee thought so, apparently, and was frequently seen to be clapping the play of both teams. A man of few words and notorious for his laconic replies, Clem, when asked if he enjoyed the game, apparently said 'yes'. Andy McLaren of Preston scored for Scotland, but it was matched by a goal from the great Raich Carter.

Scotland then went on a trip to Belgium and Luxembourg. Scotland was much loved in these countries for the part that her soldiers had played in liberating them, and the Scottish team was given a tremendous ovation by over 50,000 Belgians at the Heysel Stadium in Brussels. Scotland unluckily went down 1-2, but then went on to beat Luxembourg 6-0.

* * *

1947/48 was one of Scotland's worst ever seasons. Defeats in the autumn by Ireland in Belfast and Wales at Hampden were followed by a particularly inept performance at Hampden as they lost 0-2 to England. Loads of enthusiasm and passion were in evidence both on the terraces and the field itself, but this was not matched by any great skill or cohesion. Chances were missed in front of goal by Scotland, but England were very clinical in the acceptance of the chances that came their way. England finished the game well on top with the Hampden Roar reduced to a whimper.

The summer saw defeats in Switzerland and France after a creditable victory had been achieved over Belgium at Hampden. But Scotland were slowly beginning to gel, to learn from each other and, more importantly, the selectors were beginning to pick a team which could play together.

If 1947/48 was very bad, then 1948/49 was very good, for Scotland comfortably disposed of Wales at Ninian Park, Cardiff, then came back from losing two goals in the first five minutes to get the better of Northern Ireland at Hampden. They followed this with a famous victory over England, 3-1 at Wembley.

* * *

This 1949 game is known to posterity as 'Cowan's Wembley' in honour of the fine performance of the Greenock Morton goalkeeper Jimmy Cowan. Particularly in the early stages of the game, England threatened to overwhelm Scotland with wingers Matthews and Finney on song and supplying Milburn and Mortensen with loads of good quality balls, but Cowan defied them all with breathtaking saves. Having survived the early barrage, Jimmy Mason of Third Lanark headed Scotland in front, then after half-time Billy Steel of Derby County hoodwinked the English defence with another before Laurie Reilly of Hibs headed home a third.

Scotland were thus 3-0 up, but the game ended as it had begun with a barrage on Cowan's goal. Newcastle hero Jackie Milburn scored with fifteen minutes to go, and the last quarter of an hour saw some desperate Scottish defending and more inspirational goalkeeping from Cowan. The full-time whistle unleashed such a tide of pent-up emotion among the Scots at the ground and those following the radio commentary on the BBC's Home Service back home, that it was well into the middle of the following week before the ecstasy evaporated. Scotland then celebrated their recapturing of the Home International Championship by beating France 2-0 at Hampden, once more astonishing the world by their ability to attract 125,683 to see a friendly on a Wednesday afternoon (and using the occasion to wear again the Rosebery colours of yellow and purple).

Scotland then took a strong party to tour the United States between May and June 1949. They did not play any official internationals, merely a series of exhibition games, and they were generally very well received by the Scottish-American population. Somewhat embarrassingly, however, Scotland managed to lose one game 0-2 at the end of May to a team called Belfast Celtic. The Celtic no longer existed in Northern Ireland, having been compelled to close down after crowd trouble involving Linfield supporters, but this is their most famous result of all time.

*   *   *

The 1949/50 campaign was technically a World Cup qualifying group. Scotland and England had been invited to go to Brazil to take part in the World Cup. England accepted unconditionally, but Scotland, bizarrely and arrogantly, said that they would only go if they were the British Champions! There was no great public outcry at this, it must be said, for Brazil was a very faraway country and the World Cup meant, as yet, little to the Scottish public. The public's issue was, as always, beating England, but a little leadership might have been expected by the SFA, who gave the impression that they were concerned that the cost of transport to Brazil might be somewhat prohibitive. Indeed, a long sea voyage would not have been cheap – but there was no lack of money in the Scottish game at that point.

The campaign began on 1 October 1949 against the country now officially called Northern Ireland, for Eire or the Republic of Ireland was now recognised as a separate country and players from the twenty-six counties could not officially play for Northern Ireland. This 'rule' was honoured more in the breach than in the observance, it must be said, but it mattered little on this occasion.

Scotland utterly outclassed the Irishmen that day, winning 8-2. The hero of the hour was the East Fife centre forward Henry Morris, who scored a hat-trick. Henry was not the only East Fife man playing that day, as George Aitken also played well at centre half. Alas for Henry, however, this turned out to be his only appearance, and he thus has the rare distinction of scoring a hat-trick for Scotland on his debut and never being picked again!

Wales presented a more difficult challenge, as always. Hampden on Wednesday 9 November was dark and misty, but Scotland were professional enough to win 2-0. This time the goals came from Celtic's John McPhail and Clyde's Alec Linwood. One could hardly say that selection of the team was consistent in those days, for neither McPhail nor Linwood were playing against England in the spring and, in Linwood's case, never again for Scotland. He must have sympathised with Henry Morris.

Above Scotland playing cards before the game against England in 1950. Cards might have been a better option, for they lost 1-0.

Right 1950. Jimmy Mason, Third Lanark and Scotland, is not exactly dressed for football, but there is little doubt whose side he will be on!

Hearts and Scotland legend Willie Bauld. Willie famously hit the bar in 1950 to deprive Scotland of her chance of going to the 1950 World Cup.

England came to Hampden on 15 April 1950. If Scotland won, they would go to Brazil; if England won, Scotland would not. But what if it were a draw and the Championship were shared? In any case, Scotland were holding up the World Cup by their refusal to give a decision, and we had the ludicrous spectacle of FIFA pressing Scotland for their answer with Scotland saying 'wait', for they drew the biggest crowds in the world and, not only that, Great Britain had recently won a war! They could therefore dictate terms. The programme cover for the day shows a couple of swarthy gentlemen standing on a map of South America pleading and begging Scotland to attend!

For the game itself, Scotland picked a forward line of five Willies, as it were: Waddell, Moir, Bauld, Steel and Liddell. It was Willie Bauld, Hearts' legendary centre forward, who had the greatest nightmare. Early on, he shot straight at the goalkeeper, then after Roy Bentley had put England ahead, Bauld was through the whole defence and hit the underside of the bar. The ball came down and did not bounce into the net as it might have done, but bounced out – taking with it the trip to South America. Scotland thus lost, but England hardly made the 1950 World Cup their own, for they managed to lose to the amateurs of the USA.

Scotland at least were spared that. Instead they played three friendlies, comfortably disposing of Switzerland before another 120,000 crowd at Hampden, then

What the well-dressed Scotland footballers wore in 1951. From left to right, back row: Dowdalls (trainer), Evans, Steel, Mason. Middle row: Cox, Reilly, Redpath, Cowan. Front row: Woodburn, Johnstone, Waddell, McNaught, Young.

going on tour to draw with Portugal in Lisbon and beat France in Paris, thanks to a goal scored by Allan Brown of East Fife. Who needed the World Cup?

*   *   *

The 1950/51 season saw Scotland triumphant over the home countries, but sadly falling down twice against Austria. Before 13 December 1950, Scotland had always boasted that they had never lost at Hampden to any foreign opposition. Sadly, this proud record was surrendered to the Austrians that afternoon. Scotland lost 1-0, and the pre-Christmas Advent atmosphere would not have been enhanced by the realisation that the Austrian goal was scored by a man called Melchior, traditionally the name of one of the Three Wise Men! Christmas, of course, was not yet a major social occasion in Scotland – it did not become a public holiday until 1958 – the big midwinter festival being the New Year.

Scotland made 1951 a year for their fans to remember by winning the British Championship again. In the autumn of 1950 they had beaten Wales 3-1 and followed it with an emphatic 6-1 over Northern Ireland (with Billy Steel scoring four times) and then in April 1951 there was a repeat of their previous Wembley triumph, this time 3-2 over England. It was in fact a somewhat lucky win, for England lost Wilf

Mannion and Stan Mortensen through injury and, in these pre-substitute days, had to play for some of the game with only nine men. Scotland then beat Denmark, France and Belgium before succumbing badly to their old foes in Austria.

It was a disaster of an occasion for Scotland to lose 4-0 in the intense heat of Vienna, and particularly so for the hero of Dundee, Billy Steel, who became the first player in Scottish international history to be sent off. It was a decision, however, which owed more to the acting of the Austrians and the gullibility of Swiss referee Lutz than to any villainy of the player himself. One wonders why Scotland kept on playing so many friendlies against Austria. The countries had superficial similarities in that they were overshadowed by a large neighbour (England and Germany) with whom they were often confused by foreigners, but the solidarity stopped there, for Scotland v. Austria games were seldom pleasant occasions. (In 1963, things were destined to turn a lot worse as well.)

*　　　*　　　*

The 1950/51 season included the rare statement of a player saying that he didn't want to play for Scotland. This sort of behaviour is common enough nowadays, but in October 1950, Bobby Evans of Celtic caused a tremendous stir when he stated that he no longer wanted to be considered for the national team. Apparently he had been upset by some Press criticism of him in a game he played for the Scottish League. Fortunately the brilliant redhead was talked out of this, and kept on playing for Scotland throughout the 1950s.

Scotland, having delighted their fans with their domestic performances in 1951, went on to flop in 1952. They beat Northern Ireland, but then lost disappointingly to Wales at Hampden in November 1951 and, although the scoreline of Scotland 1 England 2 at Hampden in April 1952 looks close, in fact it was not. Scotland were well beaten that day in the rain and the wind, with the home defence having no real answer to the magic of Tom Finney of Preston North End.

The Coronation year of 1953 saw a Hibs combination save Scotland from a defeat at Wembley. A fine movement involving Bobby Johnstone and Lawrie Reilly saw Reilly score in the very last minute to salvage a point which ten-man Scotland (Sammy Cox was off injured) just about deserved. Reilly had the reputation of scoring such vital goals late in the game, and earlier in the season a similar goal by 'Last-minute Reilly' had saved Scotland from an embarrassing defeat by Northern Ireland after Scotland had been distinctly lucky to get the better of Wales.

*　　　*　　　*

The 1953/54 Home International tournament was not only the British Championship, it was also a World Cup Qualifying Section. FIFA repeated the invitation to two British teams and, this time, Scotland dropped their arrogant refusal to go unless they won the competition. This time the Championships would be held in Switzerland and, rumour had it, there might be some involvement of the new medium of communication called television. This phenomenon had come to Scotland in 1952.

Above One of Scotland's great stars of the 1950s – Billy Liddell, who came from Townhill, Dunfermline but played all his football for Liverpool.

Left 1952. Scotland v. England. George Young introduces Ian McMillan to the guest as Billy Liddell waits his turn.

Less than 10 per cent of homes in Scotland had 'the box' however, in spite of the boost in sales brought about by Queen Elizabeth II's Coronation in 1953. Yet it did seem to be the way of the future and the fans at least were very keen to watch Scotland on TV if they possibly could. Very few of them could have afforded to go to Switzerland and, apart from the finance, methods of travel were long and circuitous. It would be a possibility, however, for the more affluent to combine the World Cup with a holiday – as long as Scotland could qualify.

But Scotland had not won a game for a full calendar year, since October 1952, for the two 'Reilly draws' had been followed by a disappointing showing against Sweden. Now Scotland travelled to Belfast to play Northern Ireland. If there is any truth in the maxim that international football provides even less justice than does club football, then this was the game to demonstrate it. For long periods of the game Scotland were outplayed, with Frank Brennan at centre half looking out of his depth and Bobby Evans coming off second best in his tussles with his Celtic colleague, Charlie Tully. It was Scotland, however, who got the goals, two of them coming from East Fife's Charlie Fleming (who rejoiced in the nickname of 'Legs'). Even when the Ulstermen scored from a penalty, goalkeeper George Farm was inspired enough to prevent them scoring again, before John Henderson of Portsmouth got a fortuitous and scarcely deserved third.

Wales came to Hampden on Wednesday 4 November, attracting a crowd of 71,387. This time the punters vindicated their judgement in staying off work with 'granny's funeral' and 'sore back' complaints, for they saw a great game with Welshmen like John Charles and Ivor Allchurch as good as anything that Scotland could offer. But Scotland played like a team, passes found their man and, with a minute to go, Scotland deservedly led 3-2. With concentration impaired following the rejection of a penalty claim, Scotland relaxed and John Charles took advantage of hesitation in the Scottish defence to snatch a late equalizer.

The Welsh could not really be grudged their draw, but it meant that Scotland would have to get at least a point from the England game at Hampden if they were to qualify for the World Cup – that was as long as Wales beat Ireland. Sadly for the Welsh, they did not do so, so Scotland approached the England game knowing that they were at least second in the group and therefore they were going to Switzerland.

Scotland had done something unusual. In February 1954 they appointed a manager in Andy Beattie. Andy had, of course, played for Preston North End and Scotland before the Second World War, and his credentials were sound. But he was still the manager of Huddersfield Town and his contract seemed to be only for the England game, three pre-World Cup friendlies and then the World Cup itself. This was less than a ringing endorsement or a carte blanche, and the selectors still

Programme cover for Scotland v. England 1954.

retained the rights to pick the team! They would, of course, we were assured, consult Mr Beattie.

It was as well that Scotland did not need to draw with England that day, for they decided to put on one of their worst performances of all time. It rained at Hampden, as it had done two years previously, except this time it was heavier and the defeat was also heavier. Even the score of 2-4 is misleading as Scotland scored first and last. The first goal was lucky in that the muddy ball skidded went through a defender's legs, and the last goal of the afternoon was scored in front of a half-empty Hampden in the last minute when everyone had decided that enough was enough and that it was time to go to the pub.

It was just as well that the game was not televised. The SFA were worried in case this might affect the attendance. Curiously, they allowed the English FA Cup final of West Bromwich Albion and Preston North End to be televised, but neither the Scotland *v*. England game nor the Scottish Cup final between Celtic and Aberdeen reached the screens. Instead of the international, viewers got the Oxford *v*. Cambridge Boat Race: at least the rowing was close. So depressed was Wembley Wizard Jack Harkness that he raised the question in the *Dundee Courier* – 'Should Scotland withdraw from the World Cup?' With retrospect, it might have been not a bad idea to prevent us making fools of ourselves.

*   *   *

Scotland's approach to the World Cup was unbelievably inept. Delighted by the team's showings in meaningless friendlies against Norway and Finland, the SFA decided in the interests of economy that only thirteen players would be chosen to travel, although twenty-two would have been allowed. Fred Martin of Aberdeen was the only goalkeeper! No kit would be supplied for training, and players would have to borrow kit from their clubs. Bobby Evans went to Switzerland, but was struggling with injury and would have done well to stay at home. Lawrie Reilly was ill with pleurisy, Bobby Johnstone was injured and Rangers, indulging in one of their periodic vendettas with the SFA, announced that their players were unavailable as they would be on tour in North America!

The ineptitude of the SFA was matched by that of the World Cup itself. Each group would have two seeds (Scotland would not be a seed because they were only second in their qualifying group) and there would only be two group games. Thus Scotland would only play against the two best teams of the group, namely Austria and Uruguay. An added complication was that if any game was drawn at 90 minutes there would be extra time.

Scotland actually played very well against Austria in Zurich, in spite of the handicap of wearing, in sweltering heat, jerseys which were eminently suitable for November in Scotland. It seemed that no-one realised that, in June, temperatures in Central European countries like Switzerland were very high. In addition, there was a distinct lack of guidance from the Scottish bench. Neil Mochan of Celtic recalls that the instructions from that quarter were along the lines of repeated advice of 'C'mon

Four well-dressed Scotland players at Largs in 1954. Willie Fernie, Archie Glen, Doug Cowie and Jimmy Davidson.

Scotland! Get stuck in!' It was the same Neil Mochan who almost scored for Scotland on several occasions. In fact it was a very even game, spoiled to a certain extent by the strong-arm tactics of the Austrians after they scored the only goal of the encounter. The next and last game was to be played on the following Saturday in Basle against a country that very few people had heard of called Uruguay. They were, of course, the World Cup holders but that did not seem to matter!

The Austria game was not shown on TV. The BBC had no control over which game was to be beamed by the Eurovision link and fans saw France *v*. Yugoslavia instead. The Scotland *v*. Uruguay game would, however, be broadcast live and could be seen at 4.45 p.m. on Saturday 19 June after some cricket between Somerset and Lancashire. With hindsight it would have been better if the television had stayed focussed on the Bath Festival watching Cyril Washbrook score a century for the red rose of Lancashire.

A certain euphoria had seized the Scottish nation. The kindly Stanley Matthews of England, who had watched Scotland *v*. Austria, said that Scotland were 'unlucky', and the same Jack Harkness who had suggested after the England game in April that Scotland should withdraw from the World Cup, now said that 'Scotland are just the boys to beat Uruguay'. Clearly, curtains would be drawn in quite a few houses in Scotland that Saturday teatime, the better to enjoy the game.

Mr Beattie, the manager, sprung a surprise before the game: he resigned. He made his untimely announcement hours before kick-off, something that was less-than-ideal preparation for his players, although he stressed that he would stay until the final whistle! No-one has ever found out the real reason for this baffling move, although it would be a reasonable guess to suggest that the selectors and committee gave him less than a free hand. In any case, the game itself would very soon drown any speculation about why the manager had abandoned his post.

Once again the heat was intense and Scotland were less then suitably equipped, particularly the old heavy brown boots which covered the ankles. The first part of the game saw Scotland give as good as they got, but then two goals went in before half-time, both caused by misplaced passes. What the half-time team talk was we can but imagine. What sort of thing does a manager who is going to resign at the end of the match say to his men who are 2-0 down and suffering from dehydration and heat exhaustion? Whatever it was, it was hardly helpful as Scotland managed to lose another five goals in the second half, and the full-time whistle came as a blessed relief.

It was may be as well that the TV service of the BBC in 1954 did not do action replays or in-depth analysis by so-called experts. The programmes cheerfully rolled on, and Scottish fans were left to recover. Some, like your author (not yet six years of age) will carry the trauma of that occasion to his grave – a trauma in no way diminished by subsequent disasters. Watching a football match in a distant country on the minuscule TV screens back home (which flickered and crackled when a motorbike roared up the road outside) was an experience in itself – but what a way to begin watching television! What a way to begin watching Scotland!

*   *   *

Resilience is, however, a strong Scottish trait, and after a certain amount of introspection and cursing of Andy Beattie and the selectors, shoulders were shrugged and the nation got on with life, especially after England also exited the World Cup. The first game next season saw a totally different Scotland team persuade 53,000 people to go to Cardiff. They then beat the Welsh 1-0. Less impressive was a 2-2 draw with Northern Ireland at Hampden, but then 113,000 came to Hampden one Wednesday afternoon in December 1954 to see the brilliant Hungarians: Puskas, Hidegkuti, Kocsis and all. Hungary were the World Cup runners-up and probably the best team in the world at that time. Scotland played admirably well, but lost to the Magyars. Consolation was gained from the fact that the 2-4 scoreline was a defeat by a lesser margin than Hungary had dished out to England on two occasions in that last thirteen months!

The make-up of the Scottish team is almost unbelievable fifty years on, for there were two Anglos (from Preston North End), Fred Martin of Aberdeen in goal, and two each from Partick Thistle, Clyde, Hearts and Hibs. So much for Celtic and Rangers, and how remarkable that 113,000 Scotsmen contained not one single Old Firm bigot. It also seemed to indicate how the nation had completely forgiven Scotland for the World Cup disaster of the previous summer.

Scotland went to Wembley on 2 April 1955 with a chance of winning the International Championship. Wembley had been a happy hunting ground since the war. In fact the worst result to befall Scotland since 1934 had been a draw. But this was to be one of the many Wembley disasters that were heading our way with

The beautiful setting of Newcastle, County Down is the background to Scotland training in October 1955.

monotonous and predictable regularity. Scotland went down 7-2. The great Stanley Matthews was on song (as he often was against Scotland) but England's hero was the little-known Dennis Wilshaw of Wolverhampton Wanderers, who scored four.

      *   *   *

Scotland were always ready for more in these days and filled the close season of 1955 with four friendlies. Beating Portugal at Hampden was very satisfying, but the highlight of 1955 was a 4-1 win over Austria in Vienna which, had it come in the World Cup the previous year, would have really made everyone sit up and take notice. As it was, Scotland with Archie Robertson, Gordon Smith, Billy Liddell and Lawrie Reilly scoring the goals were very impressive, and ten days later, an even greater triumph seemed in store when Scotland went to Budapest to take on the Hungarians – and scored first! half-time came with Scotland one goal up. Unfortunately it couldn't last and Hungary eventually won 3-1, but the Hungarians once again had to admit their respect for the Scots.

Eighteen months later the Hungarian team would barely exist, for the Hungarian people had shown some dangerous signs of 'Westernising' and not appreciating their Soviet overlords. The tanks rolled into Budapest and other places in November 1956 and the gallant Hungarians were crushed. Fortunately for football, the great Ferenc Puskas managed to escape to Spain and continued his career with Real Madrid. Other Hungarian footballers were less lucky.

The mid-1950s may in some ways have been a golden age for Scottish football, but international form was unpredictable, as is always likely to happen when a committee of selectors (enthusiastic amateurs) picks a professional team. There was no long-term team-selection policy and it was a well-known fact that one good game for your club when a selector happened to be there (because he was perhaps a director of your opponents) would usually see you included in the next international.

Times were slowly changing – England, for example, had a manager with the unlikely name of Walter Winterbottom – but Scotland still retained the belief that its system was the best in the world, when one would have thought that a 0-7 thrashing from Uruguay would tend to indicate the opposite. One thing that definitely was best in the world was the attendances. Visitors to Hampden, no matter how famous or distinguished they were, were often totally amazed at the sheer size of the place and the sheer volume of enthusiastic support that there was for a team that was often depressingly ordinary.

14 April 1956 saw Hampden at its best. The weather was pleasant, the pipe bands played and community singing with *Roamin in The Gloamin* and *The Northern Lights of Old Aberdeen* kept the vast crowd happy until the game began. Both Scotland and England were level in the Home International table, Scotland having beaten Wales and lost to Northern Ireland, and England having done the opposite. On the Wednesday before the Hampden game, Northern Ireland and Wales drew – which meant that they each had three points. The Hampden winner therefore would be the Champions.

For a long time it looked as if it was going to be Scotland. In the sixtieth minute Aberdeen's talented Graham Leggat had lobbed the goalkeeper following a good interchange with Gordon Smith, and Scotland's defence, with the Old Firm duo of Young and Evans standing firm, looked solid and able to resist the English attacks

'Shortest to the right, tallest to the left...' Scotland line up in training before the game against Wales in November 1955.

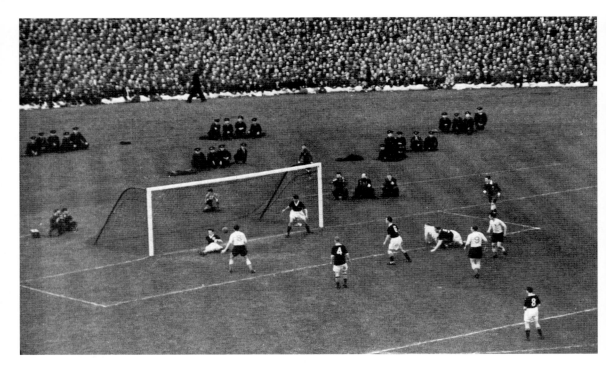

Top April 1956. Johnny Haynes is just about to score his last-minute equaliser.

Above Happy Scottish fans at Hampden Park.

Right April 1956. England's goalkeeper Reg Matthews stops a shot from Laurie Reilly.

masterminded by the teenage genius called Duncan Edwards. The Hampden Roar was gaining momentum as the minutes ticked away. Scotland's last win at Hampden over England had been in 1937, nineteen years and a world war away, and it had been a long wait.

Back home in countless living rooms, the emotions were being shared, for television, although not yet widespread, was now owned by quite a few families. There was usually at least one per street and that family were chatted up and fawned over for weeks before the international so that they would allow the neighbourhood in. In the author's case, the doctor (a football fan himself) that very morning had decided that the chickenpox had receded sufficiently for the patient to be wrapped in a blanket and carried upstairs by his father to see the game on a neighbour's TV.

What happened at 4.45 p.m. that Saturday afternoon was far worse than the (fairly mild) horrors of chickenpox. Seconds remained and Roger Byrne fashioned the nightmare with a cross to his Manchester United colleague Tommy Taylor. Taylor headed the ball down and it came to Fulham's industrious Johnny Haynes. Haynes breasted the ball down (Scotland would claim with a touch of desperation that he handled) and scored.

The silence was deafening. The referee's whistle was heard clearly even on the television as he pointed upfield. Seconds later all Scotland heard the full-time whistle and Hampden Park emptied its 132,817 spectators in the eeriest of ghostly silences. The cursing and the pointing of fingers would begin later, as of course would the English gloating, but for the moment shocked, stunned silence reigned.

Byrne, Edwards and Taylor would never again of course return to Hampden Park, for they were destined to perish in the snows of Munich in February 1958. At this time though, they were the English heroes of the hour – until somebody pointed out the statistical oddity that all four nations had three points and that therefore for

George Young with some of his trophies.
George played 53 times for Scotland.

the first time ever, the British Championship would be shared four ways. So Scotland had, after all, claimed one optimist, won the Championship! It had to be split with all the other nations of course, but Scotland were equal top.

*　　　*　　　*

Another World Cup, still two years away, was now coming into view. It would be an exaggeration to say that the Scottish authorities took the matter seriously – they obstinately refused for example to appoint a manager, although they did apparently at this stage dabble with the idea of approaching Matt Busby of Manchester United to do it on a part-time basis, as they would eventually do when it was too late. But the World Cup now created a different impression with the Press and the public, by whom it was much discussed. With the finals being in Sweden in 1958, there would certainly be television coverage through Europe, and if Scotland could manage to qualify, the games could be followed as if we were there.

Scotland's qualifying group consisted of Spain and Switzerland, one of whom would qualify. All the qualifying games would be played in the summer of 1957, except for the last one against Switzerland at Hampden in November of that year. Scotland's springboard to their qualifying ties was typically Scottish – quixotic and quirky. The games against Wales and Northern Ireland had been respectable, the

Left Tommy Docherty in 1957. Tommy became manager later in 1971, but sadly found the attractions of Manchester United to be stronger.

Opposite, above April 1957. The Scotland team in training for the game v. England at Wembley. Goalkeeper Younger seems to have cracked a joke. From left to right, back row: McNaught, Collins, Fernie, Younger, Hewie, Ring, McColl. Front row: Docherty, Reilly, Young, Mudie, Caldow.

Northern Ireland game being remarkable for its date. This was 7 November 1956, with British troops in action in Suez against the 'dastardly Nasser', as the newspapers depicted him. It was also the time that Hungary was being flattened by the Soviet Union. Scotland beat Northern Ireland (but had only drawn in Wales) and then they beat Yugoslavia 2-0 at Hampden.

All that counted for very little in April 1957. For the second time in a row Scotland lost to England at Wembley – this time by a respectable score, but nevertheless in a none-too-convincing performance. Yet the first half had belonged to Scotland. A goal ahead in the first minute through Clyde's excellent Tommy Ring, they held England comfortably until half-time, even scoring again only to see it disallowed. England slowly took command in the second half, however, and ran out 2-1 winners with Stanley Matthews outstanding and responsible for setting up the winning goal.

This defeat summed up a dismal British Championship, and it would have been difficult to be optimistic about the visit of Spain to Hampden for the first World Cup qualifier on 8 May. But Scotland, as they so often did at Hampden against difficult opposition, turned it on and won 4-2 – quite clearly their best result against foreign opposition, as the Spanish side contained men like di Stefano and Gento of Real Madrid. For a long time, a draw would have been a likely result (and a creditable one), but then Jackie Mudie, a Dundonian who played for Blackpool, scored two fine goals from passes by Celtic's excellent Bobby Collins as Scotland delighted their fans and surprised the world. Mudie had scored earlier, so this was a hat-trick,

WORLD CUP
SCOTLAND
v
SPAIN
OFFICIAL
SOUVENIR PROGRAMME

HAMPDEN PARK, GLASGOW
MAY 8, 1957 · KICK OFF 6·45 P.M.

PRICE : SIXPENCE

Left Programme cover for Scotland v Spain 1957.

Opposite May 1957. Scotland leave Prestwick Airport to fly to Switzerland for a World Cup match.

the other goal coming from a penalty expertly taken by Charlton Athletic's John Hewie, a South African of Scottish parentage.

A dangerous mood of euphoria now took over the nation, enlivened by the news that Scotland's game against Switzerland in Basle on 19 May would be televised live, or at least the second half would be. This was another boost to the already thriving world of television sales and rentals, although, 19 May being a Sunday, there was a certain amount of head shaking and tut-tutting from the Godly in a country which had not yet, in 1957, totally shaken off the shackles of Calvinism.

The game was to be played in the very same stadium as the Uruguay disaster of three years previously, but this time, Scotland had an advantage in that the conditions were more Scottish than anything else. The weather was bad and the pitch was heavy – not unlike what one gets every November. It was also a gritty Scottish performance. At times, Switzerland were undeniably the better side, but it was Scotland who had the victory. The Swiss scored first, but then Mudie equalized with a fine header. 1-1 at half-time, and television joined the game with Scotland battling to hold on to a draw. But with nineteen minutes remaining, Gordon Smith of Hibs (recognised as one of the best wingers in Scotland, although often a sad underperformer in a Scotland jersey) sent over a cross for Bobby Collins to score.

The genteele ladies of Edinburgh and Glasgow who had been to Church that morning were no doubt delighted at this (in 1957, television ownership was still mainly a middle-class phenomenon, although the lower orders were fast joining

them) although they might have been a little perturbed at the strong language used by their sons-in-law (invited as a special treat along with the children) as the Swiss pressed in the dying minutes. Tommy Younger was in good form in the goal, however, and 2-1 to Scotland it stayed.

'Wha's like us?' now chortled all of Scotland, and indeed as Spain and Switzerland had drawn, Scotland were well ahead of the field. Pelion was piled on top of Ossa in midweek when Scotland went to West Germany (sadly only a friendly this time) and actually beat the World Champions! Collins and Mudie once again got the goals, and surely they would do likewise the following Sunday when they went to Spain, to Madrid, the home of the mighty Real Madrid, for the return leg.

Watched by General Franco, Spain were under a great deal of pressure. In this grim dictatorship, under the façade of bullfighting, wine and dancing with castanets, football was becoming a mighty serious business. Franco's favourites, Real Madrid, won the first two European Cups of 1956 and 1957. No-one had yet hit on the idea of offering cheap tourist holidays to the British public, and Spain was a desperately poor country in which football was one of the few things that could excite and unite the people – even though the Catalans, who had lost the Civil War from 1936 to 1939, rallied round FC Barcelona in an unhealthy mixture of football and politics.

Scotland were not unduly intimidated by the vast crowd and were given an advantage in that once again the conditions were wet. Spain this time realised the necessity to shackle Mudie and Collins. Spain dominated this game and won 4-1, but even at that, Scotland still held the driving seat in the group because of the draw between Spain and Switzerland. It all hinged on the game at Hampden Park on 6 November 1957 between Scotland and Switzerland.

A draw might have involved a play-off, but Scotland managed to win. The large Hampden crowd and the huge radio audience had many anxious moments to endure however. It was a Wednesday afternoon and, once again, the world was amazed that the love of Scotland seemed able to persuade 58,811 to stay off their work! Scotland had an all-Clyde left wing in Archie Robertson and Tommy Ring, and it was Robertson who put Scotland ahead. The Swiss equalized, but then early in the second half, Jackie Mudie once again became the darling of Hampden when he scored following a fine drive from Celtic's Willie Fernie, arguably Scotland's finest ball player of the decade.

Then with the Swiss fighting back and forcing desperate clearances by the Scots, Scotland got a break when they scored a third goal, which to all the world looked yards offside. Alec Scott of Rangers was the scorer and the English referee would subsequently argue that Scott was not offside at the time that Bobby Collins sent in his fine defence-splitting pass. 3-1 it was, and Scotland should have been safe, but Scotland

Above November 1957. Switzerland score against Scotland in a World Cup qualifier at Hampden. Parker, Caldow, goalkeeper Younger, Evans and Docherty are all powerless to stop the goal.

Below November 1957. Jackie Mudie has just scored against Switzerland following a fine run from Willie Fernie.

have never made things easy for their fans and with ten minutes remaining, faulty defending of a corner kick gave the Swiss (and the Spaniards listening on their radios for their news programmes as they woke up from their siesta) a lifeline. Scotland held out, and much was the relief that Scotland had qualified for the World Cup finals.

This time, all four British teams were in the sixteen-nation World Cup. The ties were drawn on the basis of one British side, one Western Europe side, one Eastern Europe side and a South American team. Scotland thus got France, Yugoslavia and Paraguay, and it was generally reckoned that it was a fairly easy draw – a fatal assumption for a Scottish team to make.

Before they left for Sweden, however, there was the Home International Championship. Scotland had already played feckless draws with Northern Ireland and Wales before the turn of the year, but this meant that as long as Scotland could beat England, they might yet be the Champions. But there was another factor which entered the equation – and it was a tragic one.

One of football's saddest days occurred on 6 February 1958 when the Manchester United team were involved in a dreadful air crash in Munich on their return from a European tie. No Scottish players were among the dead, but this was hardly the point, for the whole of British football was intimately affected. When England came to Hampden in April, their team had changed considerably, but Bobby Charlton, the young survivor of the air crash, played brilliantly and inspired England to a 4-0 thrashing of Scotland.

It was an unbelievably dreadful performance with Scotland never in the game at all, as the broken-hearted thousands turned their backs and went home in a steady trickle long before the full-time whistle. Where this left Scotland as regards the World Cup, nobody knew – and nobody in authority seemed to care. In January before the Munich air crash, Matt Busby had been half-heartedly approached about leading the Scotland team in Sweden. Matt, equally half-heartedly, had given a grudging assent, but now that he was seriously injured after the plane crash, this became impossible. Amazingly, no-one else was approached, not even Scot Symon of Rangers or Jimmy McGrory of Celtic, and Scotland left for Sweden in early June without a manager, but with a certain boost to their confidence in two friendlies – a draw with Hungary and a win over Poland, two countries still reeling from their rape by the Soviet military machine which had been as efficient as it had been brutal.

The closest Scotland had to a manager was a trainer called Dawson Walker, who could confide in his captain, goalkeeper Tommy Younger or a few experienced men like Bobby Evans or Eric Caldow. Of course the selectors were there enjoying their freebies and 'helping' to pick the team. 1958 was marginally better organized than 1954 had been, but it still had a long way to go. It reeked of shambolic amateurism in a game that was becoming every year more ruthlessly professional.

*   *   *

Yet nobody could complain about the first game in the World Cup. It was a creditable 1-1 draw against Yugoslavia in Vasteras on Sunday 8 June. The Yugoslavs scored first,

Above left April 1958. Hampden Park. Tommy Docherty and Billy Wright lead their teams out. Scotland would lose 0-4.

Above right April 1958. Alex Parker clears his lines in the 0-4 defeat at the hands of England.

Left April 1958. Tommy Younger, watched by Bobby Evans and Ian McColl, saves well.

Below left April 1958. Scotland's Alex Parker can only watch as England score.

Scotland at the World Cup in 1958. From left to right, back row: Hewie, Caldow, Younger, Turnmbull, Evans, Cowie. Front row: Leggat, Murray, Mudie, Collins, Imlach.

but a good header by Hearts' Jimmy Murray put Scotland on level terms just after half-time, and with a bit of luck Scotland might just have grabbed a winner when Jackie Mudie scored late on, only to have it mysteriously chalked off. It had been a tough encounter, however, and quite a few Scots were nursing injuries.

This necessitated changes for the Paraguay game on the following Wednesday. Sadly, however, there was no great research done on the Paraguayans, who had been hammered by France in the first game. Newspapers said that they were good 'ball players' but the context was a patronising one, as if to say that 'Yes, they could pass the ball around a pitch occasionally but really they shouldn't be here on the same park as Scotland.'

The Scottish players seemed to share this attitude, and Scotland lost this game 2-3 because they underestimated two things about the South Americans. One was to the credit of the Paraguayans, and that was their speed – they were far faster than anything Scotland were used to. The other was less creditable, but sadly a hallmark of quite a few South American sides, and that was their cynical tackling and lack of scruples about using elbows and fists too, if necessary.

In addition, Tommy Younger in goal had a shocker, but even so, Scotland might yet have earned a draw but for a couple of misses late on in the game, once Scotland realised that Paraguay were not here merely to be rolled over. A more positive approach to the game at an earlier stage might have reaped some dividends, but this must go down as one of the many in Scotland's lamentable World Cup history where the players have believed the Scottish Press (which after all only reflects Scottish popular opinion) and underestimated the opposition. It was no end of a lesson, but it has never been learned.

Yet Scotland were not yet out. A win against France would earn at least a play-off, and France in 1958 were no-one's idea of the best in Europe. Orebro on 15 June saw a gallant Scotland performance and some dreadful foul play, in particular from the French although the Scots themselves were no angels. The *casus belli* seemed to be a penalty kick awarded to Scotland. Ironically, John Hewie missed it anyway, but brawls and mayhem were the order of the day, and Scotland, clearly upset by the tough tactics of the French and the woefully weak refereeing, went in at half-time 2-0 down.

But this Scottish team was not without character. Younger had been dropped and Bill Brown of Dundee was now in goal with Bobby Evans of Celtic as centre half, and captain. Evans inspired his men, encouraging them to keep calm and, although the French were the better side, it was Scotland who pulled one back midway through the second half when Sammy Baird of Rangers scored. This was of course not enough, for Scotland needed to win, not draw, and they were never close to scoring two goals. It was, however, reasonably creditable and another forerunner of a phenomenon later on in the century when Scotland start to play well at the end when the pressure is off them... and when they are more or less already out.

*   *   *

Thus Scotland returned early from Sweden. It had been a great World Cup and the television audiences had been thrilled by the Brazilians. Traditionalists in Scotland were horrified to see the abundance of passing sideways and even backwards – but such objections were quashed when it was pointed out that this was from the team which won the World Cup! Didi, Vava, Garrincha and Pelé were the heroes of all nations. Scotland clearly had a great deal to learn, but it would be a long time before the domestic game would even acknowledge that fact.

The problem was that the Scottish domestic game in the 1950s was a phenomenal success with large attendances, a very competitive atmosphere (with neither Rangers nor Celtic necessarily getting their own way) and everybody apparently talking about nothing other than football. Junior, local and schools football proliferated and thrived. A boy with no interest in football was automatically ostracized by his classmates. Was there any great need for change?

The remaining international games of the decade were the usual inconsistent Scottish rollercoaster. A fine 3-0 win over Wales at Cardiff in the autumn of 1958 was followed by a disappointing draw with Northern Ireland, and then the second-in-a-row defeat by England at Wembley in what was regarded as one of the dullest games of them all. The score was only 1-0, but Scotland looked totally devoid of any attacking capability.

By this time Scotland had a manager of sorts – albeit a part-time one. It was Andy Beattie again, the very man who had resigned hours before the Uruguay tanking in 1954. Matt Busby, having recovered from his Munich injuries, had taken the job briefly in late 1958 but soon found it too much for him and gave it up to concentrate on rebuilding Manchester United. The SFA, apparently incapable of a fresh idea, then turned back in March 1959 to Andy Beattie – to the amazement of

1959. Scotland manager Andy Beattie talks to John White, Graham Leggat, Bertie Auld, Ian St John and Denis Law.

1959. Scotland team squad in civvies before training.

Hampden Park, November 1959. Scotland come close against Wales, but the game finishes at 1-1.

Hampden Park November 1959. Graham Leggat and Ian St John (half hidden) almost score in the 1-1 draw against Wales.

everybody. Beattie's problem was that he now lacked any credibility, and he was never taken seriously by the public in his short reign before he resigned eighteen months later. He had tried to manage Scotland at the same time as Carlisle United. When he moved to Notts Forest in September 1960, Forest seemed to insist that he give up the Scotland job – which he did.

Yet Scotland, for all their travails, could delight their fans too. In 1959 they beat West Germany and Netherlands (in spite of having Bertie Auld sent off) before going down to Portugal. They then comprehensively thumped Northern Ireland 4-0 in Belfast before, in the last international match of the 1950s, drawing 1-1 with the mighty Welsh team which contained the hardy Welsh legends of Ivor Allchurch and John Charles at Hampden Park on 4 November 1959.

FIVE

Three Bannockburns and a Flodden
1960-1965

The early years of the 1960s were marked by major social change. It certainly was the era of 'The Young Ones' as Cliff Richard would sing. Cliff and Elvis Presley would vie for the attention of pop music fans, and The Beatles were only just round the corner, making their first appearance in 1962 and reaching their zenith in 1964. The Welfare State was here to stay, as indeed were prosperity and affluence. Rightly was Prime Minister Harold McMillan able to boast 'We've never had it so good', as (incredibly) in the 1959 General Election, more people in Scotland voted for the Conservatives than did for the Labour Party! War also seemed to be a thing of the past, and in 1961 came the end of National Service, the cruel system of conscription whereby young men had to serve two years in Her Majesty's Forces, whether they wanted to or not, irrespective of careers and romances – all to maintain a British Empire which was now fairly obviously being peacefully dismantled!

Less welcome was the rise of teenage crime and other anti-social behaviour. The building of huge housing schemes to replace the hideous slums was clearly a step forward. Sadly, little thought seems to have gone into the social implications of herding so many people together in good houses but in areas which lacked amenities and community spirit. Irresponsible young men now had a certain amount of money and freedom. These things were not always used wisely.

And of course there were so many more young people. The 'baby boom' of the immediate post-war years was now being noticed in secondary schools, and as the National Health Service had more or less killed off many of the pre-war childhood illnesses like rickets, diphtheria and polio, the young population was not curbed. Nor were they likely to be worked to death in slave-labour conditions in factories, mines and dockyards as their fathers and grandfathers had been.

Amid this world of change, there remained one constant factor in Scotland. Yes, it was football. Attendances were still booming and football remained the one and only topic of conversation of the working man (and even the middle-class man) at leisure. The national team was still loved as much as ever, even though success (at least permanent success) remained elusive.

There was one factor, however, that would bring a permanent change for footballers. In the early 1960s the 'maximum wage' was abolished. Hitherto there had been, theoretically, a ceiling above which clubs could not play their players. Admittedly, this restriction had been widely ignored, but now it was legally and officially possible for wealthy clubs, particularly in England, to pay players as much as they wished. The implications of this for young Scotsmen were obvious. The 'Eldorado' of England and even Europe was now even more attractive for talented young players. Loads of them would take advantage of this, thereby weakening the Scottish domestic game.

English and foreign clubs had never been all that willing to release Scottish players to play for Scotland. This would be a problem which would now intensify. There was also the factor that the many talented Scottish players did not always seem to have the commitment to their national team, sometimes giving us the impression that they were doing us an immense favour returning with their latest designer clothes to the land of their birth to play for us. There was always the emotional stuff about visiting one's mammy in Maryhill or Hamilton, yet there was sometimes less than total effort being expended on the field, under the clear instruction of the club manager not to get injured while playing for Scotland!

*   *   *

The 1960s did not start well for Scotland. The first game was a respectable enough sounding 1-1 draw against England at Hampden. What was distressing about this game was that it meant that Scotland had now not beaten England at Hampden since 1937, twenty-three years and a major war ago. What annoyed the Scots most, however, was the performance of referee Mr Szranko of Hungary who spoiled the game with his over-fussy approach and also awarded England two penalties – and a retake!

Graham Leggat, lately of Aberdeen but now of Fulham, had opened the scoring for Scotland, as he had done four years ago. At half-time, Scotland looked as if they were giving as good as they got in a stop-start frustrating kind of a game. Fatally, Scotland failed to score again, and England were awarded a softish penalty in the fiftieth minute when Dunky MacKay was adjudged to have brought down Bobby Charlton. Charlton himself took the kick and scored. It was the end of the scoring but scarcely the end of the drama, for England got another penalty near the end. This time, Celtic goalkeeper Frank Haffey was the hero as he saved it… but a Scottish defender had encroached and the kick was retaken. Hampden held its breath, fearing the worst, but this time Charlton drove the penalty wide to a tremendous roar of relief.

Hampden Park 1960. Graham Leggat scores a great goal past Ron Springett.

Hampden Park 1960. Bobby Evans rises to head clear with Denis Law watching.

Much of course would be said about Celtic's Frank Haffey the following year. What is forgotten is that in 1960, as well as saving the penalty, he also had a great game with several other fine saves. Scotland felt that this game was a moral victory and that with a better referee, things might have been different.

That may be true, but Scotland then proceeded to have a disastrous summer in 1960. They lost to Poland at Hampden, then went on a tour which saw beatings from Austria and Turkey, although they surprised and delighted everyone by drawing with Hungary – a poor shadow, it must be said of the Hungary that thrilled the world in the early 1950s and which had been so savagely mauled by the Soviet Union. The Austria game was shown on television, and viewers were appalled to see how outclassed Scotland were by an Austrian team which had already decided that it was not going to enter the 1962 World Cup because Austrian football 'was in decline'. What did that make Scotland, we wondered, as we saw Austria go four up before Dave Mackay grabbed a late consolation?

*　　　*　　　*

Inconsistency followed Scotland into the new season. Beaten in Wales, Scotland picked themselves up with a 5-2 win over Northern Ireland and approached Wembley for the England clash on 15 April 1961 not entirely without optimism. By this time, Scotland at long last had a proper manager. It was Ian McColl, still a player with Rangers at the time when he was appointed. In theory he could have chosen himself for the team (he had already earned 14 caps in the 1950s), although in practice his playing career was now beginning to fizzle out and he would pack up playing in the summer of 1961.

McColl's first game in charge turned out to be Scotland's most memorable and disastrous scoreline of all time as Scotland went down 9-3 to a very talented England side that contained men like Bryan Douglas, Jimmy Greaves, Bobby Charlton and Johnny Haynes. Mercifully, this game was not shown live on television. The radio commentary was bad enough, and those who had actually gone to Wembley suffered the horrors of hell. Yet, although this game and its scoreline broke all sorts of records, it was not as bad as it seemed. At one point Scotland had fought back to make it 3-2, then England got a goal which looked offside. For a long time after that it stayed 4-2 until both teams scored within the space of a minute to make it 5-3. Scotland finally collapsed inside the last ten minutes when another four goals were scored. If this was sad, a sadder sound was heard when the Rangers faction of the Scotland support jeered Frank Haffey of Celtic, blaming him for all the nine goals scored. It would sadly become more obvious throughout the 1960s that partisan behaviour of Old Firm fans would on occasion divide the Scottish support.

The hounding of Haffey was unfair, but sympathy for Frank tended to evaporate in later years when he appeared to make capital out of the fact that he was the chap who let in nine goals at Wembley. One particular picture of him posing under the sign on a railway platform that said '9' caused distress. No decent Scottish supporter would blame Frank for all the goals, but it was a different matter for him

Scotland v. Wales at Cardiff 1960. From left to right, back row: Duncan McKay, Gabriel, Leslie, Caldow, Martis, Dave Mackay. Front row: Herd, White, Young, Hunter and Wilson.

April 1961. Prior to the debacle. Scotland are introduced to the Duke of Edinburgh before the infamous 9-3 defeat.

Above April 1961. Haffey. McCann and Shearer watch distraught as Jimmy Greaves scores one of England's nine.

Right April 1961. Davie Wilson scores for Scotland. Sadly it was only a brief moment of joy in an otherwise devastating experience.

to be seen to be laughing about it. A defeat to England, especially by that margin, is a serious matter.

The blame of course had to be shared. It has to be admitted that men like Dave Mackay, Bert McCann and Denis Law underperformed that day, and of course the Glasgow humorists blamed it all on the fact that the ball was orange. This meant that the Rangers players Bobby Shearer and Eric Caldow were afraid to kick it lest they damage that sacred colour, whereas its very appearance scared the hell out of the two Celtic players, Frank Haffey and international debutant Billy McNeill.

The disappointment of this drubbing had to be quickly put to one side for the World Cup qualifying campaign as the 1962 event in Chile was fast approaching. Scotland were drawn with Eire and Czechoslovakia, and only one team would qualify. Scotland competently dealt with Eire in a double header in May 1961 – 4-1 at Hampden on Wednesday 3 May and 3-0 in Dublin on Sunday 7 May. The following Sunday they travelled to Bratislava to meet the Czechs. Scotland were outclassed and went down 0-4. The brilliant but irascible Pat Crerand was sent off, and it was the second depressing day in four weeks of that dreadful spring of 1961.

But Scotland fought back in the autumn of that year. On Wednesday 26 September, with an afternoon kick off because Hampden did not yet have floodlights, Scotland attracted 51,590 to see the return leg against Czechoslovakia. The rain-drenched crowd (many of whom would have some awkward explaining to do the following

Sometime in the early 1960s. Manager Ian McColl uses a new visual aid, a film projector, to his players, some of whom do not look all that impressed.

September 1961. Denis Law is congratulated after scoring for Scotland against Czechoslovakia in a World Cup qualifier.

day to employers and headmasters) were rewarded for their love of Scotland, who proved that she is not always a demanding and unrewarding mistress. Scotland, although twice down in the game and looking down and out, twice pulled back to level terms and then, following a lovely one-two between John White of Tottenham Hotspur and Denis Law of Turin, Scotland scored the winner in the latter stages of the game.

Goal average/difference did not count at this stage in the section, and so as both teams had beaten Eire, and Scotland and the Czechs had beaten each other once, a play-off was scheduled for Brussels on Wednesday 29 November to decide who was to go to Chile. In the meantime, the dangerous Scottish emotions of euphoria and optimism began to appear. Scotland had clearly bounced back from their Wembley disaster. With an outstanding half-back line of Crerand, McNeill and Baxter (which was hardly weakened when Ian Ure of Dundee occasionally got the nod over McNeill) Scotland won convincingly over Northern Ireland and Wales. The game in Belfast was a fine example of Scotland at their best. Against an Irish team which contained men like Danny Blanchflower, Bertie Peacock and Jimmy McIlroy, Scotland, inspired by Crerand and Baxter, simply annihilated the opposition, all six goals being scored by Rangers players – three by Alec Scott, two by Ralph Brand and one by Davie Wilson. The demolition of Wales at Hampden was less spectacular but no less convincing and this time it was Ian St John of Liverpool who got the goals.

Things thus looked good for that absurd play-off in a neutral country in front of a virtually empty Heysel stadium. Denis Law was brought back from Turin for the occasion, although he had missed both the home internationals. Sadly it turned out to be one of Denis's less happy days. This time it was Scotland who were in the lead twice, the goals being scored by Ian St John, but the Czechs equalized agonisingly with only eight minutes to go after the Scottish defence had given every indication of being able to ride out the storm. It was a strange goal as well. A Czech forward shot from the edge of the box, the ball hit the bar, then the post and came out. It then broke to the Czech forward Scherer (with the unfortunate Christian name of Adolf) who drove the ball through a ruck of players past the unsighted Eddie Connachan.

Even at this late juncture, Scotland rallied. The forwards had previously spurned one or two other chances which would have put the game beyond any doubt, and now Denis Law had the misfortune to see his shot go inches over the bar, and one or two half chances were also missed. The end of normal time came with the game tied at 2-2.

The late Czech equalizer meant that extra time had to be played. The rules of the World Cup now favoured the Czechs, for goal difference would come into force if the play-off was a draw, meaning that Scotland would have lost in these circumstances. Scotland therefore still had to chase the game, whereas the Czechs could now waste time and defend.

Scotland were now exhausted. Crerand and Baxter, normally the best of friends even though on opposite sides of the Old Firm divide, were great players. They were also great (although flawed) personalities, writing for example a 'ghosted' column for the *Glasgow Evening Citizen* and frequently being seen together at charity functions and other things. Sadly they fell out about who got first swig of the water bottle in the interval between full time and the start of extra time, and their play (on which Scotland depended so much) suffered. The Czechs scored twice in the extra-time period, causing tremendous distress to those listening to their radios that dull November evening, to deprive Scotland of their opportunity to go to the little known and distant country of Chile. It was so little known in fact that one player on the radio pronounced as if it rhymed with 'mile'!

It was a defeat with honour, and the Czechs themselves paid tribute to how well the Scots had performed. It was one of the many occasions in which a good Scottish team has been deprived, at an important time, of that vital commodity called luck. 'Twas ever thus, for following Scotland is so often a metaphor for life, whereby when one needs a lucky break, that is precisely when one does not get it. On the other hand, when things are going well, one has plenty of luck. The World Cup finals went ahead in Chile. England were represented, but not Scotland.

*   *   *

That this was a shame was proved in April 1962 when Scotland at long last broke the Hampden hoodoo and beat England for the first time for twenty-five years. It was an excellent game in front of the usual packed all-ticket crowd on a fine spring

Left Eric Caldow listens intently to instructions about the tossing of the coin before the start of the 1962 game against England which Scotland won 2-0.

Below Denis Law in action at Hampden Park against Ron Springett in 1962.

Sometimes better than the game itself! Dancing girls were used in 1962 to entertain the large crowd before kick-off.

day. Davie Wilson scored first, and although there was one moment of controversy when England seemed to equalize – but the ball was out of play before Jimmy Greaves crossed – Scotland remained the better team, finally confirming their victory when Eric Caldow scored a late penalty.

It was a great victory, giving Scotland the International Championship as they had already beaten the other two home nations. It was much celebrated that Easter weekend. The 9-3 thrashing of the previous season was now forgotten. There were indeed grounds for happiness in the excellence of Crerand, McNeill and Baxter, the brilliance of White and Law and the fine wing play of Scott and Wilson. But it never does to be too confident about Scotland and a defeat by Uruguay at Hampden less than three weeks later perhaps confirmed that it was possibly just as well that Scotland had missed out on that South American adventure. Yet how annoying and galling it was to see Czechoslovakia, who had only just beaten Scotland in November, reach the final and lose to Brazil!

The following season, 1962/63, saw more success in the British Championship. Wales were beaten narrowly in Cardiff, and Northern Ireland routed at Hampden in the autumn, and then on 6 April 1963 Scotland recorded their first success at Wembley since 1951. It was a new-look Wembley with a new roof, and a slick new Scotland that totally wiped out the ghosts of two years previously. 1967 was often described as Jim Baxter's Wembley; there is a stronger case for claiming that 1963 should have that claim, for he totally dominated the game.

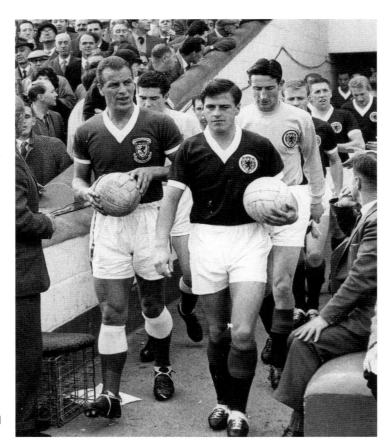

Cardiff, 1962. Captains John Charles of Wales and Eric Caldow of Scotland lead out their respective teams. Scotland would win this game 3-2.

Eric Caldow, Rangers' much loved and respected left-back was carried off with a broken leg after only five minutes – another manifestation of the Wembley injury jinx which tended to strike, particularly on big occasions like internationals and English FA Cup final day. This was before substitutes were allowed and Scotland were therefore reduced to ten men, but with Baxter on board, it was more like Scotland had twelve. Baxter scored an opportunist goal when he tackled an English defender who foolishly tried to dribble in his own penalty area, then Scotland were awarded a penalty. Caldow was the normal penalty taker, but in the absence of anyone else, Baxter himself took the spot-kick and scored, admitting afterwards that it was his first ever penalty!

As expected, in the second half England applied the pressure and it looked as if the extra man would count. The defence, however, held firm until the last quarter of an hour when Bryan Douglas, the hammer of the Scots of two years previously, pulled one back. Bill Brown, who had had some excellent seasons for the brilliant Tottenham Hotspur team of that decade, was superb in the Scotland goal, and Scotland held out to give the travelling Scottish fans something to celebrate in Piccadilly and Trafalgar Square that night.

England v. Scotland at Wembley, 1963. Gordon Banks cuts out a cross before Ian St John can get to it.

Right Wembley, 1963. Jim Baxter sends Gordon Banks the wrong way to seal Scotland's victory. It was Baxter's first ever penalty kick!

Below Denis Law celebrates Jim Baxter's goal at Wembley in 1963. Scotland won 2-1.

1963. Scotland have just won at Wembley and Davie Wilson, Willie Henderson and John White are joined by an exuberant fan.

1963 continued its course with Scotland proving as unpredictable as ever. Their first match after Wembley is almost unique in international history for it was abandoned after seventy-nine minutes when the English referee Mr Finney sent off an Austrian who refused to go! Scotland were winning 4-1 at this point, Wilson and Law having scored a pair each, and would surely have won anyway. Austria's behaviour was atrocious, but the Scottish fans had much to be pleased about with their team. It was slightly surprising that Scotland kept arranging such friendly fixtures with Austria, for relations between the teams on the field were usually anything but friendly.

On tour in 1963 the fatal Scottish conditions of over-confidence and self-destruction came into play again. Norway and Eire both beat Scotland when Scotland were confidently predicted to thump them, then Scotland proceeded to pull off one of their more remarkable results of their history when they beat Spain 6-2 in Madrid! It was no fluke and it was a strong Spanish team, but in the context of the previous defeats by what were considered to be weaker opposition in the 1960s, this was crazy, irrational, inconsistent, incomprehensible, quintessentially Scottish form. It would be repeated more than once in a World Cup context in years to come.

In the autumn of 1963, the British Government struggled to cope with the Profumo scandal when John Profumo the Minister of War was discovered to have patronised the same lady of pleasure as a Russian naval attaché. Among Scotland supporters, more hair was torn out when Scotland lost 1-2 to Northern Ireland (thus Scotland had lost to both parts of Ireland in the space of six months). As if this had never happened, Scotland then hammered Norway 6-1 at Hampden with Law scoring four goals to make amends for the shocking result in Oslo in the summer. Scotland then proceeded to beat Wales 2-1 with more ease than the narrow score-line would have suggested. Two days after this result, on Friday 22 November 1963, President John F. Kennedy was assassinated.

*   *   *

1964 was the year of the Beatles, whose long hair and working-class Liverpudlian accents attracted the disapproval of the Establishment. Their music was in full flow on the wet day of 11 April at Hampden Park when Scotland secured their first hat-trick of victories over England since the 1880s. The weather was foul, and the play was poor, with the wind and rain making life difficult for the players. Baxter was not as commanding as normal but he was still influential. The only goal of the game came after 72 minutes when Alan Gilzean of Dundee rose like a bird to head home a Davie Wilson corner. Once again Scotland rejoiced. 'Scots Wha Hae A Hat-Trick of Victories' crowed the *Evening Times* that night.

Scotland in 1964 at training before the international with England. From left to right, back row: Alex Hamilton, Jim Kennedy, John Greig, Campbell Forsyth, Ron Yeats, Billy McNeill. Front row: Willie Henderson, John White, Alan Gilzean, Denis Law, Davie Wilson, Jim Baxter.

Above right April 1964. Alan Gilzean comes close.

Right April 1964. Gordon Banks saves brilliantly from Alan Gilzean.

Below left April 1964. Ray Wilson and Bobby Moore are suitably disgusted after Gilzean has scored.

Below right Dundee's Alan Gilzean. It was 'Gillie' who scored the only goal of the game in the 1–0 defeat of England in 1964.

Right April 1964. Manager Ian McColl shows his joy at the final whistle. Scotland have beaten England 1-0.

Below April 1964. A fan joins Henderson, Forsyth, Wilson and Hamilton to celebrate Scotland's victory.

Bottom April 1964. Scots wha hae a hat-trick of victories over England! Campbell Forsyth, Alan Gilzean, Alex Hamilton, Jim Kennedy and Davie Wilson take their lap of honour in the Hampden rain.

April 1964. Manager Ian McColl greets Willie Henderson and Davie Wilson at full time. The joy of the fans is evident.

A couple of months after this fine moment for Scotland, there occurred one of Scottish football's many days of tragedy when John White (who had played so well in that game) met his death in a freak accident. He was playing golf at a place called Crews Hill at Enfield in Middlesex, when he decided to shelter under a tree in a violent thunder storm. The tree was hit by lightning and John was killed. He had played for Alloa, Falkirk and Tottenham Hotspur and was generally agreed to be the brains behind Spurs' great teams of the early 1960s. Ironically, he had been nick-named 'The Ghost' because of his slight build and his ability to appear suddenly from nowhere. His death was a tremendous blow to Scotland.

1964 was the second year of what was then called the European Nations Cup. It had been first held in 1960 and was envisaged as a tournament to be held between World Cups. In this it would turn out to be a great success, but typically, Scotland showed no interest in this tournament until some years later. This was a shame for there is no reason to believe that at this time of their history, Scotland, under the capable management of Ian McColl, might not have done very well indeed. Scotland's form was inconsistent, but like the nursery rhyme of the girl with the curl on her forehead, when they were good, they were very, very good. Spain beat the USSR to win the final in 1964… and the previous year Scotland had defeated Spain 6-2 in Madrid! In 1964 Scotland drew 2-2 with West Germany in Hanover in a pre-tournament warm-up match for the Germans. It remains galling that Scotland's many excellent players of the time were not given this opportunity.

*   *   *

There was the World Cup of 1966 to be held in England. In the qualifying sections Scotland were drawn with Finland, Italy and Poland. As early as October 1964, Scotland defeated Finland 3-1 at Hampden to open their account, but the British Championship form was disappointing after previous successes. A feckless defeat in Wales was followed by a narrow win over Northern Ireland, and then the opportunity to beat England four times in a row was thrown away.

England lost Ray Wilson to injury (another victim of the Wembley injury hoodoo) and Johnny Byrne could only limp on the left wing, but Scotland decided to play very badly and even with the benefit of a goalkeeper's own goal could only draw 2-2. A fully fit England team would have won this game, but Scotland with veteran Bobby Collins, recalled for this one at the age of thirty-four, were a huge cause of grief to the support which now expected victory over England in every game. It was a distinctly tepid Scottish performance, and the English media were quite justified in their claim that this was a moral victory.

The World Cup was now beginning to dominate international headlines. The fact that the finals were to be in England would have been no disadvantage to the Scots, for the countries were similar and in any case about half of the Scottish team played for English clubs. Travel would have been no problem for the Scottish fans, and there would have been total support and commitment from an excited nation. Scotland would presumably have been based in Sunderland and Middlesbrough, places that would have been easily reached.

As Jock Stein would say many years later 'You are allowed to dream'. Those who pinned their hopes on such fantasies would be grievously disappointed. It did not turn out to be anything like a dream. More like a nightmare, in fact – not so much in the fact that Scotland failed to qualify, more in the identity of the eventual winners.

SIX

Missed World Cups
1965-1970

It may be that one day the late 1960s will be described as the golden age of Scottish Football. Certainly, results in European competitions would tend to bear this out. Not only was there the Celtic glory year of 1967, but people tend to forget that Rangers reached the final of the European Cup Winners' Cup in that same year – and only lost it because of a bizarre team selection. Kilmarnock, Dunfermline and the two Dundee teams were also successful in European competitions, and Scottish football was treated with respect in Europe. The issues concerning the Scottish national team, however, were far more complex.

It was a great era to be alive in. Prosperity had now reached almost everybody, Beatles music was belted out of every record player and more and more working people were treating themselves to foreign holidays and cars. The Forth and Tay Road bridges were built, the Glasgow motorway was constructed, and the benign Labour Government of Harold Wilson was doing its best to see that unemployment and poverty would never revisit Scotland. Culturally and morally, the Church of Scotland was now slowly beginning to realise that it had no monopoly over people's behaviour. The contraceptive pill had been around for a few years, and the question was now beginning to be asked: 'Is sex before marriage permissible?'

The Scottish nation, of course, retained its love of its national team. In retrospect, concerning the 1966 World Cup, there are two hypotheses. It is widely believed, for example, that Scotland might well have won the 1966 World Cup – had they qualified. The other is the perceived wisdom (angrily brought up in discussions on the subject) that Scotland failed to qualify only because of the attitude and intransigence of managers of English League teams (some of them themselves Scottish) who were awkward about releasing some of their players before the vital game in Italy.

Both these hypotheses must be examined, and they are at least half-true. The first – that Scotland might have won the World Cup – is not altogether improbable. England, as we know, did so in the summer of 1966. Less than a year later Scotland were, quite clearly on the evidence of 15 April 1967, a better team than England. In theory then it is quite plausible that Scotland could have won the 1966 World Cup. But how would Scotland have fared against tricky teams like Portugal, Brazil, Argentina, West Germany and of course England themselves? Conditions would have been in Scotland's favour, but there are too many unanswered questions and questions that one will never now get an answer to. How would the comparatively inexperienced manager, John Prentice, have fared? How would Scotland's super-stars, all available presumably, have performed, and more importantly would they have displayed the right attitude? Would media pressure have got to Scotland? Would the ill-disciplined, self-destruct attitude (so evident in 1978 in Argentina) have asserted itself?

The historian must, however, address himself to facts, and here we must examine the claim that Scotland suffered because of lack of co-operation from English managers. It is certainly not without foundation in that Scotland found themselves without Law, Stevenson and Baxter for the crucial Italy game. But Baxter had only a slim chance of making it anyway, Stevenson was a peripheral player and Law, having injured his knee in a previous game, was the player on whom most arguments centred about his usefulness to the cause.

The uncomfortable fact in all this is that the managers in question were all Scottish! Matt Busby of Manchester United, Bill Shankly of Liverpool, Ian McColl of Sunderland and Tommy Docherty of Chelsea all had players whom they wanted to use on that Saturday 4 December, immediately prior to the game in Naples. It was particularly annoying for Scottish television viewers to have to listen to the exaggerated Scottish accents of all these men as they sung the praises of their native land, yet would not lift a finger to help. But it must also be said that the presence or absence of their men in Naples on 7 December 1965 was not necessarily the key point.

There were many, many other factors. In the first place the SFA did not grasp the nettle by appointing a manager, preferring to use the part-time services of Jock Stein of Celtic. Jock, only recently in position at Celtic and about to lead that club to its finest hour, could not have been expected to take the Scotland job on a full-time basis. Indeed it is to the credit of his Celtic employers that they allowed him to do the Scottish job for the duration of Scotland's World Cup campaign.

The departure of Ian McColl in May 1965 was a funny one, coming as it did a week and a half before a World Cup tie! McColl had by no means been a failure, considering that he did not necessarily have the final say in team selection. Amazingly, there were still 'selectors' in place, although one would like to think that McColl was at least consulted. The three jewels in McColl's crown had been the three consecutive wins over England in 1962, 1963 and 1964. Against that, he had failed unluckily and narrowly to take Scotland to Chile for the 1962 World Cup, but it seemed that he was worth retaining for an attempt on the 1966 World Cup. His departure was the subject of much speculation – he was, apparently, 'asked to resign' – but it was definitely odd that the SFA seemed to have no permanent replacement in mind. It may be that McColl himself was more interested in the Sunderland job, a full-time post with far higher salary, but did the SFA try hard enough to keep him?

*   *   *

Spring 1965 saw Jock Stein on a high. He had won the Scottish Cup for Celtic and then, with Scotland about to play two World Cup qualifiers, he was asked to do the Scotland job on a part-time, caretaker basis. He willingly did so. His first game on 23 May 1965 was a creditable 1-1 draw in Poland. It was a foul night in Chorsów, but it was nothing to the foul language heard in Scotland's living rooms that Sunday night. The game was broadcast on BBC Home Service in Scotland, but was cut short with two minutes to go and the score at 1-1 because the radio authorities had a religious programme to broadcast at that time! God would surely have waited, we felt, and perhaps He himself wanted to hear the final score, but it was surely the last time in Scottish history that religion was deemed by the BBC to be more important than football. In the absence of teletext (not invented for another fifteen years) we had to wait until the next TV news programme in an hour's time to hear the result. It was a long hour.

Anyway, the draw, which Denis Law earned by his equalizer, was deserved and the team then went on to record a good result in Finland. The standard of football was poor, but Scotland survived the loss of an early goal to win 2-1 thanks to goals from Davie Wilson and John Greig. So far so good, and Scotland looked as if qualification was not beyond them. Three points out of four away from home is good by anybody's standards, and of course Scotland had already beaten Finland at Hampden as well in the autumn of 1964.

But Scotland let themselves down badly in Northern Ireland in the Home International Championship in October 1965, losing a goal in the last minute.

October 1965. Alan Gilzean (punching the air) has just scored for Scotland (against Northern Ireland). Other happy Scots are Denis Law, John Greig and Dave Mackay, but John Hughes is much more phlegmatic.

The sight that really distressed the Scottish supporters was that of Denis Law at full time seeming to come off the field with a smile on his face. It was far from funny, and his sense of humour did not seem to be replicated in the attitudes of the other ten Scots.

Eleven days later came the game against Poland at Hampden Park, and it was this game, rather than anything that happened in Italy, which cost Scotland the World Cup. Scottish self-destruction is of course a constant theme in the history of our people, let alone the history of our football team. This was one of the phenomenon's more obvious examples. The crowd was 107,580 – a record for the World Cup – and they saw Scotland ahead at half-time through a goal scored by, of all people, centre half Billy McNeill. The vast masses on the primitive terraces of Hampden were cheerful and encouraging as the second half began with cries of 'Scot-land, Scot-land' resounding around the huge bowl.

Scotland were not exactly playing Poland off the park in the second half, but they looked comfortable enough. Bill Brown was confident in goal, and the Rangers wingers of Willie Henderson and Willie Johnston looked capable of providing another. But Pat Crerand, who would soon lose his place to Bobby Murdoch of Celtic, seemed stale, Bremner had lost much of his enthusiasm and Law, the European Footballer of the Year for 1965, was, as often, lethargic (and indeed had actually injured his knee). Poland came more and more into the game and predictably scored with six minutes to go. Scotland were stunned, and in true Scottish fashion, lapsed into such a catatonic state of introverted navel gazing that they immediately lost another. The incredulous Poles won 2-1. Poland then went on to lose 6-1 to Italy.

Thus it was that Scotland had to play Italy twice. If they beat them twice, they would qualify. A win and a draw would earn a play-off. It was not impossible, but very difficult, to put it mildly. Amazingly, in an eloquent testimony to the love of football, their team and to sheer blind passion and unrealistic optimism, another crowd of over 100,000 turned up on 9 November to see Scotland *v*. Italy. This time, they had cause to celebrate. Baxter was back, Murdoch was introduced and Cooke was superb as Scotland, with sheer desperation as well as passion threw everything at the Italian defence. It was after eighty-eight minutes that the breakthrough came from Rangers' John Greig, following a fine move that involved Jim Baxter and quite a few other Scotsmen.

The rejoicing in the ground and in living rooms where everybody was listening to their radios was quite unparalleled in recent history. There was now a chance, albeit still a slight one, that Scotland might yet qualify for the England World Cup. The Poland horror was swept under the carpet and even forgiven. The nation was on the march once again.

The game against Italy away from home now became the decider. Scottish games on the first Saturday in December immediately before that Italian trip were post-poned – they might have been anyway for there was much hard frost – but Scotland had no control over English games. Hence the cause for Scotland's oldest excuse of all – it was because of the English! This excuse was of course heard in Darien in the 1690s when the English refused to help the Scottish colonists when they were being attacked by the Spaniards. Here, England was refusing to help them in the World Cup. Sadly in both cases, this excuse has only partial validity, in that Scotland had got themselves into this mess in the first place.

Scotland flew out on the Monday for the game to be played in Naples at lunchtime on Tuesday 7 December. This time the game was on TV, so the nation took time off work to watch it (with various factories complaining bitterly about absenteeism, and others bowing to realism and providing TVs in the canteens). Stein did not have his sorrows to seek. The absence of Law might have been significant, but Stein could have coped with it. What was a major blow was the withdrawal of Willie Henderson with a pulled muscle ten minutes before kick-off! Stein opted for a two-man forward line of Hughes and Forrest, put Ron Yeats nominally in the forward line but to be deployed as an extra defender, and decided, apparently, to go for the draw that would have earned Scotland a play-off.

Such tactics were bound to fail – and did. It was one of the very few occasions when Jock Stein got his game plan all wrong, albeit that circumstances forced things upon him to a certain extent. Jock was a great manager, but 'Homer sometimes nods' as they say to explain a rare error. (Another occasion was the 1970 European Cup final where Celtic might have repeated their triumph of 1967 with a better team formation.) On this occasion, it might have been a better idea to use Alan Gilzean, Willie Johnston, Bobby Lennox or Neil Martin to try to grab an early goal – and then defend, but defence from the start is a game alien to the Scot and the team were well and truly beaten 3-0 and out of the World Cup. Jock Stein returned to Celtic and John Prentice was given the Scotland job. Italy came to England and famously lost to North Korea. It was hard to believe that Scotland could not have done better than Italy eventually did – or was it? This was before Iran and Costa Rica, but we remembered Paraguay of 1958!

*   *   *

Thus Scotland exited from the 1966 World Cup before it even started. Recriminations were long and loud, mainly against England and English teams for their high-handed refusal to release their Scottish stars, but the sad fact of the matter was that unless Scotland were to insist in clauses in transfer contracts that 'players shall be available ten days before Scotland games', there was little that could be done about it. The real villains perhaps were the grasping Scottish clubs who could never resist the money of English teams for their stars, apparently oblivious to the distress that it caused their supporters. Robert Burns put it rather well when he said

> *We're bought and sold for English gold*
> *Sic a parcel o' rogues in a' nation!*

The imminence of the World Cup meant that the 2 April international between Scotland and England would be even more interesting than normal, for it would give Scotland the opportunity to show what they could have done and was a chance to puncture (at least temporarily) the pride of the English. Sadly the game was a disappointment, and although there were seven goals, all of them good, England scored four to Scotland's three.

New manager John Prentice, whose first game it was, made one mistake in that he played Bobby Murdoch of Celtic. The Celtic team of this era were now beginning to emerge, under Jock Stein's leadership, into the world-class power that they would become. Prentice rightly realised that much of this was to do with the power-house Bobby Murdoch. Murdoch, however, was ill with a flu bug, but on the morning of the match, seemed better. Prentice was very keen to play him and Bobby, of course, did not want to lose the opportunity of playing for Scotland against England. He played – but was totally out of sorts, and as substitutes were still not allowed in international games, there was little that Murdoch or Prentice could do.

The losers in all this were the Scottish public. It meant that Murdoch now departed the international scene for some time – and therefore the world did not see Murdoch at his best on the international stage. It also meant that England dominated this game for long spells, going 2-0 up before Denis Law pulled one back with a header, then more goals for England meant that they retained the lead even when the hardworking Jimmy Johnstone pulled a couple back.

April 1966. Ron McKinnon and Bobby Ferguson can only look on helplessly as Hunt scores for England.

Opposite, clockwise from top left:
April 1966. Jimmy Johnstone squeezes home a goal in spite of the attention of three Englishmen.

April 1966. Denis Law heads home.

April 1966. The score is Scotland 3 England 4. Scotland almost equalize in the last minute, but Nobby Stiles heads clear.

Left April 1966. The immediate aftermath of Law's goal. Baxter runs to congratulate him, the referee points upfield and five Englishmen are dejected.

Below April 1966. Billy Bremner in action.

April 1966. Billy Bremner, wearing the England jersey, doesn't look happy. Scotland have just lost 3-4. The Englishmen are the bare-chested Nobby Stiles and the camera-shy Alan Ball.

Scotland then lost two friendlies at Hampden to Holland and Portugal, and just as we were beginning to say that it was perhaps as well that Scotland were not in the World Cup, they amazed the world by drawing against Brazil, Pele and all, 1-1 at Hampden Park, Steve Chalmers scoring a goal in the first minute. It was of course little more than a World Cup warm-up for the Brazilians, but the Brazilians were full of praise for Scotland and expressed some surprise that Scotland were not in the tournament. Pelé and company thought we were good enough!

The agonies of the average Scotsman watching the saturation coverage of the World Cup that summer on his black and white television were intense. There were some excellent games involving Hungary and Portugal in particular and TV now had a device that could instantly play back important incidents like goals and penalty-kick claims, but nothing could counter the overwhelming feeling of depression when England won the World Cup.

Sadly, there was no pan-Britannic solidarity. Crude demands from down south before the final between England and West Germany that Scotland should support 'the same team that they did in 1940' were treated with derision and scorn. Denis Law said he played golf that day, others took to the hills, but most Scots watched with bitterness and jealousy as England lifted the Jules Rimet Cup with or without the aid of that Geoff Hurst goal that never was. It was a sad moment.

To a certain extent the balance was redressed the following year when Celtic won the European Cup with eleven Scotsmen, but that was something that not all

Rangers supporters, for example, could rejoice in. But there was another moment of glory that belonged comprehensively to all Scotland. It was actually the first game of Bobby Brown as manager, John Prentice having mysteriously resigned the post in October 1966 after only a few months in office.

There had been an interregnum when Malky MacDonald had been manager in October and November 1966, but he was combining this job with managing Kilmarnock, and as others had discovered before him, it is not easy to do two jobs. Bobby Brown was summoned from St Johnstone and given the job in February 1967. Bobby Brown was an eminently likeable man, famous for his sportsmanslike behaviour when he played in the goal for Queen's Park and Rangers in the 1940s and early '50s. He did not instantly give the impression of being a strict disciplinarian, but there would be no doubt that he would carry out his duties with enthusiasm and dedication. No manager would ever have a more exhilarating start to his career.

*   *   *

It was 15 April 1967 when Scotland won at Wembley to become the first team to beat the World Cup winners. The atmosphere in the London streets was, as usual, upbeat and raucous before the game, but inside the Scottish dressing room it was full of murderous intensity as Bremner, Baxter and Law vowed vengeance for the miseries inflicted on their nation over the past two years. Plans were laid to mimic Alan Ball's high-pitched voice, to soften up Nobby Stiles with a few hard tackles and to run hard at Jackie Charlton to provoke a foul.

The game was no classic but will forever live in Scottish hearts, even though the agonies of the last fifteen minutes for those in the ground and the others listening on the radio (there was no live TV coverage for reasons of sheer cussedness) were strong and painful. Law had scored for Scotland, at last perhaps living up to his club reputation, and for a long time it stayed like that with Scotland well on top and Baxter in particular dominating things by playing keepie-uppie. Then Bobby Lennox became the first Celt to score at Wembley and Wembley erupted.

Scotland never make things easy for themselves or their fans and a moment's loss of concentration led to a goal for England. Scotland then scored again through Jim McCalliog and victory looked secure. England, however, did not want to relinquish their record easily and Geoff Hurst scored with time running out. The last couple of minutes were as nerve-wracking as any previous or subsequent ones – even in the long history of Scottish football – but Herr Schulenburg of West Germany eventually blew.

If there was anyone that deserved to be singled out for this great moment in Scottish football history it was surely Ronnie Simpson, Celtic's thirty-six-year-old goalkeeper whose selection had been widely criticized on the grounds that 'the heart was ruling the head'. Bobby Brown, himself an old goalkeeper and older contemporary of Simpson, recognised and knew Ronnie's worth. Ronnie had last been at Wembley in 1955 some twelve years previously, winning an English FA Cup

Above Scotland's famous victory at Wembley in 1967. Bobby Lennox has just scored and has disappeared among his triumphant teammates.

Left 1967. Billy Bremner and Jim Baxter celebrate the epic 3-2 win over England. Willie Wallace is assailed by a fan in the background.

Windsor Park, Belfast, 1967. Denis Law has just missed an opportunity to score. Scotland lost 0-1.

medal for Newcastle United. He would now go on to win a European Cup medal for Celtic!

This was a moment for Scotland to savour, but there would be precious few others. The Wembley game was part of the qualifying group for the Henri Delauney Cup, commonly known as the European Nations Cup of 1968. Scotland once again shot themselves in the foot. They had only been able to draw in their first game in Wales in October 1966. Admittedly, this game should never have been played for it was the day after the dreadful Aberfan disaster in which over 100 children perished when their school was engulfed in the landslide of a coal bing, and Wales (along with the rest of Britain) was in mourning. Scotland in fact were very lucky, as Denis Law scored his goal with his posterior as he slid along the ground in the wet goal-mouth!

Then in October 1967, a year later, Scotland managed to lose to Northern Ireland in Belfast. The score was 1-0 and had it not been for Ronnie Simpson saving a penalty it would have been more. All this meant that the decisive game was at Hampden on 24 February 1968 and England were in the ascendancy as they had done better against Wales and Northern Ireland than Scotland had. A draw was therefore sufficient for them and England were past masters at holding out for a draw when they had to. England scored first then, although John Hughes equalized, gained their share of the points, neutralizing the magnificent play of Chelsea's Charlie Cooke, who might have won the day for Scotland.

Thus another major European tournament had no Scotland in it. Scotland's big moment was, of course, Celtic's triumph in Lisbon the previous year. Tommy Gemmell is rightly proud of his performance and particularly the goal that he scored that night. He will be less proud, one feels, of his goal in Scotland v. USSR a couple of weeks before Lisbon. He was perfectly positioned and the goalkeeper had no chance. The problem was that the goalkeeper was Ronnie Simpson and it was scored into his own net!

*   *   *

The last two seasons of the 1960s were dominated by the desire for qualification for the Mexico World Cup. Scotland still nursed (and not without cause) the feeling that if they had qualified for the World Cup in 1966, they might have done rather well. There was therefore a certain determination to make it this time to Mexico in 1970 where England, being the previous winners, had already qualified.

Scotland were drawn with Austria, Cyprus and West Germany. While it was expected that the Cypriots would present few problems, Scotland felt that it would be a major effort to beat West Germany, while Austria were also a team with whom Scotland had had many a skirmish over the years – the most recent one being the infamous abandoned international of 1963.

The first game was against Austria at Hampden Park on 6 November 1968. Some felt that it might have been an idea to cancel Scottish fixtures on the previous Saturday to give manager Bobby Brown more of a chance to avoid injuries and to get his squad together, but this idea was not greeted with any approval from the clubs themselves, and thus Bobby had an anxious wait by the phone in case of call-offs. In this case, he was comparatively lucky.

80,856 fans were at Hampden that night. Such was the primitive method of allowing people into the ground (which was even as early as 1968 being described as a national disgrace) that the Austrians were a goal to the good before some of the fans got in, Tommy Gemmell having been caught in possession. An unpleasant phenomenon was present that night as well, not for the first nor the last time. The Scottish crowd was sadly split in two with a Celtic faction and a Rangers faction. Gemmell of Celtic was relentlessly jeered and booed by the Mount Florida End of the ground, and if that were not bad enough, the treatment meted out to Jimmy Johnstone was nothing short of scandalous, leading to appeals from the Scotland management and Rangers FC themselves for this sort of factionalist behaviour to stop. Sadly, it would be a long time before that happened.

Yet there was no division on the park, as Scotland manfully recovered from that early blow and – instead of self-justification, recrimination and finger pointing that more spineless Scottish teams had indulged in before and would do so again – buckled down to their task and got on with it. Within five minutes they had equalized, a fine goal scored by Denis Law, and then immediately afterwards they hit the bar.

Austria now settled and began to play very well, and there was no more scoring until a scrappy goal by Billy Bremner after a goalmouth tussle (or a 'stramash' as

STV's much beloved commentator Arthur Montford would say) in which Bremner himself was injured but still managed to poke the ball over the line. This was after seventy-five minutes, and the last quarter of an hour was full of chances at both ends. All in all, it was one of the better internationals that Scotland had played in for some time, and they were worth their win, not least because they had shown the qualities of grit and determination.

Disposing of Cyprus in December, Scotland then turned their attention to the arrival of the Germans in April 1969. It was of course make or break for Scotland, and this time domestic games were postponed on the previous Saturday. Amazingly, Germany had never beaten Scotland, yet they were the beaten finalists of the 1966 World Cup! Man for man, it would have to be said that the Germans looked a better and stronger team, but Bobby Brown had chosen a good side and this time, crucially, the attitude was right.

The crowd that fine April evening was only a few thousands short of 100,000, and they saw a great game which Scotland really should have won. The midfield of Murdoch and Bremner was immense, and at half-time the 0-1 scoreline was no reflection on the way that Scotland had played. Germany had gone ahead just before half-time with a fine piece of opportunism by the famous Gerd Müller, and the Germans were usually professional enough to defend a one-goal lead.

Scotland pressed relentlessly all through the second half, but it was only in the last three minutes that any reward was given for their effort. A fine move between Charlie Cooke and Bobby Murdoch saw the Celt hammer home an unstoppable shot and a Hampden Roar, of the kind that had not been made for a few decades, was heard all over Glasgow. The game was not on television, but the radio commentary was eagerly listened to and it was a long time after that goal went in before the commentator was able to speak in comprehensible English again.

The last few minutes were frantic and frenetic, and just at the death an effort by Billy Bremner was headed off the line by a German defender, deceiving those at the far end of the ground who had already erupted in joy at what they thought was a deserved winner. So a draw was all that Scotland had out of a game from which they deserved a lot more. Scottish history (both football and general), as we all know is full of hard-luck stories; never was there a better example than this.

So Scotland were still a point behind West Germany. They would now have to beat them in Germany in the autumn, but treated themselves to a confidence booster when they beat Cyprus with no real bother on 17 May. Colin Stein of Rangers scored four goals, only one short of the record set by Hughie Gallacher against Ireland in February 1929. Before that there had been the British International Championship, by now a tournament beginning to struggle against other demands and in which Scotland yet again revealed the Jekyll-and-Hyde nature of their metabolism.

This year, for the first time, the Home Internationals were all televised, and the games were played at the end of the season. Scotland's first game was at Wrexham and in a goal feast, much enjoyed by television viewers, Scotland won 5-3. Signs that the British Championship was now 'television driven' included the erection of a

April 1969. Bobby Murdoch (right) troops off Hampden Park having equalised late in the game against West Germany.

1969. Manager Bobby Browns (himself ex-Rangers) with seven Celtic players in his World Cup pool.

massive scaffold for television cameras in front of the main stand at Wrexham, blocking the view of paying customers. As far back as 1969, television was well on its way to becoming the dictator of football.

The following Tuesday in lashing rain, less than 8,000 turned up to see Northern Ireland at Hampden. This did tend to prove the point of those who did not want to see more football on television because of the adverse affect on attendances. Both the TV audience and the paltry crowd, called by the English TV pundits the 'Hampden Whisper' saw a dreadful game, arguably one of Scotland's worst ever. Both teams were flattered to get a point, and the phrase 'battle weary' was heard over and over again to justify the half-hearted efforts of some players at the end of a long, hard season.

Worse was to come. Scotland now went to Wembley, this time on a Saturday night (for the benefit of television) and horrified their supporters by going down 4-1. England took command, and Scotland simply ran away from them, obviously psyched out by the propaganda drivel that had permeated the BBC for the past week. Colin Stein scored just before half-time to make it 1-2 and give Scotland some kind of hope after a dismal first half, but the second half was worse with the Scottish midfield of Murdoch and Bremner, who had excelled against West Germany,

May 1969. Gordon Banks punches clear a corner kick with Billy Bremner and Billy McNeill in attendance.

May 1969. Scotland score against England at Wembley. Colin Stein and Alan Gilzean are the happy Scotsmen.

nowhere in sight. Only Eddie Gray of Leeds on the left wing looked as if he could do anything with the ball, and England were made to look much better than they really were, such was the lack of opposition.

*   *   *

A more important issue was qualification for 1970 in Mexico. It all hinged on the game against West Germany in Hamburg on the night of 22 October 1969. Once again, Scottish domestic games were postponed on the preceding Saturday and, as the game was on television, the whole nation was gripped with a nationalistic frenzy that had rarely been paralleled. It was one of those nights where one could walk for a mile on the streets of Edinburgh or Glasgow and not meet a soul.

Scotland really had to win. A draw would possibly see Scotland relying on a play-off – as long as they beat Austria in the other qualifying game. Bobby Brown was without Bobby Murdoch, who was at a health farm in England in an attempt to lose weight, but otherwise relied heavily on both Celtic and Rangers for his defence. Up front the double centre forward pairing of Alan Gilzean and Colin Stein looked as if they could cause problems for the Germans, no matter how good the legendary Teutonic defence was.

A fine shot of Billy McNeill of Celtic and Scotland.

It turned out to be yet another archetypal night of Scotland being the better team, but losing. Jimmy Johnstone scored first for Scotland, and although the Germans were level by half-time, it was Scotland who looked more threatening. Then disaster struck in the second half when Germany won a free kick. The ball came into the penalty area, McNeill seemed to be fouled but the ball found its way to Müller, who put West Germany ahead.

Scotland rallied again and Alan Gilzean headed a fine equalizer from a top-quality McKinnon cross. Twenty-five minutes now were left for Scotland to win the tie and, for a long time, they looked quite capable of doing so with Stein and Johnstone in particular looking very effective, but it never happened for the Scots. Then, with time running out and Scotland over-committed, Haller beat Gemmell and crossed for Libuda to give the Germans a victory that they hardly deserved. That does not excuse, however, the kick that Gemmell subsequently took at Haller. It reduced Scotland to ten men, but the gesture was born out of sheer frustration at the loss of yet another World Cup.

Scotland now proceeded to lose a meaningless game against Austria, and it would be some time before they would recover. It was a shame that the Scots did not make it to the World Cup in 1970, for there was some real talent in the team – as there had been in 1966. The world therefore did not see Scotland when they were at their best, and at a time when Scottish domestic football was doing very well for itself in European tournaments. It is a particular source of sadness that really great Scottish players like Jim Baxter, Denis Law and Bobby Murdoch were never on view at the World Cup.

*   *   *

The British International Championship of 1970 was dull. Scotland scored one goal in the three games as they beat Northern Ireland 1-0 and played scoreless draws against the other two. England were the only one of the British nations going to Mexico, and it would have been nice for Scotland to beat them at Hampden. It turned out to be a totally forgettable game of football, remarkable only for two

Alan Gilzean comes close against Northern Ireland in April 1970

How could this NOT be a penalty? Colin Stein is brought down by Brian Labone in 1970, but the referee says 'no'. The game finished 0-0.

things. One was that it was the first goalless draw between England and Scotland since the very first game in November 1872 and the other was the outrageous denial of a penalty to Scotland when Brian Labone of Everton inflicted a shocking hip-high tackle on Colin Stein when he was through on goal.

SEVEN

Respectability and a Few Shockers
1970-1976

The summer of 1970 saw England lose to West Germany in Mexico, followed a few days later by the defeat of the Labour government by Edward Heath's Conservatives. The two events were inter-connected, it was said, in that the 'feelgood' factor in England evaporated and everyone blamed England's defeat on outgoing Labour Prime Minister, Harold Wilson, and voted Tory instead. Fortunately Scotland was spared such nonsense, but there was little for Scotland to be happy about in 1970.

The years immediately following the Mexican World Cup were poor ones for Scotland. Any chance that Scotland might have qualified for the European Nations Cup of 1972 was quickly snuffed out when they lost in Belgium and Portugal in the spring of 1971, and then in Denmark in June. To a certain extent, Scotland were able to mend their reputation by winning in Scotland in all three cases, but a good team must be able to win away from home as well. The pattern always was that Scotland had great players, but could not knit together and produce a good team. With the benefit of the Hampden Roar and the fanatical and loyal encouragement that they received at home, they were difficult to beat. But away from home…

The British International Championship of 1971 was a total disaster. 0-0 in Wales in a game almost totally devoid of football, then a shocking defeat by Northern Ireland at Hampden was followed by a game at Wembley in which Scotland were completely outclassed. They were 3-1 down at half-time and it stayed that way as England knocked the ball around and Scotland's wee men like Billy Bremner and Jimmy Johnstone could not get a kick. Tony Green of Blackpool earned pass marks, but the rest of the Scotland team simply could not get going.

Scotland's manager at the time was still the extremely likeable and gentlemanly Bobby Brown. He was above all else a 'nice' man, but international football is not the place for such anachronistic 'favourite uncle' types as Bobby was. By 1971 it was

Above 1971. Jimmy Johnstone shows his prowess at Wembley.

Right Bobby Brown, Scotland's manager from 1967 to 1971. He did not enjoy the greatest of success or luck in the job.

Tommy Docherty (standing extreme right) is the manager of this group in 1971. Bob Wilson, a future TV pundit, is in the middle of the front row.

becoming apparent (and indeed blatant) that Brown did not have the mental resources nor the temperament for this job, but it was no pleasure at all to hear the chants of 'Brown Must Go' at this game. Sir Alf Ramsay, England's manager, was seen to comfort Brown at the end of the game and lifted Brown's arm to the jeering Scottish hordes.

Sir Alf was possibly being sportsmanlike, but he could afford to be, for his team were so far ahead of the Auld Enemy in everything in 1971 that for the first time we heard voices from down south questioning the wisdom of continuing this fixture, ironically when it was now almost 100 years on from its inception.

Brown did not last much longer, and for a while it looked as if Scotland had finally hit upon a winner in the choice of his successor. It fell to Tommy Docherty in September 1971 to take up the poisoned chalice that was the Scotland job. Tommy was in some ways the typical Scotsman (laced with a little of the aggressive Irishman). The Gorbals boy had fierce patriotism and loads of passion, but had hitherto displayed a distinct lack of 'stickability' in any job that he had been involved with. He already had a reputation for taking up positions and then leaving them – it was often said that he had 'more clubs than Jack Nicklaus'. Yet Tommy was proud of Scotland, he had talent and he was certainly the sort of man who could rally the country behind him. A veteran (as a player) of the horrors of the 1954 World Cup, he knew what it was like to be hurt. There was a charismatic, Bonnie Prince Charlie feel about him, but was there any backbone?

May 1972. Denis Law scores spectacularly against Northern Ireland at Hampden. Scotland won 2-0.

Manager Tommy Docherty watches Lou Macari and Colin Stein train before the England game in 1972.

Sadly the answer was 'no', not at least in a Scottish context, for within fifteen months he was off to Manchester United. This move was not exactly unpredictable given Docherty's previous form, but it did cause a great deal of distress to Scotland fans who had seen a distinct improvement in Docherty's twelve games in charge. Although three of them had been lost – to Holland, England and Brazil – the defeats seemed rather unlucky and the team had won two games in the qualifying round of the 1974 World Cup against Denmark, home and away, and were now playing with a certain amount of confidence and self-respect.

Crucially, it had seemed that Scotland did indeed have a manager who chose his own team and showed some sort of vision about building a squad for the future. Talented youngsters like Willie Morgan and Kenny Dalglish were give a run, and they repaid their manager with some fine performances. In addition, there was a certain bounce about the team that had been missing for some time.

The England game at Hampden in 1972 had been unlucky for Scotland, but England got the only goal of the game and held on to it. The game had also been a very unpleasant occasion. Fouls were frequent and Alan Ball did not help the atmosphere by seeming to use a corner flag as a handkerchief at one point. Furthermore, the Scottish crowd were nastier than they had ever been before, singling out Bobby Moore whom they called 'Golden Poofter Boy' and 'Bobby Hoor' and used some of the lyrics of *Jesus Christ Superstar*, the current hit musical:

> *Booby Moore, superstar*
> *Walks like a woman and he wears a bra.*

All this ill feeling was a little more than the primitive primeval stuff of Scotland *v.* England. It was possibly a result of the game two years previously and the 'Brian Labone penalty', but it was also the early 1970s when football crowds began to turn uglier than they had been previously. Yet there was a funny side to it as well. Emlyn Hughes of Liverpool and England tells the story about how the England team bus was on their way to Hampden and stopped at traffic lights. A group of Scotland supporters recognised the England players, made a few basic, primal gestures and hurled insults. There was no actual violence, however, other than the wee Scotsman who ran up to the bus and head-butted it! He then retreated to the admiration and cheers of his fellows!

By the time of Docherty's departure in December 1972, Scotland were at least halfway on the road to the World Cup in Germany. The game in Copenhagen saw Scotland play tough and win comprehensively and professionally 4-1. A month later, although marching orders were dispensed to Peter Lorimer, Scotland won 2-0. Lorimer had involved himself in an altercation with a Dane who had fouled him repeatedly, and he became, after 100 years, the first Scotsman to be sent off in an international played at home.

The value of these results against Denmark, much derided though they were at the time because 'it's only Denmark', would be seen the following summer when Denmark raised a few eyebrows by drawing with Czechoslovakia. This meant that Scotland need only beat the Czechs once in the autumn of 1973 to be on the plane to Germany.

*   *   *

Following Docherty's departure, which left behind a certain feeling of betrayal (in 1974 Docherty would manage to get Manchester United relegated to the undisguised delight of all Scotland fans), his successor was an unpretentious little man from Musselburgh called Willie Ormond who had played for Hibs in the 1950s. He was one of the Famous Five forward line which is still talked about in Leith, and he had also been the very successful manager of St Johnstone in the late 1960s, taking the douce citizens of the Fair City to exotic destinations like a League Cup final at Hampden and indeed several European venues.

Ormond was appointed in January 1973 and arrived just in time to see a grievous self-inflicted blow. To celebrate their centenary, the SFA foolishly invited England to play an extra friendly on 14 February. Fortunately, fog and frost cut the attendance for this meaningless fixture to 48,000, most of whom departed after England's fourth goal fifteen minutes from time. Scotland, with five Manchester United players on board, were frankly never in this match. It was said that in the 5-0 thrashing Scotland were lucky to get 'nil'. The SFA were suitably embarrassed when all that the Scottish fans could do was hurl puerile obscenities at the English.

The Home Internationals in 1973 continued to infuriate and perplex the fans. A win in Wales was acceptable, although far from emphatic, but then Scotland managed to play absolutely dreadfully against Northern Ireland and lose 1-2 at Hampden. The Wembley game saw Scotland play far better than they had in the February fiasco, and they were arguably the better team. But it was once again the professionalism (some might say the luck) of the English which won the day when Martin Peters scored the only goal of the encounter.

It was clear that Willie Ormond had a problem. A further two 1-0 defeats followed against Switzerland in Berne and Brazil at Hampden in summer 1973, but in both cases there were encouraging signs. Ormond and his men, we told ourselves, were merely attuning for the World Cup qualifiers against the Czechs in the autumn.

Wednesday 26 September 1973 was to be Scotland's day of destiny. It is difficult to overestimate the effect that this game was to have on the nation. It was, after all, sixteen years since Scotland had played in the World Cup finals – sixteen long years at that, in which all sorts of humiliations had been foisted upon us like the 9-3 hammering, England winning the World Cup and this year's dismal 0-5 defeat. Young men could not remember seeing Scotland in the World Cup finals; some who did remember wished they did not. The World Cup was quite simply something that one did not link with Scotland.

There was perhaps a political point here as well. The Scottish National Party was on the march, filling the void of those who were fed up with the establishment Westminster parties. Since 1958, the last time that Scotland were in the World Cup, at Westminster we had seen Conservative, Labour and Conservative again. These

September 1973. Jim Holton has just headed a goal for Scotland against Czechoslovakia.

sixteen years had been prosperous, but not prosperous enough, said the SNP. Oil had been found in the North Sea which the SNP felt belonged to Scotland.

The world outside the UK that winter of 1973/74 would be a difficult one. The Arabs and the Israelis had another of their wars (why couldn't they just play football like the English and the Scots did?), and as a result, oil prices rose in the west. The American President Richard Nixon, under tremendous pressure because he was slowly being found out for lying to the nation about the Watergate burglary, tried to deflect the attention away from himself by putting his forces on a 'low-key nuclear alert' and in Britain the Conservatives and the miners picked another fight with each other. It was very tempting to be like a Scottish ostrich, bury our heads in the sands of Largs or Arbroath, and say 'We'll look efter oor ain'.

It was no accident that this was the time when *Flower of Scotland* took to the TV and radio. This was sentimental pap, but it was the sort of thing that was listened to and there was a definite market for it. Soon Hampden and Murrayfield would resound obsessively to the dreary lyrics that we 'would send them homewards to think again'. Scotland even had its own pop group now, called the Bay City Rollers. Something seemed to be stirring in this nation.

The time was therefore ripe, and the nation rose to acclaim the triumph of Willie Ormond's men that September evening against Czechosolovakia. It was not a night for the faint-hearted, however. Future manager Ally MacLeod was on one of the TV programmes and at half-time, he described the Czechs in his lovely, rich, redolent

Two Scotland managers – Jock Stein and Willie Ormond.

Scottish accent as 'a bunch of crunchers'. And indeed they were, although Scotland were not unable to dish out a little raw meat themselves. For a while all looked bleak. Scotland went behind after thirty minutes when Celtic goalkeeper Ally Hunter missed a harmless drifter from Nehoda, and for a while it looked as if Scotland were yet again to fulfil their seemingly inexorable destiny of being permanent beggars excluded from the World Cup feast.

Two headers won the day. One came before half-time from Jim Holton off a corner kick, and then with quarter of an hour of the game left, Joe Jordan found the net after a move involving Bremner and Morgan. The remaining minutes were painful, as the whole nation gripped their armchairs, fearful of the expected piece of self-destructive Scottish defending, another goalkeeping error (Scottish goalkeepers were much pilloried in the English media in those days and would continue to be so), an own goal perhaps or something magical from the Czechs that would prevent Scotland from reaching the finals yet again. As the minutes ticked away, we tried not to think that the World Cup would be in Germany, that it was so near, that we could go and watch them...

100,000 implored Mr Oberg of Norway to end our agony. He would do so but not before we had a moment of real Scottish comedy and less-than-impartial television commentating. It involved the much-beloved Arthur Montford of STV. Arthur had been with *Scotsport* since its beginning in the late 1950s, and had experienced the highs and lows of watching Scotland. He was definitely one of us. He was a true fan, being an unashamed lover of Greenock Morton, and of course Scotland. His commentating clichés were the talk of the terraces. 'Up go the heads', 'What a stramash!' and 'Things getting a bit towsy' were among the favourites. His commentating that night had not been without touches of anxiety and emotion in his voice and there was an edge to his delivery. Once or twice we had heard 'Watch your legs, Billy' when Bremner was about to be tackled by a Czech, while the Czech goal had been described as a 'Disaster for Scotland', with the two Scottish goals being much praised. Now, with time passing, the veteran Denis Law, who had played well but was clearly tiring, suddenly broke through on goal. Arthur abandoned any pretence of neutrality and began shouting 'Come on, Denis! Come on, Denis!', but sadly Denis was too exhausted to take advantage of the opportunity – even with the support of the venerable Arthur.

Not that it mattered, for the final whistle blew soon afterwards and Scotland, from Thurso to Galashiels, from Kilmarnock to Aberdeen, from the Orkneys to Islay, erupted in joy. Scotland were in the World Cup proper once again, and this time there was reason to not believe that we could do well. Certainly no team on earth could ever have expected such unanimous or passionate backing from its nation. Even the normal 'Scotland knockers' who thrived on pessimism and depression – sadly another national characteristic – were, for the moment at least, stilled and joined in the national euphoria which would last for days.

Scotland still had to go to Czechoslovakia, but it was a game of no importance. Some Scots were injured, others only claimed to be and it was a weakened Scottish

November 1973. Scotland line up before the start of a friendly against West Germany at Hampden Park.

team that lost 0-1 to the Czechs, who seemed to be nursing a sense of grievance. It mattered very little. What really did matter was what happened a few hours later when Poland drew with England at Wembley, meaning that England would not be at the finals of the 1974 World Cup.

The rest of that winter and spring were passed in eager anticipation of the 1974 World Cup – although it was a dreadful time as power cuts, miners' strikes, General Elections, petrol shortages and Arab-Israeli tension distracted everyone. But the thought of being in Germany in the summer eased everyone through the difficult winter. Scotland even produced their own World Cup song, although the lyrics were buttock-clenchingly embarrassing. Using the war cry of cartoon star Fred Flintstone, it went

> *Yabba dabba dabba doo*
> *We support the Boys in Blue*
> *And it's easy, easy!*

Other stanzas contained gems like

> *Ring a ding a ding a ding*
> *Jimmy Johnstone on the wing*
> *And it's easy, easy!*

Amazingly, but indicative of the general mood of the country, people bought that record!

*   *   *

Scotland continued to be a yo-yo team with little real form to go on. In the British Championships of 1974, they managed yet again to lose to Northern Ireland but rallied well to beat Wales before, to the delight of everyone, beating England. It was a 2-0 win, both goals being deflections, but Scotland had played well enough to deserve the victory.

The match finished to scenes of general glee and the sight of Jimmy Johnstone making offensive gestures to the gentlemen of the Press! Jimmy had been having a bad time. This had been the week of his 'boating accident' at Largs, in which he had had to be rescued by the coastguard. Jimmy, free for a spell from the tyranny of Jock Stein who was his club manager at Celtic, found the more liberal regime of Willie Ormond more difficult to handle. Being out for some refreshment in the company of Denis Law and others, Jimmy had felt like a sail in a fishing boat. He had cast off, and found himself steadily heading in the general direction of America and unable to bring himself back. It was a silly, funny incident, but Jimmy had been castigated by the English and Scottish Press. Willie Ormond laughed it off and duly played Jimmy against England. Jimmy had taken the opportunity, played well and as Scotland won 2-0, felt able to illustrate by his fingers that Scotland had scored twice!

1974. Scotland have just beaten England 2-0 at Hampden and Billy Bremner and Jimmy Johnstone (who has swapped shirts with an England player) are celebrating. Earlier that week was Jimmy's infamous attempt to row the Atlantic!

So it was on to Germany via Belgium and Norway – with a defeat and a win to confuse the punters even more. The serious business would take place in the games against Zaire, Brazil and Yugoslavia. Scotland would, one imagined, beat Zaire and lose to Brazil, but Yugoslavia was the most difficult one to call. Certainly, the Tartan Army was mobilised to go there. Tickets for the games did not seem to be too difficult to obtain and Scotland would have a large and vocal support at all three matches.

It would be fair to say that Scotland did have the reluctant support of quite a few Englishmen. Englishmen do not reciprocate with a feeling of hatred to Scotland the feelings that Scotsmen have for England. There is a tendency to support Scotland, albeit in a patronising sort of a way. There was in 1974 an advertisement on TV about an Englishman who moaned about everything to do with Scotland… until he saw the beer, saying 'Your beer is good'. Similarly, there was a general tendency in Newcastle, Manchester, London and Birmingham to admit that, in the absence of England, it was permissible to support Scotland.

This did, however, have its lunatic element on the World Cup TV football programmes. We had the embarrassing spectacle of Englishmen wearing tartan jackets when they were doing their stint on the studio panel – something that everyone cringed at – and being introduced as 'Brian McClough', etc. Worse still was the almost universal description of the Scottish nation as the 'Jocks'. Some Scottish people felt they were being mocked, but most found the whole thing so offensively and infuriatingly banal that they waited until the actual kick-off time before putting on the television!

Scotland's World Cup started with Zaire. A 2-0 victory on 14 June seemed satisfactory, but it was one which Scotland would bitterly regret a week later, for they simply had not scored enough goals. There were perhaps two reasons for this. One was the undeniable fact that the poorer teams play better in their first game, (and Scotland would suffer likewise in future World Cups), but the other was perhaps a certain tactical naivety in that the Scots did not seem to be all that aware of this 'goals' factor. Scotland were 2-0 up at the halfway stage with goals from Lorimer and Jordan, but they visibly took their foot off the pedal in the second half when more goals should have been pursued.

Still for the moment all was well. Frankfurt on Tuesday 18 June 1974 probably saw Scotland's best ever performance in a World Cup, when they earned a goalless draw against the mighty Brazil – and really ought to have won. Billy Bremner, in particular, had a great chance but the ball fell badly for him. Scotland were, in the opinion of everyone, the better team. Brazil were reduced to fouling to stop Scotland on more than one occasion, but the goal would not come for the Scots. It was indeed difficult not to be proud of one's nation that night – but the fact remained that they had not won and Yugoslavia had thumped Zaire, so that Scotland would have to beat Yugoslavia on the afternoon of Saturday 22 June.

It was one of those days where everyone will remember what they were doing. All of Scotland seemed to stop. Golf courses were distinctly empty, traffic in Edinburgh and Glasgow was light and some people even postponed their weddings by a few hours so that everybody could see this game. (Sadly, the author of this book was a guest at a wedding that day of people who obstinately refused to postpone or delay. It was no real surprise then that, with such an attitude, the marriage did not last long and the couple divorced acrimoniously a few years later! Hell mend them, as the Scottish phrase goes.)

Scotland had the opportunity to progress to the last eight of the World Cup, and to date this has been our best chance. For a long time in the intense heat of Frankfurt, things were looking well, with Scotland ignoring the intense provocation of the coarse Yugoslav tackles, and playing their own game. But they did not score, and the longer the game went on, the more Scotland began to get desperate. Questions began to be asked as to why Jimmy Johnstone was not being deployed. He was on the bench and warming up. He looked just the man for a situation like this.

Elsewhere, things were for the moment working for Scotland. Brazil were playing Zaire in Gelsenkirken and the Africans were defending brilliantly to hold the Brazilians to 2-0 late in the game. This would probably have allowed Scotland a play-off at least, even if the game remained 0-0 against Yugoslavia. But there are moments of destiny which one cannot really do an awful lot about. The Ancient Greeks envisaged the Three Sister Fates: one who spun out the thread, another who took it in and a third with a pair of scissors who decided when enough was enough. This all happened to Scotland in the space of a few minutes.

In Gelsenkirken, the Zaire goalkeeper allowed in a goal which bordered on the unbelievable. It was a weak shot by an exhausted Brazilian from a tight angle and all the 'keeper had to do was stand beside the post and he would have stopped it. Curiously, in the long history of suspected bribery involving goalkeepers, no-one seems to have questioned this particularly absurd, yet so significant, goal.

The Scottish players apparently did not know of that, but, soon afterwards, they did know that they themselves were 1-0 down. Seven minutes remained when the overstretched defence was caught out, Scotland conceded a goal and effectively

World Cup 1974. Joe Jordan comes close for Scotland against Yugoslavia, but the game ends in a draw which is not enough for Scotland to qualify.

The undefeated Scots return from the 1974 World Cup.

went out of the World Cup. It mattered little that, almost at the full-time whistle, Joe Jordan at last scored for Scotland as there was barely enough time to centre the ball and restart the game.

Thus Scotland came home, the only unbeaten team to bow out of 1974 World Cup. It was the closest that Scotland were ever likely to come, and although fingers were pointed at Billy Bremner for over-elaboration with the ball when more goals needed to be scored against Zaire and at Willie Ormond for not using Jimmy Johnstone against Yugoslavia, in truth the nation was really very happy with the squad. Respectability had been achieved and quite a few foreign journalists and a few grudging English ones had to agree with Willie Ormond when the loveable Musselburgh man said ungrammatically but sincerely 'the lads done well.'

*   *   *

Scotland proceeded to continue their bewilderingly unpredictable form, this time all the more infuriating for the undeniable fact was that they were a good side. It would have been nice, for example, to qualify for the European Nations Cup finals, as they were then called, in 1976 but a careless defeat at the hands of Spain in the very first game more or less put paid to that, however well they played afterwards. It was a classic case of Scottish self-destruction.

'The boys done well!' – Willie Ormond (centre) is justly proud of his boys as they come home from the 1974 World Cup in Germany.

In front of 94,331 people at Hampden, Scotland took an early lead through Billy Bremner, then were awarded a penalty. Tam Hutchison (who would have an interesting career in that he would score for both sides in the 1981 FA Cup final) missed it, and then Scotland immediately began to argue with each other instead of concentrating on the task in hand. Spain scored before half-time and, with the sting obviously now out of Scotland, scored in the second half as well.

The return match at Valencia was unlucky. Scotland scored first again, but Spain, with the crowd at Valencia almost on their and the referee's backs, scored a dodgy equalizer which Willie Ormond was subsequently taken to task for complaining about. Thereafter, although Scotland beat Denmark home and away and drew creditably with Romania on two occasions, this was not enough and there was no Scottish representation in the 1976 European Championships.

*   *   *

There were two bad events involving Scotland in 1975. One was the 5-1 thrashing against England at Wembley, which was totally unforeseeable in the context of the recent form of both teams. On this occasion, the man who had to carry the can was Stewart Kennedy, the goalkeeper of Rangers. It was of course very unfair in the same way as it was unfair that fingers should be pointed at Fred Martin of Aberdeen

1976. The Celtic connection. Dalglish and McGrain hold up the British International Championship Tournament trophy.

in 1955 and Frank Haffey of Celtic in 1961. It is, of course, very convenient to blame a goalkeeper and to forget that the other ten men on the field also let their country down. In this case, it seemed that Scotland were overconfident, lost two goals in the early part of the first half and lacked the moral fibre to fight back.

But at least this was only a disgrace on the park. In September 1975 in Copenhagen after a very creditable 1-0 win, some Scotland players disgraced themselves in a Copenhagen nightclub. The ringleader seemed to be Billy Bremner, but Willie Young, Arthur Graham, Joe Harper and Pat McCluskey were also involved. Bremner almost appeared to admit guilt when he said there was 'no fight and no trouble about the bill' (thereby implying that there was), before going on to add 'anyway what we do in our spare time is nothing to do with anyone else'.

Yet this was while they were with the Scotland party! Not for the first time had Willie Ormond's lax approach to discipline come to grief – one recalled the Jimmy

Johnstone incident with the boat at Largs in 1974, and a minor incident in Oslo in the same year – and the result was that the players were banned for life. There was something in tune with the rest of the 1970s in this ugly incident . The 1970s were the time when hooliganism and violence on and off the field were at their height, but there was something intrinsically Scottish about this inability to cope with freedom and alcohol abroad.

Scotland now had a problem with credibility and, for a while, attendances dipped alarmingly (11,375 to see Romania in December 1975 and 15,531 to see Switzerland in April 1976) as the nation seemed to turn its back on its team, but it is to the immense credit of Willie Ormond that he managed to turn things round and to win the British Championship for Scotland in 1976. Grit and determination were at long last in evidence as both Wales and Northern Ireland were dealt with, and then, for a change, it was an England goalkeeper who was lampooned in an international.

Ray Clemence was undeniably one of the better of the many good England goalkeepers of that decade. With the score at 1-1 at Hampden, Clemence let a weak Kenny Dalglish shot trickle through his legs to give Scotland a win that they actually did deserve. It was a gift, but thereafter the Scottish team buckled down to it, worked for each other and wiped from the national consciousness the disasters of 1975. It was the first time that Scotland had beaten all three countries since 1963, and it did show that Scotland could sometimes show some spirit and resilience.

May 1976. Danny McGrain, in an England jersey (having swapped at the end of the game) holds up the British International Championship trophy. Scotland have just beaten England 2-1.

There was a postscript to this game and the Ray Clemence incident. Years later, on a train, the author met Don Revie, the England manager at the time of the 1976 game. Don chatted amiably about this and that, singling out team managers who faked injuries for players to avoid international matches as the main bugbear of an international manager, and then talking about England v. Scotland games. He talked about 1976 and said that on the morning of the game, a member of the back-room staff who knew about such things said that he had done a computer check on Clemence and that he was on a 'triple critical' biorhythm the following day. This would mean that Clemence would be very likely to make mistakes, and that it might be an idea to drop him and play someone else in goal. Don's reaction to this was dismissive and derisory and Clemence played. Subsequently, Clemence was indeed blamed by everyone for both Scottish goals. Don had a twinkle in his eye as he told that story. Maybe he was having the author on or maybe the author's biorhythm meant that he was more likely to believe rubbish that night?

EIGHT

Argentina
1978

Some years before the 1978 World Cup, there appeared the song *Don't Cry For Me, Argentina* sung by Julie Covington. It was part of the Eva Peron musical *Evita*. Later, the film would feature Madonna in the eponymous role. The story was based on the tragic life of the wife of the Argentine dictator of the early 1950s, Juan Domingo Peron. Eva herself had distinct parallels with Lady Diana Spencer in that she was beautiful, cared (apparently) for the underprivileged and died young, but the song was beautiful, and the name Argentina ('the land of silver' in Latin) still conjured up something exotic, distant and beautiful. When Scotland qualified for the 1978 World Cup in Argentina, it would have been a fair bet to say that less than 1,000 of Scotland's population of five million had ever been there or indeed had ever harboured any intentions of going there.

It is difficult to resist a historical parallel with the Darien fiasco of the 1690s. In 1693 a previously reputable Scots businessman called William Paterson launched a scheme to colonise Darien on the Isthmus of Panama. Paterson had previously founded the Bank of England and the original intention had been to join forces with the English and the Dutch and perhaps cut a canal through the isthmus to connect the Atlantic and the Pacific Oceans, the easier to facilitate trade between East and West. When the English and the Dutch pulled out of this scheme, Paterson was all the more enthusiastic, for this would be the beginning of the Scottish Empire in the same way as England was already settling in India and North America, and the Spaniards in South America.

Paterson persuaded many Scots people to part with £5 and some to sail with him from Leith in 1698. It was total blind optimism. Paterson himself had never been there before, and very few others had. He was going on 'hearsay' evidence. Some Scots died on the voyage, others died soon after arrival as there was no immunity to foreign diseases. To make matters worse, the climate was the very antithesis of the Scottish one and the native Indians and the Spaniards were far from friendly. The English refused to help because they were trying to build friendly relations with the Spaniards, and the whole thing collapsed ignominiously, the only saving grace as far as national pride was concerned being the opportunity that we could blame the English for it all.

This scheme probably was more deleterious to Scotland's psyche than the Battle of Flodden, the Glencoe Massacre, the Jacobite Rebellions, the Highland Clearances and the establishment of the Glasgow slums all put together. Yet, it might have worked had it not been for the fatal Scottish flaws of inadequate preparation, uncompromising faith in Scottish ability to solve all problems and the penchant for self-destruction. As we shall see, the parallels with Argentina in 1978 are eerily accurate.

*   *   *

1976 and 1977 were good years for Scotland. Great players abounded – Dalglish, Rioch, Gemmill, Jordan, McGrain, McQueen – and Scotland not only beat England in both years but also recovered well from defeat in their first World Cup qualifying match in order to reach Argentina. The loss to Czechoslovakia in October 1976 in Prague was hardly disastrous, for Czechoslovakia (managed incidentally by Josef Venglos who became Celtic's manager in 1998/99) had been the beaten finalists of the 1976 European Nations' Cup.

The other nation in the three-team qualifying section was Wales. Scotland beat them on 17 November 1976 at Hampden. It was not exactly a vintage performance but it was professional enough after Wales gifted the Scotland an own goal. Manager Willie Ormond was delighted, but in May of 1977 he suddenly left his Scotland job to take a post with Hearts – a strange place for a former Hibs hero.

The replacement was Ally MacLeod, an effervescent character who had won the League Cup for Aberdeen, thus ending a long period of underachievement in the north east. The character of MacLeod was crucial to the World Cup campaign. He was an instantly likeable fellow, very patriotic and enthusiastic. He had been a cult figure in Aberdeen because he actually encouraged the punters to talk to him in the street. As soon as he was in the Scotland job, he immediately won the affection of the country by winning the British International Championship with a rare victory at Wembley, the first since the famous triumph of ten years earlier.

World Cup qualification was helped by a freak result when Wales stunned the world by defeating Czechoslovakia 3-0 at Wrexham in March 1977. This meant that the three results had cancelled each other out, and that Scotland could qualify inside the British Isles if they beat Czechoslovakia at Hampden and Wales in Wales (as we thought the venue might be).

In the meantime, the summer of 1977 was a good one for Scotland. A win over Switzerland was then followed by a 0-0 draw against Wales in the Home International Championship (not the World Cup qualifying group), in which the phrase 'cat-and-mouse tactics' might justifiably be used to describe both teams'

Ally MacLeod in 1977 soon after his appointment as manager of Scotland.

approach to the game. Then Scotland beat Northern Ireland 3-0 with Celtic's Kenny Dalglish grabbing two goals, before earning a famous victory in early June by beating England at Wembley.

It was a good 2-1 victory, with England ill-deserving of their late consolation goal through a soft penalty, but sadly this match will be remembered for all the wrong reasons. It was the day that the Wembley turf was desecrated by Scottish fans and the goalposts snapped in two as the tartan-bedecked hordes climbed on top of them. There was no real malicious intention in all this, but it was an image which did Scotland no good at all and probably did more than anything else to encourage England fans to try to get a little revenge on future occasions. In the long term, this day was the catalyst to the stopping of the fixture altogether.

But Scotland were on a high and, very imaginatively, had arranged a tour of South America to play Chile, Argentina and Brazil. The 1978 World Cup would be in Argentina, of course, and it was an excellent (and uncharacteristic) piece of forward thinking. It also revealed a certain amount of optimism that Scotland expected to be at the 1978 World Cup. The Argentinians were delighted to see the Scots, for there had been a question mark over whether they were to be allowed to stage the

The unacceptable sight of Scottish fans, as they break the goalpost at Wembley while celebrating their defeat of England in 1977.

World Cup, given their human rights record and the military government's tendency to eliminate those who disagreed with them.

There was indeed opposition to this tour back home. The game in Chile would be played in the Estadio Nacional of Santiago, where less than four years previously following the bloody coup of 11 September 1973, Pinochet's thugs had massacred hundreds and possibly thousands of supporters of the deposed Salvador Allende. The political prisoners had been detained in the playing arena and actually shot in the dressing room that Scotland would use! It was a chilling thought, and historians would parallel Pinochet's repression with that of the Duke of Cumberland after Culloden in 1745.

Showing admirable determination, Scotland continued with the fixture and commendably won 4-2. Three days later in Argentina, Scotland took on the home team containing Passarella, Luque and Ardiles. MacLeod's men drew 1-1 in a game which would have a good chance of being considered one of their best ever results on foreign soil. In fact it was a game of two late penalties, the one for Argentina giving every sign of being an appeasement offering for Scotland's a few minutes earlier. Both were converted, Scotland's by Don Masson, and the game finished as a draw. The Argentine Press and public were very impressed with the Scotland team.

It was a game, however, in which Willie Johnston would begin his unfortunate dealings with the country of Argentina. Willie, a hard working, likeable player, although generally regarded to be on a shorter fuse than most, would hit the headlines in a world-shattering way the following year. This year, he contented himself with being sent off, adding to many such unhappy experiences that he accumulated in a long and varied career with Rangers, West Bromwich Albion and Hearts.

On to Brazil and once more a creditable performance in the Maracana. Scotland lost 0-2, but were hardly disgraced and Brazil's goals were late in coming. Scotland thus returned home with every reason to be proud of themselves. They had played well in that distant continent – the only snag being that it was now felt that no more work needed to be done on South American football. The research had already been prepared for the big exam, as it were. All that was required was to get there, and all would be well.

21 September 1977 saw the Czechs at Hampden. In a game that was reminiscent of the 1973 encounter, Scotland won 3-1 with all the Scottish goals coming from the air. Bruce Rioch was outstanding as captain, Kenny Dalglish (who was now a Liverpool player rather than a Celtic one) was brilliant, but the Man of the Match was West Bromwich Albion's Don Masson. On a night on which there were no failures at all, and on which the Scottish substitutes bench apparently joined in the singing of *Flower of Scotland*, the Hampden Roar was heard in full volume once again. The following day the nation talked positively and animatedly about football. Now all Scotland had to do was beat Wales.

Wales, for reasons best known to their legislators, opted to play this crucial fixture in England, at Anfield, Liverpool. This was presumably with the intention of making more money for themselves, but it remains a mystery why they couldn't have asked the rugby authorities for the use of Cardiff Arms Park where *Land of My Fathers* might have drowned out *Flower of Scotland*. As it was, most tickets fell into greedy Scottish hands and as Anfield was now the home ground of Scotland's key player, Kenny Dalglish, it was a massive misjudgement by the Welsh. Scotland became more or less the home team.

MacLeod was also lucky with injuries. Only Danny McGrain had to call off with a mysterious, but long lasting foot injury. Rioch's replacement by Lou Macari was hardly a loss. Don Masson was promoted to captain and he clearly relished the job. The character of Masson would be a significant one in the World Cup campaign, as we shall see.

Even in the Beatles' heyday of more than a decade previously, Liverpool had never seen such hysteria as the Scots brought that night. Welsh supporters were hardly visible for their 'home' game, and Liverpool's famous 'Kop' was taken over by the tartan-clad brigade. Liverpool's legendary manager Bill Shankly, who had galvanised Liverpool during the 1960s, was moved to say that Anfield had never seen anything like this.

The Scottish crowd played a significant part, for the game hinged on a penalty. Welsh centre half David Jones and Scotland's Joe Jordan went up for a ball and the referee thought that it was the hand of the Welshman who punched the ball away. In fact, television pictures in slow motion proved that Jordan was the guilty party, and had this been a predominantly Welsh crowd of 10,000 or so at Wrexham, it probably would never have been given. Don Masson scored from the spot.

If there was some legitimate doubt about that goal, however, there was nothing that could be said to take away the second one, which was a superb Dalglish header. Following this clear-cut goal it seemed as though Scotland had done just enough to deserve their victory – however much the English Press tried to pretend otherwise. England had their own problems, because, for the second time in a row, they failed to qualify for the World Cup finals.

*   *   *

For 1978, most Englishmen were sympathetic to Scotland, although a substantial minority were not – even though most Scottish players played in the English League (which the BBC kept telling us was the best in the world). It was no uncommon phenomenon in those desperate times for England to hear a Scottish player in the English League being booed by opposing fans – just because he was Scottish! Yet there was interest and love for Scotland as well, as witnessed by the amazing popularity of Paul McCartney's ballad *Mull of Kintyre*, which became very popular during that winter of 1977/78.

In Scotland, the national mood between October 1977 and June 1978 varied between the euphoric and the ecstatic. There was little happening on the domestic front to hold any interest in a singularly insipid season, and conversation centred almost exclusively on Scotland's chances in the World Cup. Ally MacLeod not only caught the mood, he typified it, telling everyone that Scotland would win the competition. Respected football journalists said that as Scotland had one genuine world-class player in Kenny Dalglish and several who were almost as good, Scotland must win the World Cup – or at least were in with a good shout. Such is the propensity for people to believe anything if they want to believe it, that nobody laughed at the time.

To be fair, not everyone thought that Scotland would win the World Cup, but nobody predicted what would actually happen, and moderate opinion tended to go for a respectable Scottish performance with Scotland ending up at least in the quarter- or the semi-final stages. Ally remained upbeat and supremely confident. Presumably, the famous Scottish general Douglas Haig felt similarly on the eve of the Battle of the Somme in 1916.

The image that haunts all Scotsmen is that of Kenny Dalglish jumping over advertising hoarding at Wembley because he had scored a goal for Liverpool in their European Cup final victory over Bruges a few weeks before the departure to Argentina. Sadly it seems in retrospect to typify and encapsulate Scotland's contribution to the world. Yes, there was genius in Scotland and yes, we could reel off a list of things from telephone to television that had been invented by Scotsmen – but sadly, only in England or the USA and with the co-operation of other nations, seldom in a totally Scottish context. Dalglish could win trophies for England's Liverpool, and jump over hoardings to show his glee. But could he ever do this for his own Scotland?

*   *   *

1978. Ally MacLeod (with a cardboard Rod Stewart) leads his men in singing the cringeworthy World Cup song of that year.

The draw for Scotland's group seemed kind as it contained Holland, Peru and Iran. Holland were good, but few problems were expected with Peru and Iran. Sadly, little research was done on them (in the same way as William Paterson in 1693 failed to do his homework on Darien). Scotland would manage to cope with everything that anyone could throw at them. Ally's army was on the march!

> *We're on the march with Ally's army*
> *We're bound for the Argentine*
> *And we'll really shake them up*
> *When we win the World Cup*
> *For Scotland are the greatest football team!*

sang Andy Cameron, better known as a comedian than a singer. The song was a huge hit, and contained another verse which stated that 'England cannae dae it, cos they didnae qualify'.

Alarm bells should have sounded in the Home International Championship. All of Scotland's games were to be played at Hampden Park (travelling to Northern Ireland was still considered unsuitable for security reasons in the wake of the relentless troubles) and the performances could best be described as insipid: 1-1 against both Northern Ireland and Wales (the Welsh game characterised by a hideous own-goal mistake by Manchester City's Willie Donachie) was followed by a terrible performance against England as Scotland seemed disjointed and disorganized and reaped their due reward when England's Steve Coppell sneaked a late winner.

Even then there was no humility about the Scottish management, the Scottish players or the Scottish crowd. Banners were displayed asserting the world dominance of the Scots, even a few funny ones like 'Joe Jordan shoots faster than the Argentine secret police' or that 'Joe Jordan strikes faster than British Leyland' – a reference to the chronic labour problems in the motor industry in that decade. *God Save The Queen* was roundly booed and that dreadful dirge *Flower of Scotland* was given a good airing. The atmosphere was upbeat, hysterical, confident – and totally divorced from reality.

On the pitch itself, even when things started to go badly for the Scots, Ally MacLeod obstinately refused to bring on Rangers' Derek Johnstone when the Scottish forward line persisted in its dysfunctional decline late in the second half; the crowd sang the banal 'You didnae qualify' and 'We're going to Argenteen' to the tune of *We are the Champions* instead of having the decency to be quiet at such an appalling display. Then, in a shocking and almost incredible display of sheer gall (mingled with not a little bad taste), the Scottish players, without any great hint of discomfiture came out to greet their fans after the final whistle!

This should have been embarrassing but it wasn't, and the Sunday papers continued the hype with only a few, wiser elements in the Press warning that there was here serious cause for concern. The time was when a defeat from England plunged the country into Stygian gloom. In the 1890s, for example, the Press would freely use words like 'mourning' to describe the national mood after a defeat by the Auld Enemy. Not this time! The commonly felt emotion was that these games were merely pre-tournament friendlies, which highlighted weaknesses perhaps, but in the grand scheme of things did not really matter.

It is important to stress as well that this was a national phenomenon. The know-all 'I knew it would go wrong' was only really heard after the disaster. The mood of the nation was indeed not unlike that of the Darien fiasco of the 1690s where everyone was convinced that all would, of course, work out well, or the Sicilian Expedition of 415 BC, when Alcibiades persuaded the Athenian Assembly that even though Athens was locked in a life-or-death struggle with Sparta, it would be an appropriate time to build a new Empire in the West in Sicily. The fleet sailed out festooned with flowers and everyone convinced that the return would be even better. Similar was the mood in Scotland in early summer 1978.

There was, for example, the farewell itself. At Hampden Park, players were taken round on an open-topped bus before setting out for the airport, as patriotic music blared and even more tartan scarves and tammies were sold. An example of the inability to think things through was seen in the case of centre half Gordon McQueen. McQueen was injured and in the event did not take part in any of the three games. He was nevertheless taken along and was seen to be hobbling as he made his way to the aeroplane. Contrary to later stories, he was not carried out on a stretcher… but he certainly did limp. More seriously, there was no other specialist centre half with his heading ability in the party!

How we all cheered, and settled down to wait for Scotland's first game on Saturday 3 June 1978. A few had gone to Argentina, but there were hardly enough to be called 'Ally's Army'. Most of the nation (and this would include those who normally hated football) wore something tartan and looked forward to watching television. It is to the eternal shame of this author that he bought a tartan rosette and pinned it on his six-month-old daughter, the better to encourage her to understand that her nation would soon be crowned the best on the planet.

*   *   *

Above 'Goodbye-ee-ee'. Dunblane Hydro, 1978, on the eve of departure to the disastrous Argentina World Cup. The players look less then impressed with the required pose.

Right 1978, on the eve of departure to Argentina. Ally MacLeod looks relaxed and confident at Dunblane Hydro.

Almost immediately on arrival, the problems began. These problems centred on moaning about accommodation at a place called Alta Garcia. It was apparently not up to what had been expected by mollycoddled professional footballers who were used to better things. Not only that, but there was a fence around their 'hotel', which was more like a 'hostel'. Much of this is to be expected in a third-world military dictatorship, as Argentina undeniably was in the 1970s, but it came as a shock to the Scots. Stories however soon found their way back to the Scottish newspapers about 'escapes' and 'nights on the town', as well as more lurid additives like players being stopped at gunpoint by trigger-happy Argentinian police. Not all these stories were necessarily true, but smoke without fire is indeed a rare phenomenon.

MacLeod's party lacked the discipline that other more successful teams had. Apparently, the great Jock Stein, although occasionally excessive and even obsessive in his teetotalism, nevertheless made strenuous efforts with his Celtic and Scotland teams to ensure that everyone toed the line. He would sit in the lobby of the team's hotel in full view of the front door, so that he could see who was going out and coming in and, being himself an insomniac, would stay awake drinking tea and patrolling the hotel corridors until he was convinced that everyone was safely in bed. This approach seemed to be lacking in 1978, and the wilder elements took advantage.

An example of the negative publicity on the home front during the disastrous World Cup in Argentina.

So was Scottish self-destruction already present before a ball had been kicked? Not according to Mr MacLeod, who still exuded confidence, and the first game against Peru on 3 June couldn't come quickly enough. It appears that little, if any, research had been done on the Peruvians. We knew that they wore white shirts with a red diagonal band and that they had a chap called Cubillas who had played for them for many years. Other than that, little was known by either the Scottish public, the players or the manager. It didn't seem to matter.

The tense and excited nation put on its television sets that Saturday evening and watched Scotland take an early lead when Jordan was on hand to score when the goalkeeper couldn't hold a Rioch drive. This was good, but almost immediately Peru's midfield took a grip of the game as Rioch, Masson and Hartford (all of whom had been out of form for some time) struggled. Peru equalized before half-time at the crucial point when Scotland might have rallied under the influence of a half-time talk.

The real tragedy of Scotland often lies in the fact that opportunities are given but cannot, for one reason or other, be seized. It is like a drowning man who is thrown a stick, and all he has to do is grab it. But will he? Or someone suffering from a depressive illness. Cures and solutions do present themselves. Can the patient use them, or will he continue to sink into the mire of his own self-inflicted hell?

The stick was indeed thrown to the drowning man that night in Cordoba. All that was needed was to seize it and be rescued. Scotland were awarded a soft penalty early in the second half, but it was given to the off-form Don Masson to take. Masson had been outstanding in the qualifying games, but was now clearly finding this adventure too much for him. He had been one of the main complainers about the conditions. It would surely have been better to give the penalty to someone like the ultra-professional Kenny Dalglish, who had been in form for Liverpool and indeed won the European Cup for them that season. Kenny was also a very disciplined character who shunned strong drink and went to bed at the proper time. In that sense he was a real child of Jock Stein.

But Masson it was who took it. His effort was weak and almost immediately Peru surged forward. Cubillas, the old man of Peruvian football, scored twice, one of the goals coming from a free-kick, and Scotland lost 1-3. While the BBC gloated, it seemed as though MacLeod was immediately a changed man. Gone was the jaunty self-confidence to be replaced with the particular depression that a working Scotsman feels about going to his work on a rainy November Monday morning. Except that this was the Argentine in June.

Pubs were silent places all through Scotland that night. Most Englishmen had the good sense to hold their tongues, but those who didn't were given a frosty silence rather than any old-fashioned beating up. A visit to a chip shop anywhere in Scotland that Saturday night would see gaunt, sunken, sullen faces with glazed eyes not unlike those that war veterans would recall seeing in the ranks of Rommel's Afrika Corps in Tripoli and Cape Bon in 1943. What had happened to Scotland's new golden age? The world was over. We had been kidded on. We had been taken comprehensively to the cleaners. We had blown it.

The following day, ministers in Church made brave jokes about football to their disillusioned congregations and the *Sunday Post* – couthy, Scottish and comforting as always – pointed out that it was only one game. Perhaps a lesson had been learned. It fooled no-one. We knew that we had blown it, and that a quick departure home was perhaps the best idea. It would have saved a lot of further pain, anguish and agony.

*   *   *

Then came the scandal which would rock Scotland and the world, and make Scotland even more of a laughing stock than she already was. To incompetence on the football field would be added the charge of cheating. It transpired the day after the Peru game that Willie Johnston had taken an illegal substance before the match. It was probably taken without any deliberate attempt to cheat, but the world would not see it that way. In a laudable attempt to prevent the draconian penalty and banishment from the tournament, the Scottish authorities took the law into their own hands and sent Johnston to pack his bags and fly home. Ironically, all this meant that even if Scotland had beaten Peru in that ill-starred match, Peru would have been awarded a 2-0 victory. And cynics wondered what kind of pills Johnston had taken. Were they tranquillizers or perhaps sleeping pills? And had other members of the team also been on barbiturates? Judging by the way they played...

Years later to justify, rationalise or, more likely, to laugh off this catastrophe, MacLeod told a story of how they disposed of the rest of these pills. On a bus journey, they threw them into a field of cows. On the return journey a few hours later, the same cows, who had been placid and tranquil on the first journey, were all frisking about and charging about the field.

Even before Iran took the field against Scotland on Wednesday 7 June, Scottish public opinion was outraged. MPs asked questions, sponsors withdrew their support and relatives of the players were abused in the streets of Glasgow as the country searched for someone to blame for the national humiliation. The culprits were no one other than the Scottish public itself for its gullibility and for going along with this crazy ill-thought out euphoria which the media and SFA themselves had engendered.

The Iran game was even worse than the Peru encounter. MacLeod made changes but failed to introduce the obvious improvements of Graeme Souness and Derek Johnstone. Donachie, Jardine and Robertson were brought in, the midfield was tinkered with and the forwards were left alone. Scotland's goal was an own goal – another example of how the breaks can be given by the gods of football, and another instance of a stick being thrown to the drowning man – but Scotland were so lethargic and disjointed that they could not capitalize. Even a 1-0 victory in these circumstances would have given the team a slight chance of qualification, but Iran equalized in the second half and might indeed have won the game. Dalglish, of whom so much had been expected, was humiliatingly substituted, but the end

The quintessential face of Argentina 1978 as Ally MacLeod cannot bear to watch the Scotland *v.* Iran game.

of this spectacularly awful game came with the score still rooted at 1-1. More than one journalist used the word 'catatonic' to describe Kenny's awful performances, so much at odds with the way he had played for Liverpool earlier that year.

Ally was seen with his head in his hands, the Scottish fans hurled abuse at their own team shouting to them 'You only want the money' (unbelievably, rumours had leaked out that the players were unhappy with their wages after the Peru game) and the whole nation back home was sunk in a despair so total that it was honestly asked whether football would ever be the same again. Fortunately, resilience has always been a Scottish characteristic, as indeed has been the ability to laugh at oneself. The nation survived. Other more volatile countries with Latin temperaments, perhaps, or with traditions of political instability might have done something more drastic than the dour, phlegmatic Scots did. No-one was shot or hanged. It was, however, a profoundly sad point in many people's lives.

Those who chided their weeping children with things like 'Grow up! Learn to take a defeat! Don't take it too seriously' were of course the ones who had taken it too seriously themselves. Those who adopted the 'I knew this would happen' line were the same people who had bought tartan bonnets and scarves earlier. But everybody was now agreed that this was more than just a defeat – it was a national humiliation and disgrace. The crowing from south of the border was intense.

*   *   *

Back in Argentina, Scotland, when all was more or less lost and the pressure was off them, got it right at last and showed the world what they might have done! Fear of a real hammering deterred many Scots from watching their televisions on Sunday 11 June when Scotland were due to play the mighty Dutch side, which had reached the final in 1974. It was a fine night and dogs were taken for walks and gardens tended to. Those who practised these mundane pursuits missed one of Scotland's greatest ever games, which, in another context would have entered the Hall of Fame along with the Wembley Wizards of 1928 and 1967.

Scotland, with Souness at last on board, took a grip of the game and won 3-2. Dalglish came to life and it was an earnest Scottish performance. Archie Gemmill's goal which made it 3-1 midway through the second half will be deservedly talked about for all time, and for a spell it opened up the possibility of a 4-1 scoreline – which would have qualified Scotland against all the odds. Sadly, Johnny Rep ran up and scored almost immediately and the 'miracle of Mendoza' that Archie McPherson talked about on the BBC did not take place. Scotland were out.

If anything, this result exasperated and infuriated the supporters more than the previous two matches, because it showed that Scotland were not necessarily a team of no hopers. It was annoying and frustrating to see Holland reach the final (for the second time running) after losing to Scotland, but the victory did nothing to hide the size of the Scottish calamity. The galling thing was what could have been. The team returned home not to a heroes' welcome, nor even to a hostile reception, but to something even worse than that – the sound of silence, with only a few baggage handlers and a small band of diehard supporters at the airport noticing their arrival. They resembling the dwindling band of those who aided Bonnie Prince Charlie escape to Skye and then France in 1746.

It was no end of a lesson. The nation had been publicly disgraced. MacLeod stayed on as manager for a while, when it was obvious that he would have to be replaced. Some players were publicly sacked. 'Those who have expressed publicly their wish never to play for Scotland again will be accommodated in their desires' said a tight-lipped, angry Ernie Walker, secretary of the SFA, and others simply dropped out of the scene altogether.

It marked a total change in attitude in Scotland. It was no accident that the Scottish National Party, which throughout the 1970s had been boisterous and blinkered with some of its more radical slogans, now became quieter, more introspective and more thoughtful. Almost alone of all 'nationalist' parties in Europe and elsewhere, the Scottish National Party is not jingoistic, right-wing or bigoted, but before Argentina, it was tending in that direction.

Nine months later, on 1 March 1979, a referendum was held on whether Scotland should be allowed its own devolved Parliament. Scotland voted 52 per cent to

48 per cent in its favour, but that was not enough, for there had been a stipulation that 40 per cent of those entitled to vote would have to say 'Yes', and only 32.9 per cent of the electorate did so. Although the whole idea of 'devolution' had been a national bore for many years – and this in itself may explain at least some of the apathy – another factor surely was the lack of national self-confidence brought on us by the Argentina humiliation. Had the referendum been held a year earlier, i.e. during the pre-Argentina hype, it would have been a totally different story.

The loss of the referendum vote played a part in the fall of the James Callaghan Labour Government, and its replacement by the horrors of Margaret Thatcher who, with no great support in Scotland, proceeded to butcher so much of the country for the next twenty years.

> *Fareweel tae a'our Scottish fame*
> *Fareweel our ancient glory!*
> *Fareweel even tae the Scottish name,*
> *Sae fam'd in martial story!*

Football did not, of course, suffer any real permanent loss in Scotland, although the atmosphere was now much subdued. With Jock Stein as manager, Scotland played noticeably less flamboyantly and with a great deal more circumspection. The Scottish public had had its wings clipped, publicly and painfully, and it would be a long time before national self-respect was regained.

NINE

Respectability...and Tragedy
1978-1986

It was clear that Ally MacLeod could not last long as Scotland's manager as his credibility had been irretrievably impaired. Indeed, the very credibility of Scottish football itself was in dire peril. Yet three months after the fiasco, MacLeod was still there as Scotland opened their campaign for the European Championship to be held in Italy in 1980. The group was a very difficult one, comprising Austria, Norway, Portugal and Belgium, and would have been recognised as tricky even if Scotland were on form.

The defeat in what turned out to be MacLeod's last match was another of these exasperating Scottish performances. It was played on 20 September 1978 in Vienna and when the Scottish team (not, in all honesty, radically different in personnel from the Holland game in Argentina) went three goals down, then they began to play well to come back and almost earn a draw. This game was a microcosm of Argentina, indeed a metaphor for Scotland itself – lose, then play brilliantly, so that everyone went around talking about what could have been.

MacLeod went quietly after this game, and his replacement was the only man that it could have been – Jock Stein. Jock was already considered the elder statesman of the nation. He had been seen frequently on the TV screens during Argentina, radiating dignity and majesty, and cowing the TV journalists into agreeing with him. He had been supportive of MacLeod, at least in public, saying things like 'Once they cross that touchline, there is nothing that a manager can do' to cheer up the hapless Ally, but everybody was aware that most of the problems would not have arisen had Jock been in charge. Several of the troublemakers and the under-performers would not have been there in the first place, discipline would have been far stricter and the whole nation's feet would have been kept far more firmly on the ground.

Jock had enjoyed phenomenal success with Celtic, taking them from being a small club with a big support to being European champions and sustaining their success in Scotland. He had departed from Celtic Park earlier that summer, having apparently reached his peak. He had sustained serious injuries in a road accident in 1975 and a feature of his management in the 1970s had been his inability to keep star players. Macari and Hay had gone to England at the beginning of the decade, Connelly, a potential world-beater had not been able to cope with the emotional demands of the game, and, most recently, Kenny Dalglish had left for Liverpool.

The drain of talent from Scotland to England was hardly new, but what was noticeable was that Stein had been unable to impose his presence on these players and cow or bully them into staying with Celtic. This may be because the 1970s generation was the first that had actually been born into the Welfare State. They had therefore grown up with their own ideas and a refusal to be afraid of bosses and managers. There were also, undeniably, a large number of young men 'on the make'. If they wanted to go to England, they would go. Money was more plentiful down there. How would Stein cope with this breed of talented Scottish young man?

Following his departure from Celtic Park in 1978, Stein himself was trying English football, this time with Leeds United, but the call of Scotland was just too much for the intensely patriotic Stein, and more particularly his wife, Jean, who was not adjusting very well to life in England. She had never wanted to leave Scotland in the first place. Her experiences of life in Wales in the brief spell that Jock played for Llanelli in the early 1950s had not been happy ones.

It would of course have been very easy for Stein to play up to a 'Scotland's Man of Destiny' role and take an 'all my life has been nothing but a preparation for this moment' stance, but this simply was not Jock's style. He had seen too recently the problems that occur when emotion is allowed to take over from reason. His return to Scotland after his forty days in charge of Leeds was deliberately low key, but he did say that the important thing for Scotland would be the World Cup. 'Judge me on the World Cup' he would say. By that, he meant, presumably, qualification. He did not, one would have imagined, envisage winning the competition.

*   *   *

Stein won his first game, against Norway, at Hampden on 25 October 1978, his old protégé Kenny Dalglish scoring twice in a 3-2 win. That Scottish fans were willing to give Stein a chance was seen in the agreeably large attendance of 65,372. Unfortunately, public relations were not what they could have been and as several of the turnstiles were not manned, the crowd took a considerable time to be admitted. Clearly the authorities had not reckoned on such an attendance. It was another Scottish own goal at a time in their history when they needed, above all else, good public relations.

Scotland then had hard luck in Portugal in late November. They lost 1-0, but fought all the way and most independent observers thought that they deserved at least a draw. Two defeats meant that Scotland's chances of qualification for the 1980 European Championships were now slim.

The next international games were played in May and it was the Home International Championship. The winter of 1979 had been a hard one, and amazingly some Scottish domestic games were still being played in the month of May, so that neither a Celtic nor a Rangers player was available. It was a disaster of a tournament for Scotland. It opened with a comprehensive defeat by Wales in Cardiff, which was followed by a pitiful 1-0 win over Northern Ireland at Hampden; then we had yet another Wembley sob story. Scotland were winning 1-0 late in the first half thanks to a crisply taken John Wark goal, and as half-time approached, Stein walked from the bench towards the tunnel. Seeing this, the Scottish defence relaxed and, in the inordinate amount of time that the referee added on for injury time, England equalized.

This was rough justice on Scotland who in fact should have been far ahead at half-time. A goal before half-time has a tremendous psychological effect, however, and Scotland's midfield of Souness, Hartford and Graham, which had done so well in the first half, now collapsed in the second half and England won deservedly 3-1.

A week after that, in a high-profile friendly, Argentina came to Scotland and the Hampden crowd got their first look at a prodigy called Maradona, as well as some of the star-studded team which had won the World Cup a year previously. The defeat was by a respectable scoreline of 1-3, but then Scotland finished a difficult season on a high note by going to Norway to beat the home side 4-0, reviving briefly the flickering hope of qualification for the European Championships.

Such hopes stayed alive, but only just, when Austria came to Hampden and left with an undeserved point, but everything collapsed in a double header against Belgium who beat Scotland 2-0 and 3-1, when once again Kenny Dalglish's magic failed to materialise. But then, as was their habit, having been vanquished and with the pressure off them, Scotland decided to show the world what could have been when they beat Portugal 4-1 at Hampden in March. It was a great pity that only 20,000 were there to see this game, for Scotland played superb football.

* * *

There would be no European Championships that year – Scotland had never qualified for that – and it was perhaps just as well. Five games were played in that summer of 1980 and only one game won – that against Wales at Hampden. The worst game of all was the pathetic performance against England at Hampden: 0-2 actually flattered Scotland, so out of touch were they. Clearly, if there was to be any resurrection under Jock Stein, it was not yet happening. But the following season a new World Cup was opening up – and Jock had always said that he wanted to be judged on that.

It was indeed a relief for the people of Scotland not to be involved in that European Championships of 1980. The standard of football was not great, England received their predictable comeuppance, and the tournament was eventually won by West Germany. Belgium, who had beaten Scotland twice in the qualifying section, surprised a few people by reaching the final.

* * *

Jock Stein keeping a close watch on Andy Gray's shooting practice.

The 1982 World Cup finals to be played in Spain would contain twenty-four teams, for no other reason than that more money could be generated that way. It took little account of the logistic problems of arranging the finals with twenty-four teams, when sixteen or thirty-two would have been far more sensible. The draw decreed that Scotland were in a qualifying group of five teams, but that two would go through. Northern Ireland, Portugal, Israel and Sweden would be Scotland's opponents. In one of Stein's greatest achievements, Scotland not only qualified but in fact topped the group, having the luxury of being able to lose the last game against Portugal and knowing that it did not matter.

The influence of Jock Stein was seen throughout the two years of the qualifying games. Out of the window was the gung-ho super-optimism which had been the downfall of Ally MacLeod and others, and replacing it was the thoughtful, low-key approach with total respect given to opponents, and much research done on them. In addition, Jock had used the two years from 1978 to 1980 to evaluate his squad and to bring together a group of players who would be able to replicate, on an international stage, their club form. Crucially, the players now had the right attitude. The two dire years since 1978 could be seen as a course of treatment to recover from the sickness of the Argentina World Cup. It was painful at the time, but necessary.

Sweden were professionally dealt with twice, away and at home, with a year in between. In some ways, the 1-0 win in Stockholm in the opening group game was the best result and the goal scored by Aberdeen's Gordon Strachan was a good one. Strachan had been well groomed by Stein for international duties, and, for all his personality quirks, he became a good player who never let Scotland down. The 2-0 win at Hampden over the Swedes a year later was in some ways less satisfactory, for Andy Gray made a bizarre and foolish comment that he had conned the referee into giving him a penalty, when it would have been a lot better to keep his mouth shut, for it took away from what was a good victory.

Israel on 25 February 1981 saw a good Dalglish goal give Scotland the points, and a couple of months later, Scotland beat them 3-1 at Hampden when it should have been by a wider margin. As everyone was taking points from each other in this rather balanced group, it did not matter too much that Scotland only drew with Portugal and Northern Ireland at Hampden, although Scotland do always feel that they should be able to beat the Ulstermen.

Scotland remained unbeaten, and they went to Belfast on the night of 14 October 1981 knowing that a draw would be sufficient to guarantee qualification. Northern Ireland had a good team, with men like Jimmy Nicholl and Martin O'Neill who would have influence on the Scottish game in years to come. In addition, Billy Bingham seemed to have been able (like no-one else could) to unite that unhappy

1980. Goalkeepers in training – Alan Rough and Billy Thomson.

October 1981. This Scotland foursome of Ray Stewart, Kenny Burns, Frank Gray and Asa Hartford prepare to fly to Belfast to play Northern Ireland in a crucial World Cup qualifier.

country – which frequently in those days gave the impression of being on the brink of bloody civil war – and the Irish played with a hunger and a desperation of the kind that one would frequently have associated with Scotland in other times. Bingham seemed to be one of the few Ulstermen who didn't care about anyone's religion in that he was quite happy to make Martin O'Neill, a practising Roman Catholic, his captain.

The Ulstermen, whom Scotland had beaten 2-0 at Hampden in the British International Championship in May, played ferociously that night in Belfast but Scotland, with Strachan exceptional, took all that Northern Ireland could hurl at them and earned a 0-0 draw. It was a game remarkably bereft of Scottish defensive errors – and those that were made were quickly covered up by teammates. It was typical of Scotland of that era – cool, professional, very Stein-like - but how often could one in the past (or the future) describe Scotland like that?

*   *   *

In 1981, Scotland had already achieved a great feat even before qualification for Spain. They had beaten England at Wembley for the first time since 1977. It was an undistinguished game, the only goal coming from a penalty sunk by Notts Forest's John Robertson, and Scotland, with Aberdeen's double centre half pairing of Miller and McLeish outstanding, well able to resist any attempt by England to get back into the contest. It was a distinct improvement from the previous week in Swansea, where Scotland had gone down yet again to Wales, the cause not being helped by Joe Jordan being sent off for his second bookable offence.

But these games were now insignificant compared with the undeniable fact that it was Spain for Scotland in 1982. Before that could happen, however, there was a major diplomatic and political problem for the British countries whose government and people found themselves at war with Argentina. In early April 1982, the fascist junta had occupied the Falkland Islands – apparently to divert attention from their own economic incompetence and repression of civil rights – and the British Government under Margaret Thatcher, with the greatest of relish, sent a task force to reclaim their territory.

Thus during the months of April, May and June 1982, British troops were in action against Argentina. This posed all sorts of questions about the World Cup, but fortunately, the tournament continued. What saved it was that no British nation would meet Argentina until the later stages of the competition. Had they been in the same group, it would have been a different matter altogether. The cynics would also say of course that a British or an Argentine withdrawal from the World Cup would have lost too much money! It would have indeed been better if differences could have been settled on the football fields of Spain rather than the battle fields of Goose Green and Two Sisters.

The superior British troops, professional and well equipped, soon drove out the reluctant conscript 'Argies' (as the popular press dubbed them) out of the Falklands, but the final surrender of the Argentinians did not come until the tournament had begun. Just to make 1982 a bad year for Argentina, they didn't win the World Cup either and England fans would sing 'Argentina, Argentina, what's it like to lose the war?'

Italy in fact were the eventual winners. This time Scotland's showing was respectable and not unlike that of 1974. Before Scotland flew out, they played their annual fixture against England. It was the 100th match of this fixture (for although it had been first staged in 1872, one has to allow for war years), and both countries were led out by an old timer – George Young for Scotland and Tom Finney for England. Scotland once again disappointed at Hampden by going down 0-1, and never look-ing as if they were likely to get into the game. It was a 'duller' for the Scottish players and fans, but at least it kept feet firmly on the ground for the World Cup.

*   *   *

Scotland's opponents in the group stages were New Zealand, Brazil and the USSR. It was generally agreed that if Scotland could beat New Zealand, then perhaps draw with Brazil… they could qualify. Scotland were unlucky in that they played New Zealand first, and it is the popular wisdom that the weaker countries raise their game in the first match before being 'found out' later. In spite of this factor, and the poor result against England, there was a note of cautious optimism radiating from the Scottish camp.

Today we're off to sunny Spain. Frank Gray, Asa Hartford, Alan Hansen, George Wood, Davie Provan and George Burley about to set out for the 1982 World Cup.

Gordon Strachan lays down the law to the stewardesses as Scotland embark for Spain for the 1982 World Cup. Just as well that Big Jock (extreme left) is looking the other way.

The contrast between Spain in 1982 and Argentina in 1978 could not have been more marked. Nobody complained about the facilities, discipline was strict, Stein adopting the same methods that he used in his Celtic days – i.e. sitting with a pot of tea near the front door of the hotel so that he could see who was going out and in. Everyone worked hard for each other and the final failure was at least after an honest and determined effort.

The Falklands War had just finished the day before Scotland played New Zealand and Brazil had also beaten the USSR that night. This made it clear, therefore, that to qualify, Scotland would probably have to get the better of the Soviets, assuming they beat the All Blacks and lost to Brazil. New Zealand contained men who would in normal circumstances have been Scotland supporters. Several were Scottish born and names like Mackay, Malcolmson, Boath and Hill had a Scottish feel to them.

The game was played on a hot night in Malaga and Scotland won 5-2, a feature of the game being the excellence of Scottish set pieces. Scotland had conceded two goals and, indeed, at one point in the second half, New Zealand (having been three down at half-time) pulled things back to 3-2. Yet it was a reasonable start to the competition, and Scotland could look forward with confidence to the next two games. Unlike four years previously, it was not the case that the country was in disgrace right from the start of the tournament.

It was now to Seville for the game against Brazil. *'Quien no ha visto Sevilla, no ha visto maravilla'* – 'He who has not seen Seville, has not seen a marvel' – and indeed that night provided an excellent example of what football should be about, as the fans of both football-mad countries mingled happily and danced sambas and strathspeys in indiscriminate harmony with each other. It was all the more remarkable when one considers that only days previously Scotland had been at war with Brazil's neighbours, with whom the Brazilian Government (officially at least) sympathised. Seville's love affair with the Scottish nation, as exemplified by their reception of the Celtic fans in 2003, began that night.

On the field, Scotland did not do so well and ultimately they were completely outplayed by an excellent side. Yet for fifteen glorious minutes, Scotland were ahead through a goal scored by Dundee United's David Narey. Narey, an accomplished defender, found the ball at the edge of the box and lashed home an unstoppable shot; just for a spell, we thought we were the best team in the world. It only lasted for a quarter of an hour until the roof fell in, but what a wonderful quarter of an hour it was!

Brazil eventually won 4-1, but this goal of Narey's became famous. It might have been called the 'Jimmy Hill' goal. Jimmy Hill was an English pundit, already despised for his apparently patronising attitude to Scotland. There was probably no real harm in the man, nor any evidence that he disliked the Scots, but on this occasion he described this goal with astonishing insensitivity as a 'toe poke', a phrase normally reserved for a tap in from two yards.

From now on, Jimmy became the man who was hated north of the border. A chant grew up and increased in vehemence until Jimmy disappeared off the TV screens. It was vitriolic, homophobic and repetitive, yet heard wherever the Tartan Army travelled to. It went along the lines of

> *We hate Jimmy Hill!*
> *He's a poof! He's a poof!*

Quite a few Scotland supporters were embarrassed about this chant, particularly when their young son asked the inevitable question, but everyone agreed that the phrase 'toe poke' was ludicrous in the context of that brilliant goal.

By the time that Scotland played the USSR back in Malaga on 22 June, Scotland knew that a draw would suit their opponents, who had done better against New Zealand and Brazil. Yet a win did not seem beyond Scotland, for the team had played well in patches against Brazil, with redhead Gordon Strachan of Aberdeen catching the eye.

For the USSR game, Stein banked on Joe Jordan, the man who in many ways typified Scotland. Loads of effort and stamina, good in the air, Joe was capable of a brilliant goal or two, but too often let himself and his country down by missing chances that he would take at club level. On this occasion, however, he vindicated Jock's judgement by grabbing an opportunity provided him by Steve Archibald and after fifteen minutes of play put Scotland ahead. For a long time after that, Scotland remained in front and it was beginning to look as if they might just sneak through to the later stages of the World Cup.

Enter stage left the indigenous Scottish fault of self-destruction. First, Alan Rough was at fault for not staying on his line to save a chip from Chivadze. This meant that Scotland would not qualify unless they got a winner, and they were now visibly beginning to tire in the intense Andalusian heat. Stein brought on Danny McGrain in place of the exhausted Strachan and Alan Brazil for the similarly drained Jordan in an attempt to get that elusive winner.

For a while it looked possible, until the moment came that will haunt Willie Miller and Alan Hansen the rest of their lives. The ball was near the touchline about halfway up the field and both of them decided to go for it, without taking the elementary precaution of saying 'Mine'. They both missed the ball, collided with each other and allowed the disbelieving Shengalia to run in on goal unmolested and score.

Scotland were now out, and it was typical of Scotland's habit of doing well in a losing cause that they then scored through Souness (in circumstances reminiscent of 1974 when they had no time left to get another). It was a desperately awful way to go out of the World Cup. It would have been far better to suffer a 6-0 tanking.

Phrases like 'going out with our heads held high' and 'regaining respectability' were naturally thrown about Scottish society for the next few weeks. Such clichés normally mean very little, unless of course you have ever come back home with your head not held high and respectability lost. This had clearly happened in Argentina in 1978, but this time no-one had taken illegal substances, no-one had moaned about the accommodation and underperformed as a result and no-one had behaved like a spoilt brat. The nation was not the laughing stock of the rest of the world, as it had been so obviously in 1978.

The Scottish nation is inured to disappointment. It will take heartbreaks and come back from them; it has had loads of experience in doing just that. In 1982, the Scottish players were able to look their nation in the eye. We could forgive them much for that. Jock Stein had not yet replicated on the international scene the phenomenal success he had had with Celtic, but he was worth another go.

*   *   *

Next came the European Championships of 1984. Scotland continued their lamentable inability to qualify. It was a tough section, consisting of East Germany, Belgium and Switzerland, and for Scotland it was the same old story of respectable performances at home, but an inability to do anything on their travels. The 2-0 victory over East Germany at Hampden on 13 October 1982 was a good start, but by Christmas, Scotland had lost in Switzerland and Belgium, the Belgian game being notable for a brilliant goal scored by Dalglish in a losing cause. Scotland needed to beat Switzerland at Hampden in March, but could only draw. In fact they were 2-0 down, but came back to equalize and a great goal was scored by Charlie Nicholas.

It was this goal more than anything else which possibly persuaded Arsenal to buy him from Celtic, and after his move to England, the talented Charlie never regained his form for Scotland. When Scotland played England at Wembley in 1983, having already drawn with Northern Ireland and beaten Wales, Nicholas was on the verge of his transfer to Arsenal. He played woefully and, to the embarrassment of everyone, had to be substituted as Scotland went down 0-2, a scoreline which slightly flattered the Scots. In the catalogue of Wembley disasters, this one was a 'collector's item'.

Scotland then did something unusual and innovative. They went to Canada to play three games against the host nation in a series, not unlike the Test Match arrangements that one has in cricket. Scotland won all three games very comfortably, raising their profile in a nation that is undeniably pro-Scotland anyway, then beat old foes Uruguay at Hampden in a friendly in September, raising hopes that qualification for the European Championships might yet not be totally impossible. Alas, a feckless draw against Belgium at Hampden was followed by a defeat by East Germany in Halle, and Scotland were once again absent from the European feast.

*   *   *

The British Championships of 1983/84 made a welcome departure from the previous system, which had been in place since 1969, of all games being played at the end of the season. Scotland went to Northern Ireland in December 1983, then Wales came to Hampden in February and the season was brought to an end with the visit of England to Hampden on 26 May. Sadly, this were the death throes of the tournament. Scotland and England simply did not make enough money out of

Wales and Northern Ireland. There was also the problem of terrorism associated with Northern Ireland. Although Scotland would continue to play England for the Rous Cup for a few years, the Home International Championship, which had been running for almost exactly 100 years since 1884, was sadly shelved at the end of this season. Wales and Northern Ireland quite rightly felt betrayed by all this.

Scotland had every cause to be embarrassed by an abysmal performance on their final visit to Belfast for British Championship business, for they lost 0-2. They beat Wales at Hampden – once again reflecting the Scottish trend of being virtually unbeatable at Hampden but very poor away from home – and the England game was one of the lowest-key games there had ever been between the two nations as a tame 1-1 draw was played out with all twenty-two players looking as if they wanted to be somewhere else. Indeed it was elsewhere that Scottish sporting fans had to look in 1984 for any cheer, as the Scottish rugby team managed to win the Grand Slam for the first time for almost sixty years!

The World Cup remained the most important competition. Scotland were desperate to qualify for Mexico in 1986. Mexico had hosted the tournament as recently as 1970, and the 1986 hosts were supposed to be Columbia, but such was the political instability in that poverty-ridden country that the venue was changed. Not that Mexico was without problems, for that nation suffered an earthquake in the run up to the tournament, and its ability to hold the event was, for a while, put into doubt.

The World Cup was crucial to Jock Stein. He had said 'Judge me on the World Cup' in the context of 1982, and now that he had failed to deliver qualification for the 1984 European Championship, he would certainly be judged by a critical public on the 1986 World Cup. Observers had noticed that he was certainly slowing down – he was after all over sixty – and his limp was even more pronounced, but he still retained that massive presence and the aura about him that convinced that all would be well. The atmosphere still changed when he walked into a room or even appeared on a television screen. This was, after all, the man who had produced one of Scottish football's greatest moments in the 1967 European Cup: the nation was still waiting for its international glory.

Iceland, Spain and Wales were the opponents in the qualifying section. The winners would qualify as of right and the team that was second might well have some sort of play-off arrangement. With his assistant Alex Ferguson, the successful manager of Aberdeen, Stein started off well. A 6-1 friendly victory over Yugoslavia in September gave the team confidence, and then Scotland thrashed Iceland 3-0 in the first World Cup game, the highlight being a brilliant long-range goal from the fast developing Paul McStay of Celtic.

Then on 14 November 1984 we saw a really good Scottish performance as Spain came to Hampden and were humbled 3-1. Maurice Johnston was on song with the first two goals that night, and we also saw some of the Dalglish form that was so obvious for Liverpool. A brilliant goal, just after Spain had pulled one back and were even threatening to equalize, had the Hampden crowd in uproar at such magic. Scotland thus finished 1984 having played two games and won two – but the snag was that both these games had been at Hampden. Could they reproduce·this else-where?

The answer seemed to be 'no', for Scotland then lost in Seville in early 1985. No-one could criticise the performance, because Scotland played well enough and held Spain until half-time before losing the only goal of the game. The referee came in for a certain amount of criticism from Jock Stein for his lenient treatment of Spanish defenders like Jose Camacho and the notorious Andoni Goicoechea, and Jock also added the bizarre (although totally credible) complaint that goalkeeper Jim Leighton had been pelted by oranges. 'But that's Spanish football for you' said Jock with a smile.

He would have less cause for smiling after the next game, for it was a major disap-pointment. Wales came to Hampden on 27 March 1985 and shocked 62,424 fans by winning 1-0. Liverpool's Ian Rush scored the Welsh goal before half-time, and the second half was a long catalogue of Scottish ineptitude in front of goal with Kenny Dalglish coming in for a certain amount of stick from the Hampden crowd for once again failing to reproduce his club form.

This rare failure of Scotland to win at home clearly put qualification in jeopardy. A defeat in Spain (and a narrow, unlucky one it was) was hardly a disaster, but losing to Wales at Hampden was a different matter. A certain amount of justified gloating was heard to come from the valleys that night, but it was wailing and gnashing of teeth from the Scottish heartlands.

The Home International Championship had gone, but Scotland were still to play England for the Rous Cup, in honour of Sir Stanley Rous, the famous referee, legis-lator and administrator. This game should have been played at Wembley, but for security reasons it was played at Hampden on 25 May 1985. This was the day that Glasgow saw the ugly side of English football hooliganism as youths with National Front and other fascist insignia descended on Glasgow with their foul chants against 'Jocks' and ethnic minorities. Some of the 'Jocks' resented this sort of thing, and several parts of the environs of Hampden saw an unacceptable amount of violence.

On the field, Scotland had reason for happiness when a Richard Gough header secured a long overdue victory over England. It was the first victory over the Auld Enemy for four years and would turn out to be Scotland's last one against them until November 1999. It was thoroughly deserved on this occasion, and those who braved the Hampden wind, rain and the neo-Nazi thugs that day had much to be happy about.

Three days later, Scotland returned to World Cup duty, this time in Iceland. On paper, this should have been a very easy exercise for the Scots when one consid-ered the relative strength of the two teams. Scotland shocked the watching TV audience back home by an appallingly inept performance, in which players who had performed so well against England looked as if they had never met each other. The only excuse was that Liverpool players were not there as they were due to take part in the ill-fated European Cup final of 1985 in which people met their death at the Heysel Stadium – but then they had also been absent from the England game. Scotland stuttered and stumbled and when the goal did come from Jim Bett four

May 1985. A rare but gratifying sight of a Scotsman lifting a trophy. Scotland have just beaten England at Hampden, and Graeme Souness lifts the Rous Cup.

minutes from time it was scarcely deserved. Indeed, Iceland had a good chance immediately afterwards but missed it, and Scotland, with or without justice, flew back home with three points.

The other games in the group had been haywire also in terms of form, and the result was that Scotland, Wales and Spain were all level on points, as Scotland approached their last game against Wales on 10 September 1985. A win would mean that Scotland would qualify as of right, whereas a draw would land them in the play-offs.

The Welsh, still nursing their sense of grievance for been abandoned as far as the Home International Championship was concerned, in addition to their feelings of being cheated in 1977 for a previous World Cup qualification, approached this match with the intensity that they normally reserve for rugby. They would not make the error of playing the game in England as in 1977 and the game would go ahead at Ninian Park, Cardiff. They might have made more money if they had held the game at a larger English venue, but national pride dictated that it would be at home proper.

They were not successful, however, in keeping Scots supporters down to their allocation. Scotsmen wanting to see their team play will find ways of obtaining tickets, even if it means arriving in the Principality days in advance and putting on Welsh accents in order to convince ticket offices that they were home supporters! One went too far and was refused tickets when he called the girl 'Bach' and the gentleman 'Boyo' in an unsuccessful attempt to convince.

Be that as it may, Scotland supporters inside the ground far exceeded the 12,000 that had been officially allocated to the Tartan Army. It looked as if Scotland accounted for about 25,000 of the 39,500. It even appeared that the ground contained far more than its capacity, as there were several parts of the stadium that looked dangerously overcrowded – something that folk worried about in 1985 in the aftermath of the Bradford and the Heysel tragedies of that year.

Jock Stein certainly tended to worry about large crowds – he had confided to Leeds manager Don Revie at half-time of the famous European Cup semi-final of 1970, between Celtic and Leeds at Hampden, that he was worried about the swaying of the crowd on the East Terracing – and many of those close to him had worried about his health with the changes in the colour of his face, his increasing irritability and his limp which was now more pronounced than ever. Yet there he was on the field at Ninian Park that night, signing autographs and on one occasion helping out the Welsh with their practice!

The ball that the Welsh team were using had disappeared into the Scottish crowd and showed no signs of coming back. Wales' goalkeeper Neville Southall of Everton approached Mr Stein very politely to ask for his good offices in getting the ball back. Stein immediately went to the Scottish crowd and made gestures in the shape of the ball to ask his Tartan Army if the Welsh could have their ball back. It was a great tribute to the man that the ball came back immediately. Neville said 'Thank you, Mr Stein' and the practice continued.

The game itself was one of the most tense that even the Tartan Army had ever experienced. Those watching at home on TV would admit that such was the emotion that they even on occasion flicked over to BBC 2 or Channel 4 to relieve themselves momentarily of the tension and to convince themselves that there was another world away from football, but even the sight of a young woman taking her clothes off in a soap opera is less appealing ultimately than the sight of Scotland playing for World Cup qualification.

The Tartan Army were cowed into some sort of submission within the first quarter of an hour when a good Welsh move caught Scotland out, and Mark Hughes scored a goal that had not been undeserved. The rest of the first half saw Scotland unable to get through a strong Welsh midfield and defence and at half-time the score remained 1-0 for Wales, enough to deny Scotland their trip to Mexico.

Such was the tension in the Scotland dressing room that nobody in particular noticed the change in Jock Stein. He was not shouting and screaming, but that was not his style in any case, at least not with Scotland. He preferred the quiet word, the piece of advice 'Try to get past him on the inside', the encouragement. That was it this time – a few pats on the shoulder and a reminder that one goal would change it all.

Jim Leighton, the goalkeeper, had an eye problem and had to be substituted by Alan Rough, then the hardworking Gordon Strachan, who had run himself into the ground for an hour, was replaced by Rangers' Davie Cooper, an old-fashioned

Scottish winger whom some of the elderly brigade compared with Alan Morton. Davie did indeed upset the Welsh defence but their defence remained solid, as the tension on the field, the touchline, the terracing and the television screens rose to a virtually unbearable level.

Ten minutes remained and pessimism began to appear in the Tartan Army. But suddenly it all changed. Graeme Sharp knocked a ball down to David Speedie, who hammered it goalwards. The ball struck a Welsh defender on the arm, and the Tartan Army behind that goal screamed for a penalty. Mr Keizer of Holland had little doubt. He immediately pointed to the spot.

The Welsh complained vigorously, as one would have expected. It was one of these difficult decisions where the ball hits an arm. Sometimes a referee gives them, sometimes he does not and the Welsh would claim afterwards that the screams of the Tartan Army massed behind that goal must have affected him. Perhaps they did, but Davie Cooper took the penalty well.

So the score was 1-1, and the tension, already at fever pitch, was cranked up another notch. This scoreline would grant Scotland a play-off against some distant southern hemisphere team, but they had to hold out for the remaining ten minutes. Some supporters watching at home prayed, others hid in garden sheds, others went to the toilet – but at the ground there was no escape. The minutes passed slowly as Scotland retained possession and a group of photographers gathered at the touchline to get a picture of the Scotland bench in their moment of triumph.

TV screens were now being beseeched and shouted at to persuade the referee to blow for time. Eventually, after a couple of desperately agonising moments of injury time in which the exhausted Welsh tried anything, and in which Scotland almost scored again, the final whistle came. Those who were too busy embracing each other did not notice the camera shot of Jock Stein being carried up the tunnel. Those who did thought that he must have been hit by a missile hurled by a frustrated Welsh fan. In the meantime, it was hysteria unconfined.

The players came off the field understandably joyful, but they found distress in the Scottish dressing room as efforts were being made by paramedics to resuscitate Jock Stein, who had suffered a heart attack. It was to no avail, and half an hour after the final whistle, he was pronounced dead. Thus it was that at one of the greatest moments of his illustrious career, Jock Stein died still a few days short of his sixty-third birthday. The nation was plunged into mourning, but laudably no games were postponed in his memory. He would not have liked that. It would have been an insult to him, for football was all he lived for.

*   *   *

In the meantime, once the shattered supporters returned and the dignified funeral obsequies were carried out, there remained the question of Scotland qualifying for Mexico. Alex Ferguson was given the job. He did not flinch from it and said that the nation required him and the players to 'Do it for Jock'. It turned out that Australia

Scotland's management team in 1985, Jock Stein and Alex Ferguson.

were what stood between Scotland and Mexcio. They had beaten Israel and were aspiring for qualification for the second time, having played in Germany in 1974. They had no great pedigree as a football nation, being more interested in cricket and rugby, but Australians love their country and would be hard to beat at any sport. Their team also had a fair number of expatriates who had played professional football in the British Isles.

Scotland played a friendly against East Germany – a miserable goalless affair with Jock Stein clearly on the minds of players and spectators – before the first of the play-offs to determine which team would make up the twenty-four in Mexico, the other twenty-three having already been decided. It was Hampden Park on Wednesday 20 November 1985 where Scotland took a decisive 2-0 lead: one a free-kick scored by the hero of Cardiff, Davie Cooper, when the Australian defence failed to line up properly, and the other a fine goal by newcomer Frank McAvennie of West Ham. McAvennie might have scored another near the end, but the consensus of opinion was that two goals would suffice.

Wednesday 4 December, with a breakfast time kick-off in Scotland, determined the fate of the nation. Loads of people were late for work, and many shops and offices simply bowed to realism by either providing a television or by not opening till later in the morning. Apparently, at half-time there was almost a power cut because of the demand as everyone started to make themselves a cup of tea. It was hardly the first time that a nation had been brought to a standstill by a football match, but it was the first and only time that it had happened so early in the day.

Genteel English cricket fans are not unknown to arrive late at their offices because of having been listening to a Test Match from Australia, but on this occasion, Scotland was more or less totally paralysed.

The 32,000 crowd at Olympic Park, Melbourne contained a few Scottish supporters. The natives did not appreciate their presence and became a bit restive at times with one or two arrests, but the game itself was uneventful, although goalkeeper Jim Leighton was called upon to make a few saves. Scotland, without really overstretching themselves, weathered the storm and safely gained a 0-0 draw.

It was not exactly triumph and ecstasy on the streets of Glasgow and Edinburgh that grim December morning, but there was a certain amount of euphoria and satisfaction that Scotland had qualified for the World Cup for the fourth successive time. As a veteran fan would remark 'I'll hae tae bide alive till the summer noo – just tae see hoo they dae'. It was good that Scotland had, in spite of everything, managed to produce the World Cup goods yet again. Jock Stein would indeed have been happy.

TEN

Two more World Cups
1986-1990

No matter how unorthodox Scotland's qualification for Mexico 1986 may have been, there was once again the four-yearly visitation of World Cup fever upon the nation. This time, there was also a certain feeling that Scotland owed something to Jock Stein to make something of themselves. They must not end up as respectable failures as in 1974 and 1982 and certainly not repeat the disgraces of 1978.

Alex Ferguson, in temporary command, was already recognised as a great manager. His triumphant years were yet to come in charge at Old Trafford, but he had already shown at Aberdeen that he could challenge the Old Firm. In 1983 he had brought European glory to Pittodrie when he won the (now defunct) Cup Winners' Cup. Could he do something similar with Scotland? Certainly he would have the backing of the country. Another dreary dirge had hit the nation about the 'Long Road to Mexico', but it sold well and proved, if there ever was the slightest doubt, that there is a vast reservoir of goodwill towards the football team. Crappy music is certainly not a turn off as far as Scotland fans are concerned.

The run up to the World Cup saw good wins over Israel and Romania and a creditable draw with Holland, but a sad defeat in the Rous Cup game against England was a blow to confidence. It was also yet another blow to the oldest international fixture in the world, as it was played on a Wednesday night at the end of the season. Both teams were at less than full strength, with players absent from both sides – 'injured' with the none-too-subtle encouragement of their clubs – and it was England who won 2-1.

Ferguson raised a few eyebrows by not taking David Speedie and Maurice Johnston to Mexico. The impression was certainly given that the non-inclusion of Johnston may have been something to do with disciplinary rather than footballing reasons, for Johnston had had an excellent domestic season for Celtic.

Kenny Dalglish, now nearing the end of his lengthy career, was unavailable through injury. No-one really thought that Scotland were going to win comfortably in '*El Grupo de Muerte*' as it was called, consisting of Denmark, West Germany and Uruguay.

The good news was that there was no scandal involving Scotland, no disgraceful performances against poorer opposition, no feeling of shame to be Scottish. In all three games Scotland played as well as could be expected, but lost to Denmark and West Germany and in the last game could not get the better of Uruguay. Scotland possibly deserved a draw against Denmark and West Germany but simply lacked the fire power up front. Possibly if Mo Johnston had been there, it might have made a difference. Against West Germany they scored first through the excellent Strachan, but could not capitalise. The Germans equalized a few minutes after Strachan's goal, went ahead after half-time and then held on to their lead.

Funnily enough, these two adverse results did not knock Scotland out. Some of the best teams placed third could also qualify, thanks to this crazy idea of having twenty-four teams in the tournament. A combination of results elsewhere meant that if Scotland could beat Uruguay, then they could yet get through. Uruguay – there was a name from the past. One recalled their 7-0 win over Scotland in 1954 and shuddered. Uruguay had, however, not been a great side since the early World Cup years, and there was no reason to doubt that Scotland could beat them.

Ferguson made the bold decision to drop Souness for this game. Souness had recently been appointed player-manager of Rangers back home, and was already reversing the Scottish talent drain by bringing players like Terry Butcher of England to come and play for a Scottish team. Souness' own best playing days were probably behind him now. Some people thought that this was a piece of one-upmanship by Ferguson, the real agenda being that he and Souness would be competitors in the Scottish Premier League the following year, as managers of Aberdeen and Rangers respectively. This is unfair on Ferguson. Souness had disappointed in the two games played so far, and it was not unreasonable to drop him in place of someone else.

The game was a catalogue of horror for two reasons. One was the sheer viciousness of the South Americans, but the other was that Scotland, in spite of the apparent advantage of playing against ten men for eighty-nine minutes, allowed themselves to be intimidated and were unable to score just the one goal that would have seen them through to the next phase. Realising that Gordon Strachan was the danger man, Uruguay's Jose Batista tried to put him in a wheelchair in the first minute and was promptly sent off. But this did not stop the foul play, and sadly Scotland simply lacked the skill to show the world that good football could beat hackers.

It was a particularly unpleasant game of football, and Scotland were on the plane home within twenty-four hours, but not before Ernie Walker, Scotland's secretary, used words like 'cheats', 'cowards' and 'the scum of world football' to describe the Uruguayans. Significantly, he was not taken to task for these words. Yet the saving grace of Scottish football has often been its sense of humour. A radio programme was made and someone sounding like Ernie Walker said 'The World Cup? I've never seen anything like it! The hacking, the spitting, the jersey pulling…' 'You mean the Uruguayans?' asked the interlocutor, 'No, Graeme Souness, when we told him he had been dropped!'

*   *   *

Thus ended Ferguson's reign as Scotland's manager – a disappointing experience in an otherwise very rich career – but there was still the demise of England to be waited for. It came with Maradona's infamous 'Hand of God' – an example of blatant cheating, but one which gave rise to an interesting insight on the Scottish psyche. Picture the scene: it was a douce Edinburgh household one Sunday night, about a week after Scotland's demise. The family was middle class, practised Christian values, possibly even voting now and again for the Conservatives, and it was a friendly, polite, well-balanced atmosphere. The author was visiting there with wife and young children, and the paterfamilias of the Edinburgh household asked if the author minded watching the England *v.* Argentina game. This was surprising, for the gentleman concerned had never previously expressed any interest in football. The TV duly went on. Wives and children went out for a walk, for it was a fine Sunday evening. The ninety minutes were thus spent by two gentlemen (who really had not known each other very well previously) in a frenzy with unbridled passion, hatred, narrow-mindedness, xenophobia and jealousy, with even the occasional bad word passing the lips. Maradona was praised to the heavens and the downfall of the English was greeted with rapture and joy. Ten minutes after full time, when wives and children returned, the two gentlemen were calmly drinking coffee and talking about income tax, holidays and new organists for the church.

The burden of the Scotland job now passed to Andy Roxburgh, who had done very well with the younger teams. He was a fine coach and diplomat, but possibly suffered in some people's eyes because he had never been the manager of a top club. His remit would be to get Scotland to the 1990 World Cup, which would be the fifth in a row and a landmark in world football, for very few teams qualified with such regularity.

It would also be nice to see Scotland qualify for the European Championship, an honour which had consistently eluded us. This time Scotland were drawn against Bulgaria, Eire, Luxembourg and Belgium. Qualification did not seem an impossible task, but Scotland got off to a poor start by only drawing 0-0 with Bulgaria at Hampden to the disappointment of the 35,000 crowd – an attendance that was 20,000 down on what would have been expected ten years previously. The dullness continued with a visit to Lansdowne Road, Dublin and another 0-0 draw. Such things did the reputation of international football no good at all, but Scotland at least managed to beat Luxembourg 3-0 at Hampden before the end of 1986.

The game which ruined Scotland's chances was the visit of Eire to Hampden in February 1987. It was the first time that Irish supporters had visited Scotland en masse and for a long time they managed to outshout the Scots. Jack Charlton was doing well to build up an Irish team. Not all of them were totally Irish, it has to be

Andy Roxburgh, Scotland manager from 1986 to 1993.

said, but on this occasion they outplayed Scotland, and even though there was only one goal in it (an early Mark Lawrenson counter) Scotland were at times outplayed in this game with quite a few of the Scottish team looking as if they wished never to play for Scotland again. In some cases their wishes were granted.

Worse was to come when Scotland went to Belgium and collapsed 4-1 to a Belgian team which was itself no great shakes. The loss of an early goal was counteracted by a Paul McStay strike and if anything Scotland looked slightly the better team as the first half came to an end. But the second half saw the roof fall in and Scotland went down to three good goals. The Tartan Army, present in agreeably large numbers, was reduced to baffled, bewildered silence at how a team that contained men who played so well for their clubs could be so ineffectual when the same players were asked to play for their country.

Thus international football in Scotland was at a low ebb in the summer of 1987 when the Rous Cup was revamped to include Brazil as well as Scotland and England. Hardly surprisingly, Scotland lost to Brazil (0-2) but the fans were more prepared to forgive a defeat to a team like Brazil than they were the miserable goalless draw against England a few days earlier. The game, played at Hampden on 23 May in front of 64,000 spectators, was distinctly devoid of any meaningful football. It was played by two tired teams who both needed their holidays. They had been heavily committed for their clubs, and a friendly international match (however well it was disguised as a Rous Cup game) was not what any of them really wanted. It showed, if anyone had any doubt about it, that the regular Scotland *v.* England international was on its way out.

Something that had hastened this decline was what had been happening in club football in the past year. Rangers had won the League that year for the first time since 1978, something that brought a great deal of belated joy to the Ibrox fans. But it had not been done by the Scottish brilliance of a Bob McPhail or a Jim Baxter as had happened in the past. One could not even say that religious bigotry was a large part of the equation, except in the eyes of a few of their followers. This Championship had been won by the naked spending of money in what would became known as the Souness Revolution.

It meant that Rangers fans would now look to English and foreign stars to produce the goods for them, and it therefore followed that the traditional Rangers links with Scotland were irretrievably loosened. It also meant that the chances of a young Scottish star getting a game for Rangers, and therefore being exposed to competition at the highest level, were much diminished. Celtic and the rest of Scottish football would soon follow suit in this deplorable trend.

*   *   *

The autumn of 1987, with Scotland effectively out of the European Championships, saw the resurrection of another Scottish trait, namely the ability to play well and show people what could have been done once they are out. A win in a friendly over Hungary was encouraging, and then the Hampden crowd (down to 20,000 – a miserable fraction of past glories) saw Scotland beat Belgium 2-0. Six months previously this team had lost 1-4 to Belgium in one of the worst displays in recent memory. This performance was totally unrecognisable. Admittedly there were changes in personnel (as indeed there should have been), but it was the spirit and the passion and the determination about this team which made one think that playing for Scotland now began to mean something again.

A month later Scotland went to Bulgaria. That dismal and depressing country, with its poor standard of living and thraldom to Soviet tyranny had never before been host to the Scottish international side, but this was now a big occasion for the Bulgars. They seemed to be on the brink of qualification for the European Championships and the atmosphere in the Vasil Levski Stadium that night was electric. Only 49,000 were there, but that was a big crowd for Bulgaria and a big crowd for that stadium. Their expectation of victory was tangible, and not unlike the atmosphere at Hampden in days gone by.

The game kicked off in the early evening Great Britain time, and was duly televised to Scotland. But there was probably more interest in another country – namely the Republic of Ireland. If Bulgaria won, or even drew, they would qualify. If Scotland could win, then Ireland would go to the European Championship finals in West Germany. It would, however, have been a very confident (and slightly irrational) Irishman who had any great faith in Scotland.

But this Scottish team was now not without character. They absorbed all the hysterical pressure that the Bulgarians, with the backing of their fans, hurled at them. Jim Leighton in goal had a few great saves, and slowly the defence began to get the better of the Bulgarian forwards, notably Hristo Stoichkov, who had been so dangerous in the early stages. The game seemed to be heading for a draw. The very few Scottish fans in Sofia were surprised to see Paul McStay being substituted by Andy Roxburgh. His place was taken by Gary Mackay of Hearts, a hard-working character but without as yet any great credentials for being seen as an international class player. It was, however, Gary Mackay in his first international who delighted the Hearts fans at home and came close to becoming the uncrowned King of Ireland that night when he scored the late winner that allowed the Republic to qualify.

O'Connell Street in Dublin that night celebrated – a rare event in a country which is nothing like as football mad as Scotland – and glasses were raised to Gary Mackay and Hearts. Scottish newspapers the following morning were equally delighted, but there was still the nagging, annoying factor about Scotland. Why did they only produce the goods when it was too late? Why could they not score goals so that they themselves might qualify?

If anyone actually imagined that Scotland were on the way to recovery as an international power, they were in for a fairly rude shock when they went to Luxembourg three weeks later. It was a European group match technically, but in practice by now a friendly and Scotland managed to achieve a 0-0 draw against the Duchy of Luxembourg – whose entire population is about half the size of Dundee's.

Draws now became the order of the day as Scotland played absurd friendlies against Saudi Arabia (for money, presumably), Malta (for no obvious reason other than practice), and then a more sensible one against Spain. A fifth draw on the trot was registered in the Rous Cup game against Colombia, where the talking point was the hairstyle of Carlos Valderrama, for there was little else to get excited about.

Then it was off to Wembley for what would be the last trip there under the current set-up. It was a low-key affair with England being professional enough to score early on and then hold on to what they had. Scotland might have snatched an equalizer near the end from Kevin Gallacher of Dundee United, but it was not to be. The crowd was less than Wembley's capacity – another clear indication that this fixture was finished. The days of the biennial trek of Scots to Wembley were well and truly at an end – something that had been clear for well over ten years.

*   *   *

Scotland thus spent the summer of 1988 as television spectators yet again of the European Championships, but there was one moment which brought joy to Scotland and Celtic supporters in particular. This was when the Republic of Ireland with three Celtic men on board (Bonner, Morris and McCarthy) beat England – a result which saw almost as much joy in Scotland as it did in Ireland. It was a fine way for Ireland to say 'Thank you' to Scotland and Gary Mackay for what they had done in Bulgaria the previous November. More tellingly, it showed what could be done by small nations – given the right level of commitment at player and managerial level.

Scotland supporters could be forgiven if they stifled a yawn at the start of the 1988/89 season. Yes, it was the start of another World Cup campaign. Could

Scotland do it again and qualify for five World Cups in a row – which would, apparently, be some sort of a record? Manager Andy Roxburgh clearly thought so. He had shrugged off his depression at the dismal performances in the European Championship qualifying section of the past two years, and was now frequently on our television screens. Very articulate and likeable, Andy, who had been no bad player himself, clearly knew a great deal about Scottish footballers and the Scottish psyche. He was also quite blatantly a Scotland fan, being seen wearing tartan ties and scarves. Could he deliver?

He certainly started off well with an excellent victory in Norway. Scotland scored first but then lost a goal on the stroke of half-time. This might have been the prelude to a typical Scottish collapse in the second half, but not this time. The Aberdeen duo of Miller and McLeish held the line very well, and when Maurice Johnston scored halfway through the second half, Scotland played some fine possession football and survived the few scares that came their way.

Yugoslavia, a country that now no longer exists, but which in 1988 contained Serbs, Croats and Bosnians and many others who were about to begin an incomprehensible war against each other, now came to Hampden. It was a fine game, and Scotland were disappointed only to draw 1-1, for they had a few other chances as well. There would be a violent sequel to this match, for a Yugoslav 'football supporter' came into Scotland with the fans, watched the game, then promptly headed for Kirkcaldy where he assassinated somebody. This was a grim harbinger of what was soon to happen on a massive scale in Yugoslavia itself.

Roxburgh now took his team to Italy. Italy was, of course, where the 1990 World Cup would be held, but whether a game three days before Christmas in bad weather in Perugia would tell us anything about conditions in high summer in eighteen months' time was open to question. Scotland lost 2-0, but it was only a friendly.

Serious World Cup business resumed on 8 February 1989 in Cyprus. This was a remarkable game, played in early afternoon British time, which Scotland won 3-2 after being 1-2 down. Scotland were indebted to referee Herr Kirschen of Germany for allowing an inordinate amount of injury time. Scotland had equalized early in the second half, and the rest of the game had seen some fairly blatant time-wasting on the part of the overwhelmed Cypriots, as Scotland pressed and pressed but could not find a winner. Balls were kicked out of play, Cypriots lay down clutching limbs, fouls were committed just to get the game stopped, and these Fabian tactics seemed to have won the day when the usual ninety minutes came and went.

In 1989, there was not yet a man with a board who told players and spectators how many minutes were to be added on. It was all at the referee's discretion. No-one would have blamed Herr Kirschen if he had blown for time. After all, he would still collect his fee. But he was clearly a conscientious man, and refused to blow, no matter how impassioned the pleas were from the desperately impatient Cypriots. Eventually, in the ninety-sixth-minute of the game, Richard Gough scored a winner for Scotland. The Cypriots complained and the other teams in the group moaned, but justice had been done.

Scotland were now on the crest of a wave and, a month later at Hampden Park, played one of their better games of recent years to beat France 2-0. The French side were not as good as they would become, but they did have Patrick Battiston, Laurent Blanc, Frank Sauzee and Jean-Pierre Papin. Scotland, however, had Maurice Johnston and his two goals saw Scotland home in front of 65,000 delighted fans.

More joy, but this time somewhat muted, came when Cyprus arrived at Hampden. Queen's Park's ball boys were all very efficient and did not allow time to be wasted as it had been so blatantly in Cyprus, and although Scotland won 2-1, the feeling was that Scotland should have scored an awful lot more. Yet Scotland had now won three World Cup games in a row, had won four games out of five and drawn the other. This had to be World Cup qualification form.

Almost as a sideshow, an era came to an end on 27 May 1989 when Scotland played England at Hampden Park for the last time, unless they would be drawn together in either the European or the World Cups. Since 1872, they had played each other in every peacetime year, but now this fixture was almost a hindrance, shoved away to the end of the season when the weather should have been more conducive to other pursuits. Scotland themselves, lacking the 'World Cup' impetus which seemed to motivate them so much in these days, played poorly and lost 0-2. They were duly rewarded for this performance when only 9,000 turned up four days later to watch Scotland beat Chile 2-0 in the other game of this little-coveted and little-lamented Rous Cup.

As far as World Cup qualification was concerned, it was as well that Scotland had done all the hard work the previous season, for they now proceeded to horrify their fans by playing atrociously. They started off needing one point from three games. It was the same old Scotland story. Do not ask Scotland to do anything easy, for over-confidence, arrogance, complacency and carelessness will take over. In Zagreb against Yugoslavia, Gordon Durie put Scotland ahead before half-time, and things looked secure. But then the Yugoslavs equalized and Scotland proceeded to score two own goals to prove the point that 'self-destruction' was alive and well in Scotland!

Two chances remained. One was against France in Paris in October. *Rothman's Football Yearbook* is very euphemistic when it makes a comment that Scotland's midfield 'failed to exert any dominance'. A more accurate, but less kind comment, would be that they were never in it, and that (as often happens when Scotland are doing badly) they visibly sagged, leaving their fans to wonder whether they even wanted to go to Italy for next year's World Cup.

So it all came down to the wire. The last game of the section was against Norway at Hampden on 15 November 1989. Again, all that was required was a point. 63,987 forgiving spectators turned up at Hampden and once again the nation closed down so that the rest of Scotland could watch the game on TV. Neutral observers would estimate a reasonable result being 4-0 for the Scots, who had after all defeated the Norwegians in Norway the previous year.

But this reckoned without Scotland's propensity for making life difficult, nay, unbearable for their fans. McCoist scored on the point of half-time. Hampden erupted and the TV audience made themselves a cup of tea, secure in the knowledge that unless Scotland lost two goals, they would be bound for sunny Italy in June. The Norwegians tried, but after a stormy spell early in the second half, Scotland settled and as full time approached, the noise level grew as anxiety gave way to confidence and even to that most dangerous of Scottish emotions, euphoria. The 'Mexican Wave' was in evidence, whereby each section of the crowd in turn stands up and gives a wave – usually a sign that the football was becoming boring. *Flower of Scotland* was beginning to do its dreary and predictable rounds of the Hampden terraces, telling us that King Edward was away home to think again. In addition, there were a few less acceptable chants about the English and the twentieth-century Royal Family, currently disgracing themselves in all sorts of sexual shenanigans.

One minute remained when Erland Johnsen of Norway, who had had a fairly undistinguished game so far, shot from a distance – more in hope than in confidence. Jim Leighton, normally Mr Reliable personified, had the ball in his hands but allowed it to squirm into the net. Hampden was stunned. It was a terrible goal to lose, almost unbelievable in fact, but what was very credible was the fact that if Norway scored again, Scotland would be out of the World Cup in the greatest 'throwaway' of all time. Scotland had been asked to gain one draw in three games. Now even that minimal demand was in jeopardy.

One will never forget the sheer desperate all-engulfing silence that enveloped Hampden as referee Listkiewicz of Poland allowed injury time. Punts up the field were greeted with applause, throw-ins were cheered, but when the game did come to an end, the atmosphere was not delight that Scotland had yet again qualified for the World Cup, but instead tangible relief that the country had not made itself the laughing stock of the world. The veteran supporter, who in 1985 had said that he would have to make an effort to stay alive to see the 1986 finals, had actually made it through to 1989. Now he said the same thing about 1990… and he would indeed live to see the finals in Italy, but he had very nearly been denied that privilege.

Scotland making itself a laughing stock is no new phenomenon. That would, of course, eventually come in the finals themselves, but in the spring of 1990 Roxburgh arranged five friendlies and a motley collection of results were produced. A win over Argentina and a defeat to East Germany took place before the Pittodrie crowd in Aberdeen were horrified and appalled to see a 3-1 defeat by Egypt. This was followed by a draw with Poland and then a lucky win over Malta. It was difficult to see any sort of pattern in all this, but we consoled ourselves with the thought that the World Cup would be different.

*   *   *

Scotland would play in North Italy (Genoa and Turin) and would face Brazil (for the third time in World Cup finals since 1974), Sweden and Costa Rica. Most people reckoned that we would lose to Brazil (no disgrace in that), that Sweden were within our capabilities, and that as long as we remembered Paraguay and Iran and took lessons from these grizzly historical memories, Costa Rica would present us with very few problems. We sat down to watch what would be a feast of football.

It was probably the largest-ever exodus of the Tartan Army. The combination of a civilized country with loads of other attractions, fine weather and the all-embracing national euphoria encouraged more and more fans to go to Italy. They didn't all have tickets, but went anyway, reckoning that they would be able to watch the games on large-screen TV or in bars, if they couldn't get in. Once again the behaviour was impeccable, and Scotland would have no reason to feel ashamed of their fans. The team was another matter.

First up at teatime on Monday 11 June 1990 was Costa Rica. This was the day on which Scotland finally lost her credibility, the day on which the general public of Scotland got fed up with the national team and the day when the jibes of England and the rest of the world became simply too much. The nation has never really forgiven the team for this humiliation, which still rankles well into the next century.

Geography teachers in schools all gave their pupils a lesson on Costa Rica. It is situated in Central America and its name in Spanish means 'rich coast'. Indeed, it might have been a rich coast (the Scots certainly thought so in the 1690s when the Darien Scheme was mooted) but sadly it lies in a part of the world which depends on the grace and favour of the United States of America. Costa Rica has a population of about three-and-a-half million, poverty is widespread (although by no means the worst in that part of the world), and its economy depended on three things – bananas, coffee and tourism. Its cause was not helped by the cheap world price of bananas and coffee, and its shocking crime rate did little to encourage tourists.

The Costa Ricans had done well to qualify. Unlike one of his infamous predecessors, Roxburgh did some research on them, and what happened cannot really be blamed on Andy. He seemed to pick the right team, but as previous Scottish managers could have told him, whenever his eleven men crossed the white line, there was nothing that he could do.

The Tartan Army was in Genoa in strength. Of the 30,000 crowd, about 25,000 must have been Scottish, for very few people from the banana republic could afford to make the long and expensive trip. Back home, Scotland ground to a halt as firms bowed to realism and stopped early to allow their workers to watch the game with the teatime kick-off. The rush hour out of Edinburgh and Glasgow, normally a nightmare, was a dawdle that night, for most workers stayed in the metropolis to watch the game on a pub TV or had left a lot earlier. The weather was beautiful, and unless you were in such a pub, the city centres were absolutely idyllic. Peace and quiet reigned in Princes Street Gardens, with only a few Japanese or American tourists around, wondering where everybody was.

It would remain quiet an hour and a half later as Scotland managed to lose 1-0. The first half had been unimpressive, but this was the start of a World Cup and no-one was all that worried about the slow start, as long as the notches were cranked up a little in the second half. But it was Costa Rica's Cayasso who scored soon after the interval and Scotland were catatonically paralysed for a while. Even after the initial shock wore off, the lack of fight was astonishing as the world once again laughed at Scotland.

Anger was not one of the main emotions that night in Scotland. It was more a sort of torpor, a kind of belief that Scotland were not meant to win even against Costa Rica, and a determination that a pursuit which caused so much distress as this must really be abandoned and replaced by gardening, chess, amateur dramatics or hill walking. The weather was excellent. What about a game of cricket, tennis or golf? Deep-sea diving perhaps? Anything other than football!

It was also the night on which the Tartan Army was put to the test. Thousands of them in Italy itself might well have turned nasty, such was the mood of frustration and the feeling of having wasted their time and money. Wine, consumed in large quantities, might well have fuelled passions and anger. But it didn't. Scotland, in contrast to England, had and still have well-behaved fans. It was a pity they did not have a team worthy of them.

Back home, over the next few days, recriminations were furious. Fingers were pointed at Roy Aitken, whose form had suffered since he left Celtic, at Alan McInally, who played for Bayern Munich and really should have done better and at Paul McStay, who was in danger of assuming the mantle of Kenny Dalglish in that he seldom replicated for Scotland the form that he showed in abundance with his club. Roxburgh too took his fair share of flak, but cheerfully accepted that fans had the right to be angry. There really could be no excuse for this display, and to Roxburgh's credit, there was no whining about ground conditions, brutal opponents or poor refereeing. As patriotic as anyone, and as hurt, Andy promised more in the remaining two games.

The next game was against Sweden on the night of Saturday 16 June. Little was now expected against the team that contained the baby-faced Tommy Brolin and who had lost (honourably) to Brazil in the first game. Many supporters organized their own TV boycott by simply watching another channel or going out for a walk that lovely midsummer evening, Roxburgh made several changes, some of which smacked of panic. Out went Gough, Bett and McInally with McStay relegated to the bench, but a certain solidity was given to the side with the appearance of the excellent Murdo MacLeod and Craig Levein.

It was typical Scotland and a good performance after the cause had been lost. While any chance of progression had not been totally thrown away against Costa Rica, it was certainly rendered a wheen more difficult. Yet this was a good, hard-working professional performance. Stuart McCall silenced his detractors by scoring in ten minutes, and this time Scotland did not crack. In fact it was Scotland who scored again, through a penalty (taken under immense pressure) by Maurice Johnston – although a man who had actually changed sides from Celtic to Rangers must have considerable nerve – and he slotted it away. Only ten minutes remained at this time, but Scotland would not be Scotland if they didn't make things difficult for themselves. A moment's loss of concentration gave Sweden a goal, but mercifully only one, and Scotland had a victory.

To say that the nation went mad with joy would be an exaggeration, but life was visibly better. One fan, amorously taking his lady friend for a walk trying to avoid any television, walked into the beautiful sunset with her. They met no-one for a couple of hours, until a boy with a transistor radio started to go potty because Scotland had won 2-1. The lover immediately combined rapture with romance by bursting into song with

Roamin' In the Gloamin'
On the Bonny Banks o' Clyde
Roamin' in the Gloamin'
Wi' a lassie by my side.
When the sun has gone to rest,
That's the time that I love best,
Oh it's lovely Roamin in the Gloamin!

They got married six months later, and were spotted at Hampden Park at the Faroes game of 2002 with two boys, the whole family tartan bedecked.

The following day, a lovely Sunday morning, as complete strangers walked their dogs, they would say things to each other like 'Better lest nicht' to be answered by 'Aboot f…in' time tae'. Any euphoria had to be tempered by the thought that Scotland would have to get at least a draw against Brazil on the following Wednesday. Granted, Brazil had been none too impressive against Costa Rica or Sweden… but they were still Brazil.

Once again, frustration was the order of the day. Scotland played well and did not do anything wrong against Brazil. They held out for eighty minutes and only went down to a late goal in which goalkeeper Jim Leighton had not looked too sharp. It was, however, not the defeat to Brazil that knocked out Scotland. It was the Costa Rica disgrace. Once again Scotland were on the early plane home, having blown it. Suicide had been committed in the first game. We really had to stop doing that.

It must also be recorded that this was the year in which England almost reached the final. One must admit that they played well, if unspectacularly, to reach the semi-final and only lost to West Germany on penalties. One is always sorry for someone who misses a penalty in a shoot-out, but our sympathy was tempered with the thought of what life would have been like if the unthinkable had happened and England had won the World Cup. As it turned out, the Argentinians behaved like spoiled brats in the final, Maradona was in tears and the Germans lifted the trophy.

ELEVEN

The Crest of the Broken Wave
1990-1998

The 1990s saw a change in Scotland. As Burns said about the death of his friend John Rankine 'Alas! Alas! A devilish change indeed'. Quite simply, Scotland ceased to matter to many football fans. Not only did they cease to matter, we now saw some Rangers fans openly supporting England, wearing white England tops to games and rejoicing, for example, in Scotland's defeats. It would be the forerunner to the crowings of triumph in 2002 when they sang songs like 'There's no Tartan Army in Japan'. Changed days indeed from the 1930s where Rangers fans used to boast about being Scottish, singing songs like 'The Wells o Wearie' and 'Loch Lomond', in contrast to their Irish and alien opponents!

Gates at Scotland games were low. This was not helped by a bizarre and erratic ticket-selling policy of charging the earth for some games and then allowing parents and children in for £2 at others. In 1994, for the first time in twenty years, Scotland failed to qualify for the World Cup finals; they did make it to the European Championships of 1992 and 1996, but that was scant consolation. By 1998 it seemed that normal service had been resumed as Scotland qualified for the World Cup finals but blew things badly once they got there.

Apathy certainly ruled. There were several clearly defined reasons for this. One was the Costa Rica result: Scotland once again became the laughing stock of the world – a role that Scotland had apparently relished and even enjoyed on several occasions in the past – but something more serious happened with this one. The Scottish public really did switch off. In fact the team performed creditably after that, beating Sweden and playing well against Brazil, but the battle had been lost. The Scottish public apparently thought that Costa Rica was one defeat too far. There were limits to what they were prepared to endure. Costa Rica was the time that the message really got through, that Scotland really, for all its continuing national obsession with the game, were really not very good at football.

Another thing that affected Scotland was the loss of the British International Championship, and in particular the deprivation felt to the sense of national identity by the loss of the England fixture. The tournament disappeared in the mid-1980s, and even the Scotland v. England game had been struggling for some time, usually stuck away at the end of the season and with many players coming up with weird excuses for not wanting to play. The actual loss of the fixture was a blow to Scottish nationhood, however, in that during the years from the 1920s until the 1970s, the England games – with tartan-bedecked people filling trains and buses to Wembley one year and Hampden the next – were the occasion when the nation could be Scottish and proud of it. It was a sad fact that Scotland was not Scotland unless England were also around.

In tandem with football woes there were several other blows to Scottish nationhood. Politically, Scotland had to accept the diktat of Conservative England. Culturally, New Year used to be a very Scottish occasion, but as the festival became universalised (ironically with the advent of the Edinburgh street parties), traditional Scottish music began to be replaced with more depressing material. Even Burns Night was spoiled as glory-hunting singers tried to prove that they were better than Burns himself by inventing their own tunes and words for beautiful traditional airs.

In football itself, the Scottish dimension to Scottish football had been much diminished. This process had started as early as 1986 when a desperate Rangers Board of Directors hired Graeme Souness to be their player-manager. Souness himself is, of course, very Scottish, but very early on he began to hire English and foreign mercenaries. Lamentably, Celtic followed suit and soon too did other Premier League clubs, under the naïve misapprehension that all foreigners were automatically good players. Some clubs, notably Rangers and Celtic, were taken to the cleaners by such players and their grasping agents. How long, for example, did Sebastian Rosental play for Rangers, and how did Rafael Scheidt do for Celtic?

This meant that young Scottish players were not given the opportunity of a run in Scottish football. It also meant that the talent drain of young Scottish football players to rich English clubs (once the cause of Scotland managers tearing their hair out in despair) now stopped – simply because there were not enough good Scottish-born players around. When it came to picking the Scotland team, quite a lot of the fans had never heard of the players concerned. Long gone were the days when arguments went on from January of each year about what Scotland's team should be against England in April. Was Bobby Evans a better centre half than George Young? What about Ian Ure and Billy McNeill? Or Eric Caldow v. Harry Haddock? Jimmy McGrory or Hughie Gallacher? All these pub, factory floor and playground arguments now came to a stop. The question now was 'Who is Neil Sullivan?' or 'What team does this David Hopkin play for?'

Yet some good things happened in the 1990s. The Scotland fans were widely recognised as the best behaved in the world, and a complete contrast to the English fans who sacked and ravaged any place that dared to stage an international against

England. Scotland had a Travel Club organized for away fixtures, and the Tartan Army now consisted of men, women and children, who normally supported comparatively civilized teams like St Johnstone, Raith Rovers, Dunfermline, Hamilton, Forfar and Ayr. Although it would be a lie to say that total alcohol abstinence was practised, the drunkenness was good natured. Friends were won for Scotland all over Europe and the world. The image from 1992 of the Scottish supporter in his kilt who pointed to his cheek so that the nice-looking Swedish police lady might kiss him – with the good lady obliging – is an enduring one.

The Celtic *v.* Rangers factionalism within the Scottish support was now gone. Players were no longer booed just because they were of the Roman Catholic religion, although that sort of thing still happened in Northern Ireland. One hopes that most of the Old Firm supporters still supported Scotland, but they seemed to be far more interested in people like Brian Laudrup and Henrik Larsson – not without cause, for both were fine players – and left the Scotland supporting to Scottish supporters. Thus, although the Scotland support was small (average perhaps 20,000 for home games) it was a very sincere following, and one that the nation had every reason to be proud of.

*   *   *

The post-Costa Rica era began on 12 September 1990 in front of only 12,801 when Romania came to Hampden to begin the European Championship qualifying section, a group which also contained Switzerland, Bulgaria and San Marino. Only one team was destined to qualify, and as Scotland had never before achieved that, there was little reason to suppose that they would do so now.

The 12,801 who almost got lost in Hampden's huge space that night saw an honest, hardworking and brave Scottish team come back from an early goal to beat Romania 2-1. This was a fine performance as Romania, with excellent players like Hagi and Lacatus, had really caught the eye in the World Cup. Andy Roxburgh was quite rightly proud of his team.

It was enough to up the attendance to 27,740 on 17 October to see the next game, this time against Switzerland. Once again, Scotland delighted their fans to win 2-1 in another hard-working rather than inspirational game of football. So far so good, and the next game involved an away trip to Bulgaria. Memories of the last time that Scotland had been there came back as people recalled Gary MacKay's late winner, and this time Scotland once again did well to return with a 1-1 draw – a totally creditable result, even though it was disappointing to have been ahead for so much of the game before going down to a late equalizer.

It was also a question of late goals when Bulgaria came to Scotland in March. The game had been distinctly dull and looked as if it were petering out into a draw (that would not have been the world's greatest disaster for Scotland's qualification prospects). Celtic's John Collins came on as a substitute with less than quarter of an hour remaining and almost immediately grabbed a goal. The Hampden crowd of 33,119 (disappointing in the context of the good form that Scotland had enjoyed recently) came to life and were on the point of roaring Scotland to a great victory when Kostadinov levelled for Bulgaria just at the death. 'Lucky Bulgars' – or something like that – was commonly heard as the disheartened Scottish crowd trooped home that night.

Scottish qualification (and the winning of a difficult section) was still feasible for the as-yet-undefeated Scotland side. There was, however, a small nation called San Marino to deal with. The first of May 1991 saw Scotland's first ever trip to San Marino and a crowd of 3,512 to see a shocking game of football. The agonies of the first half were shared on television by the watching Scottish nation, as Scotland once again showed their total inability to raise their game against poorer opposition. In fact, they lowered it. Nightmares of Iran and Costa Rica began to appear again, but Scotland eventually got a penalty, gratefully sunk by Gordon Strachan, and then Gordon Durie added a second.

Scotland now faced the summer with 8 points from 5 games (2 points still for a win), one point behind Switzerland who had played one game more. But Scotland's goal difference was not as good, and we remembered the 1974 World Cup when Scotland had failed to advance because of not scoring enough against Zaire. Scotland's chronic inability to thrash minnows was now reappearing with a vengeance.

But the team had character. The trip to Switzerland on 11 September 1991 appeared at half-time to have been a total waste of time and money for the large numbers of the splendidly organized Tartan Army, as Scotland were two down. Although the goals were lucky ones, the Swiss seemed to be totally in command and such was Scotland's pedigree of playing away from home that nobody would give Scotland much hope. But Gordon Durie pulled one back immediately after the restart, and then sheer persistence and hard work saw Ally McCoist score the equalizer almost at the death.

No-one was kidded into thinking that Scotland had qualified. They still had to go to Romania. A victory there would possibly have done the trick, but this time Scotland had little luck, losing 0-1 to a penalty granted by the German referee which might not have been given to an away team. It is, of course, a fact of international life that home teams get more penalties than away sides!

Qualification was now very problematical, especially after San Marino's visit to Hampden yielded only four goals, when many more were required. Scotland were thus obliged to sit it out and watch what happened in Sofia on 20 November. Bulgaria could not catch Scotland, but if Romania won by two goals, then they would win on goal difference and once again the fault would be Scotland's inability to hammer poorer countries, in this case San Marino.

For a while the news from that game was not good, for Romania were one-up at half-time, but fortunately Sirakov of Bulgaria scored the next goal, and the game finished 1-1. Scotland were through by a somewhat fortuitous route, but no-one should minimise Scotland's achievement in winning what was a very difficult group indeed. A certain amount of self-respect had been deservedly won back for the nation by Andy Roxburgh.

*   *   *

Before the European Championships of 1992, Scotland went on a tour of North America and, fortunately, Scotland beat both Canada and the United States. They also beat Northern Ireland in a friendly, and drew with Finland and Norway. The wisdom of playing international friendlies at a time when the calendar was already overloaded with other things was questioned when one saw the attendances at Hampden to see Northern Ireland and Finland – 13,651 and 9,275. Clearly, such quaint anachronisms as international friendlies were being rejected by the public.

Despite such apparent indifference, the Tartan Army marched to Sweden in large numbers in the summer of 1992, there to complain vociferously about the scandalous price of Swedish beer, but otherwise to behave impeccably and to be a colourful asset to the tournament. Scotland's opponents were to be Holland, Germany and the CIS. Political happenings in the very recent past had accounted for the renaming of the last two countries. The Berlin Wall had come down in 1989, and Germany was now reunified for the first time since Hitler. Thus it was no longer West Germany and East Germany but simply Germany.

Around the same time as the fall of the Berlin Wall, the Soviet Union had also imploded on itself for no other reason than that the Russian Communists could no longer hold on to their disparate and polyglot Empire. The next time that a World Cup would be held, the nations of the former Soviet Union would all play under their different banners, but as they had started the qualifying stages of these European Championships together, they had to continue – although they refused to be called the Soviet Union. For this tournament, they were renamed as the CIS, which sounded like a Scottish insurance company but in fact was the Confederation of Independent States.

It was a strange tournament. The standard of play was really rather low and the eventual winners were Denmark, a team who had not originally qualified. They had been allowed to enter to replace Yugoslavia, a country which no longer existed and indeed was now the scene of a succession of extremely bloody civil wars. There were only eight teams in the tournament, and Scotland, some people said, played some of the best football of the lot. They certainly played better than did England, whose participation in the tournament was a disgrace.

Scotland had the advantage that nobody gave them much chance and they had no minnows to contend with. Their first game was against Holland, and although Scotland were penned back for the first fifteen minutes (as we all held our breath to expect the inevitable thumping), Scotland finished the first half at least the equals of the Dutch. It was only a late Dennis Bergkamp goal which gave Holland a win over a very brave Scottish team, who deserved at least a draw.

More bad luck came Scotland's way against Germany. Riedle scored Germany's goal in the first half, and then their second goal was scored by Stefan Effenberg thanks to a wicked deflection that completely deceived Andy Goram. Even the German commentators and journalists said that Germany were lucky to win that game, for Scotland once again played well, even when 0-2 down – circumstances which in previous years had been the catalyst for a total Scottish collapse.

Then, out of the tournament and with only pride at stake, Scotland played a brilliant game against the CIS and won deservedly 3-0. Inspired by Paul McStay, who had a fine tournament, Scotland really impressed the pundits, and such was the good behaviour of the Tartan Army that the neutral Swedes took Scotland to their hearts and applauded them off the park at the end of the game. Scotland flew home, disappointed but not dejected, and the general opinion was that they had deserved better. Andy Roxburgh deserves great credit for what he did with that squad, a feature of which was the almost total lack of 'superstars'.

*   *   *

World Cup time came again and the question was asked 'Would Scotland qualify for the World Cup for the sixth successive time?' Some recalled Costa Rica and asked whether we wanted them to or not! This year, the World Cup was to be held in the USA, a strange venue perhaps, for the States had obstinately refused to become as passionate about football as the rest of the world, but it was felt that there was certainly loads of money there, and that the 1994 World Cup might just be the stimulus that football needed.

Scotland, following their success in 1992 in Sweden, might have been entitled to feel optimistic, but their qualifying section consisted of Estonia, Italy, Portugal, Switzerland and Malta. Hampden Park was out of action as it was undergoing one of its periodic redevelopments, this time being converted into an all-seater stadium. Scotland's home ties therefore were played at Ibrox and Pittodrie. This was a pity, for there were problems involved with both stadia.

Ibrox was, of course, anathema for half of the nation, being the home of Rangers (and in any case lacked a little of the necessary atmosphere for a Scottish occasion). The lack of atmosphere was even truer of Pittodrie, which was small, distant and unable to host a crowd of more than 21,500. In addition, Aberdeen fans, although as knowledgeable and patriotic as anyone else, had the reputation of lacking passion. 'You can tell when they are getting excited. You can hear the sweetie papers rustling' someone said unkindly.

Scotland certainly missed the 'Hampden factor' in their qualification group, for of the five home games played, Scotland only managed to beat Estonia and Malta. The three 'big' home games against Portugal, Italy and Switzerland were all drawn, and miserable draws they were as well. Scotland would have been expected, on her past record, to beat at least one and possibly two of these teams on home soil.

But it was the away form that really sunk Scotland. They started off badly by losing in Switzerland on 9 September 1992 and never really recovered from that. The score was 1-3, but the way that the Scots were outplayed that night put a large question mark over their commitment and indeed credibility as World Cup challengers. Richard Gough was sent off, and one cannot really afford to go down to ten men in international football.

The real moment of truth came in April 1993 when Scotland went down 0-5 in Portugal. It was seldom that Scotland, although frequently defeated away from home, were on the receiving end of such a tanking, but the truth was that the scoreline reflected the play. Scotland were, in a word, outclassed. Ironically, Portugal

Three goalies take a break from training in 1992 from top – Gordon Marshall, Henry Smith and a young-looking Andy Goram.

would not qualify for the USA either – something that says a great deal about Scotland!

This was all very disheartening after such a creditable performance in Sweden in 1992, and it had its effect on Andy Roxburgh. For some time, he had been flying the distress signals saying things on TV like 'International managers have a sell-by date' and then he had a none-too-subtle dispute with Rangers' Richard Gough, which

September 1993. Coach Andy Roxburgh and captain Gary McAllister training at McDiarmid Park.

really should have been kept quiet. Gough ended up saying that he never wanted to play for Scotland again under Roxburgh – and never did after the Portugal thrashing. Gough appeared oblivious to the part he himself had played in the national disgrace, both against Portugal and by his red card in Switzerland.

Soon after Scotland's draw with Switzerland at Pittodrie in September 1993, which mathematically killed off what lingering hope Scotland might yet have had of making it to the USA, Roxburgh announced his resignation and the job eventually passed to Craig Brown, who had done very well with the Under-21 team.

* * *

Roxburgh's departure put Scottish international football under another cloud. He had done a reasonable job under difficult circumstances and had managed the team for 61 matches, the same amount of games that Jock Stein had been in charge for. But the major disappointment was that the summer of 1994 saw World Cup finals being played for the first time since 1970 without Scottish participation. If there were any consolation on offer, it was that England didn't make it either (in circumstances even more heartrending for them than Scotland's agony was for us) and

Left The notorious but talented Duncan Ferguson at training in 1993. Behind on the left is Dave Bowman.

Right Scotland's team manager from 1993 until 2001, Craig Brown, relaxes on the golf course.

thus we were reduced to supporting Jack Charlton's Republic of Ireland side, who did very respectably and reached the quarter-finals.

Not for the first time, we asked the question of how it was that a nation like Ireland – by no means a football-mad country in the sense that Scotland was and with no great domestic League structure – could do what Scotland couldn't? We now looked to Craig Brown to supply the answer to that question. The European Championships of 1996 were to be held in England. It would be nice if Scotland could be there.

Scotland certainly got off to a good start in Helsinki when they beat Finland 2-0, goals coming from Duncan Shearer of Aberdeen and John Collins of Celtic. The Faroe Islands were then pasted 5-1 at Hampden before Scotland had to face the two really difficult teams in the group – Russia at Hampden and Greece in Athens. Possibly more disappointment was felt with the draw against the Russians at home than with the defeat away from home, because it is of course home form which was traditionally Scotland's strength. A good goal by Scott Booth was cancelled out by slackness in the defence allowing Radchenko to equalise, and Scotland could not get back into the game after that.

The week before Christmas 1994 brought the defeat in Greece, Scotland losing to a penalty in the eighteenth-minute. Yet Craig Brown was not despondent, and he was certainly a man who took his football seriously and possessed a wide knowledge of world football. Scotland travelled to Moscow on 29 March, knowing that it was now absolutely vital to bring something back from that game. No pretence was made of trying to entertain the Moscow public, and Scotland ground out a 0-0 draw, thereby cancelling out Russia's draw at Hampden the previous November.

Scotland then went to San Marino and the Faroes in the spring of 1995, and won 2-0 in each case. We were grateful for the wins, although the football played might have been a good deal better. In between these two games, Scotland took part in a bizarre tournament called the Kirin Cup in Japan. They drew 0-0 with the hosts at Hiroshima, but then beat Ecuador 2-1. The team was understrength as not everyone wanted to go there and there was still domestic football being played. It did, however, say something about Craig Brown's determination to broaden horizons.

*   *   *

The 1995/96 season had barely begun when Scotland had to play two crucial games. Fortunately, both were at Hampden and it was felt that if Scotland could win them, then they would probably qualify for England. The more difficult game was against Greece and it came first. Greece had defeated Scotland in Athens the previous December, but this time, on a balmy Scottish night, Scotland won through. Craig Brown also showed that he had a Midas touch regarding substitutions. With the score at 0-0, a scoreline which would have favoured the Greeks, Brown pulled off the ineffective Duncan Shearer and replaced him with Ally McCoist. McCoist then scored with his first kick of the ball. Thereafter, Scotland held out in spite of some late Greek pressure.

Scotland now had to beat Finland at Hampden. Russia were top of the group, having beaten Greece in Greece, but Scotland could now finish second and therefore qualify. Once again it was Scott Booth of Aberdeen who got an early goal against Finland, but this time Scotland stayed on top, rendering qualification likely.

It more or less became definite on 11 October 1995, on the night that Scotland were playing a meaningless friendly in Sweden. They lost that game, but the country was less concerned with that than they were with the news that Russia had beaten Greece, effectively winning the group for themselves and giving Scotland second place. Scotland now beat San Marino 5-0 at Hampden in the last match of the section.

Thus was interest temporarily restored in the Scottish international team. The very fact that the tournament was to be held in England was a great stimulus, and the interest was intensified after the draw on 17 December which paired England and Scotland together along with Holland and Switzerland. It was nobody's idea of

Pat Nevin, Gordon Durie and Scott Booth, training at McDiarmid Park.

an easy group, but there was a realistic approach to it. Euphoria and over-confidence no longer appeared in the Scottish vocabulary.

Scotland's approach to the Championships was, however, less than impressive. Four games had been arranged, but it was questionable whether these fixtures were going to tell us much about how the team would fare in England. Australia came to Hampden in March and surprised quite a lot of people by the quality of their play: Scotland were indebted to an Ally McCoist goal to win the game.

Scotland then went to Denmark, who of course had won the European Championship in 1992, and never recovered from being two goals down within the first half-hour to the Laudrup brothers. The 0-2 defeat was discouraging, but there followed a somewhat pointless pre-tournament tour of the United States. Scotland lost 1-2 to the home team, thereby of course emulating England who had also lost to the USA (once in the 1950 World Cup and the other time in a friendly as pointless as this one), and then Scotland went to Miami to meet Colombia and lose to them as well.

This was embarrassing, but Craig Brown maintained his insouciance, saying that these games were all for trying out some ideas, and for bonding with his players and so on, and that Scotland would be seen for their true value in England in the European Championships.

*   *   *

'Football's coming home' was the theme tune of this Championship, for England claimed to be the genesis of the game. It would have to be admitted that the tournament was very well organized. There were now sixteen teams in the finals and it was very high profile. Scotland's games were to be played at Villa Park and Wembley, and concern was expressed about security and how easy it would be for Scotland and England fans to organize their own Battle of Britain whenever they met. No-one need have worried. Everyone behaved well, and those of the Tartan Army who could not get tickets were happy to watch the games on TV.

The first games in the group were cagey ones, with two draws in games that were frankly disappointing. England drew 1-1 with Switzerland, and Scotland drew 0-0 with Holland at Villa Park on Monday 10 June. The Scots had every reason to be happy with this. Chances were available at both ends, but in small doses. Scotland were not outplayed and could now approach Wembley for Saturday's game against England on equal terms. Before that happened, however, Holland had beaten Switzerland 2-0.

It was like old times again with Scotland going to Wembley. The differences were that there were not nearly as many Scottish fans as there used to be and the weather was good. It was a brilliantly hot, midsummer day, and it was perhaps with this in mind that Craig Brown seemed to prefer going for a defensive formation, bringing in Tosh McKinlay of Celtic as extra cover, and leaving the front two of Spencer and Durie instead of bringing in another attacker. McCoist was on the bench and came on in the second half.

Scotland held their own in the first half, and much was the speculation in TV studios and elsewhere whether a draw would suit Scotland, given that they only had the talented (but now disheartened) Swiss to play. But it all went wrong for Scotland in the middle part of the second half. First Alan Shearer scored, and then came the minutes that will live with the hard-working Gary McAllister for the rest of his life. Scotland were awarded a penalty, and the luckless midfielder missed it. Hardly had the groans died away than England were two up with a brilliant goal.

Paul Gascoigne was the scorer, and the really hurtful thing about the goal was that he was an Englishmen who now earned his living playing for a Scottish club, namely Glasgow Rangers. Even more hurtful was the sight in pubs and streets of Scotland of Rangers supporters cheering and applauding this wonderful strike. That beautiful summer day was a very sad one in the history of Scottish football. The loneliest man in the British Isles that night must have been Gary McAllister. Everyone misses a penalty now and again, but poor Gary had to miss one on that occasion and at that vital time of the game.

But all was not yet necessarily lost. Holland and England had four points, and Scotland and Switzerland one each. If Scotland could beat Switzerland, then as long as someone won the game at Wembley between England and Holland (and it wasn't drawn), then Scotland might still qualify on goal difference. After their brave, gallant and unlucky performance against England, it was felt that Scotland deserved a second chance. Craig Brown certainly felt so, and kept his composure and his dignity. UEFA rules meant that the games had to kick off simultaneously on the

A broken Tartan Army! Despair is the order of the day after defeat by England at Wembley in Euro '96.

night of Tuesday 18 June. Brown at last recalled Ally McCoist (he had been under intense pressure to do so and had yielded to a certain extent by bringing him on as a substitute in the second half at Wembley) and the irrepressible Ally rewarded him by scoring after thirty-seven minutes. Scotland went in at half-time leading 1-0, as indeed were England leading Holland 1-0.

The Tartan Army now had no choice. They had to abandon the habits of a bigoted lifetime and support England! Scotland's goal difference was 1-2, whereas Holland were still 2-1. The second half was spent in an atmosphere of unbelievable tension, which affected every part of the British Isles, as first Sheringham scored for England, then Shearer scored. This made Holland's goal difference 2-3, but it was not enough, for they would still qualify on goals scored. But then Villa Park erupted as transistor radios told them that Sheringham had scored again. Scotland were now marginally ahead, and it stayed like that for another fifteen minutes.

Scotland could have solved their own problems by scoring again, but no further goals looked likely against the stuffy Swiss defence. And then the transistor radios gave out the bad news that Patrick Kluivert had scored for Holland. This would make Holland's goal difference 3-4, as distinct from Scotland's 1-2. If only Scotland could get another goal!

But it was not to be. The bubble had burst, and both games finished without any further scoring. It was, yet again, another Scottish heartbreak to go out on goals scored, not even goal difference. England had done their best for Scotland (and themselves) but Scotland were on the way home again. The tournament would eventually be won by Germany, who beat the Czech Republic in the first major tournament to be settled by sudden death or the Golden Goal (i.e. the first goal scored in extra time).

*   *   *

France now became the focus for the world's attention, for the 1998 World Cup was due to be played there. Traditionally, France was not as football daft as some other European countries like Italy and Spain, but they were a popular choice for World Cup hosts. They did a good job, and of course capped it all by winning the tournament themselves with a very impressive squad of players.

Scotland found themselves in a qualifying group with Austria, Sweden, Belarus, Estonia and Latvia. Only one nation was guaranteed qualification. The second-placed nation might have to involve itself in a play-off. Scotland did very well in this group, and although they finished second, they did not have to take part in the play-offs, for they were adjudged to be the 'best second' team of all the groups. Indeed, but for one ludicrous situation and a certain amount of skulduggery behind the scenes, Scotland would possibly have won their group.

Arguably their first game was the most difficult, against Austria in Vienna on the night of Saturday 31 August 1996. The game was dull, but Scotland were not in the slightest bit worried about that, for they earned a 0-0 draw. The boos of the crowd were music to their ears at the end, and Craig Brown knew that his first World Cup venture was well begun.

Scotland were due to tour the Baltic countries to play Latvia on Saturday 5 October and Estonia on Wednesday 9 October. The game in Riga was another good Scottish away performance. A 2-0 win was characterised by a particularly well-taken goal by Darren Jackson of Hibernian, and Scotland looked everybody's favourites to beat the Estonians as well.

But then things became silly. Scotland went to Tallinn and were immediately unhappy about the floodlighting. The lights were low, looked more than a little dangerous and would have been distinctly ineffective in that the game would have to be played in very dim light – a point accepted by the television companies as well. Scotland immediately lodged a protest and suggested that the game be played in the afternoon instead, when floodlights would not be necessary. The Estonians seemed to accept this in the first place, but then declared that they would not play in such circumstances.

It was unclear whether this change in circumstances had been ratified by FIFA, but Scotland thought that the verbal agreement was sufficient and duly turned up to play the game in the afternoon. The referee and his linesmen were there, the Tartan Army were there (not, it must be said, in huge numbers but in sufficient numbers), the television cameras were there – but there were no Estonians who had refused to turn up, claiming that their floodlights were adequate (then weakening their case by saying that replacements had been delayed). Clearly, having just been released from fifty years of Soviet tyranny, the Estonians were not going to be browbeaten by a rich Western nation like Scotland.

Scotland duly stripped and, at kick-off time, walked on to the field in their Scotland strips, waved to the crowd, took a kick-off when the referee blew his whistle, then immediately saluted the Tartan Army, believing that Estonia's default had earned Scotland a 3-0 victory – which is what apparently happens in those extremely rare circumstances. Such nonsense was food and drink for news programmes (apparently making it to CBS news in the United States, for example) and will be great fun for the next hundred years or so in sports quizzes. 'What happened next' seemed to be designed for just such a bizarre occurrence. It was indeed fairly difficult to parallel, although once in Scottish history, in the Scottish Cup final of 1879, Rangers had refused to play against Vale of Leven and the Cup had been awarded to the Vale of Leven. In 1996, Scotland felt that they had indeed won this game 3-0.

On 7 November, FIFA showed their ability to be taken for a ride by decreeing that the game would have to be replayed, on 11 February 1997 on neutral territory in Monaco! This decision lacked common sense, credibility, equity or wisdom. They had backed down to the smaller country, clearly afraid that they would be seen to be backing the 'giant', but had handed Scotland a sop by saying that the game would have to be played at a neutral country.

There was a body of opinion that felt that Scotland should themselves turn awkward about this and refuse to play, but fortunately it was decided that they should compete, albeit with a bad grace. Craig Brown remained calm and dignified, for indeed he had more urgent matters on his mind, namely the impending visit of Sweden to Ibrox. Rangers ground was being used because Hampden was yet again getting one of its facelifts in another phase of the tedious redevelopment of what was to become known as the National Stadium.

Sweden arrived on Sunday 10 November 1996, and it was felt that this would be a real test of Scotland's World Cup credentials. Scotland started well, with a good goal scored by Bolton Wanderers' John McGinlay, but the rest of the game saw a real end-to-end contest, with Scotland indebted to a stout defence and some inspired and occasionally lucky goalkeeping by veteran Jim Leighton, once of Aberdeen, Manchester United and now of Hibernian. Sweden threw all they could at Scotland that day, including the introduction from the substitutes' bench of an unknown called Henrik Larsson, but Scotland held firm and Ibrox heard the final whistle with a tremendous amount of relief.

Craig Brown had cause to celebrate Christmas 1996 with joy, for Scotland had won two games and drawn one. But he now had a double header against Estonia, one in Monaco and the other at Rugby Park, Kilmarnock. The Monaco ground had excellent floodlights and the Kilmarnock game was to be played in daylight on a Saturday afternoon, so there would be no problem there. Where there was a problem was in the way that Scotland played in Monaco in front of a pitiful attendance in a large stadium of 4,000. One or two Scottish players seemed to be allowing their justified resentment at scandalous treatment to get the better of them to the detriment of their playing ability, as the Estonians earned a 0-0 draw.

Scotland, however, made no mistake in Kilmarnock, winning comfortably 2-0. Using this as a springboard, they then went on to play a really good game at Celtic Park four days later as they defeated Austria 2-0. Kevin Gallacher scored both goals for Scotland and his second goal in particular was a real gem. It seemed that little could stop Scotland from qualifying if they kept on playing like this.

In late April, however, Scotland went to Gothenburg in Sweden and paid the penalty for poor marking as Sweden scored twice and looked like adding more in the last half-hour. Showing a little character in adversity, Scotland rallied and pulled a goal back late in the game through Kevin Gallacher, too late though to save any points.

Scotland still had to face Belarus, one of the many nations formed from the break up of the Soviet Union. They were unknowns, but Craig Brown was very punctilious in doing his homework and Scotland ground out a 1-0 win in Minsk in June. Gary McAllister scored a penalty, (one presumes he was happy about that) but that was all that came Scotland's way as hard work was required to register Scotland's second away win of the competition. It was a good win as well, for Scotland now finished off their campaign with two home games.

It was now becoming clear that Austria, especially after their win over Sweden on 6 September 1997, would win the group – in fact the only nation they had lost points to was Scotland – but that Scotland were likely to qualify automatically as being the best team placed second. All they had to do was to beat Belarus and Latvia at home. It did not seem a tall order.

Scotland should have played Belarus on 6 September 1997 at Pittodrie. The problem was that Princess Diana had met her untimely death the week previously and the funeral was scheduled for that day. For a while, the SFA laudably refused to be bullied into changing the date on the grounds that the much lamented (in England) Princess did not seem to have all that much to do with Scotland and that a minute's silence before the start would suffice.

But eventually under pressure from the British Government and facing a revolt of some Rangers players (who were presumably trying to appease the Orange and Royalist elements in their own support), the SFA backed down and played the game on Sunday 7 September. This decision did not please Belarus who, like most of the Scottish public, took a little convincing that this decision was necessary.

Be that as it may, Scotland scored early at Pittodrie and then turned on the heat in the second half to beat the Belorussians 4-1. All that remained now were the Latvians. This game was originally scheduled for Easter Road, Edinburgh in Scotland's praiseworthy attempts to move the games around the country in the continued unavailability of Hampden Park. It soon became clear, however, that Easter Road would be far too small for the expected large crowd, given the huge interest in the game and the resurgence of enthusiasm for the team which Craig Brown's erudite and restrained leadership had deservedly earned. Celtic Park was given the nod instead.

Scotland duly won 2-0 and it was difficult not to feel pride that day as the team took its dignified lap of honour and the fans clapped and cheered their heroes.

That is the closest we have ever come to it! Craig Brown touches the World Cup, as Paul McStay looks on.

Seldom was a bad word heard from the totally civilized support. It would have been hard to imagine any trouble in that august stadium that Celtic Park was now fast becoming. Misbehaving by wrecking goalposts or doing any of the mad crazy things that had befouled the name of Scotland twenty years ago was quite clearly a thing of the past.

The contrast with England could hardly have been more starkly delineated. On that same October day, England too qualified for the World Cup finals. They did so by drawing 0-0 in Rome with Italy, but that was hardly the main story. The main story was the running battles between English and Italian fans, which led to more than one MP asking in the House of Commons whether England's qualification for France was necessarily a good thing. Scottish MPs on the other hand had no such problems in accepting their nation's involvement in the competition.

Over the winter and early spring, Scotland played five friendlies, losing two and drawing three, but once again Craig Brown reassured us that they were all learning processes. Once again he went to the USA, this time doing marginally better than he had done in 1996, earning draws with both the USA and Colombia. An issue developed when Brown did not pick Ally McCoist, and the media made much of it – especially when Ally joined the media himself. He was nearing the end of his career, certainly, but it might have been an idea for propaganda or nuisance value to include him with a view to deployment as a substitute. As it was, it strengthened

Above May 1998. Scotland playing in the unlikely venue of the RFK Stadium, Washington against the USA. Kevin Gallacher is the Scotland player on the ground.

Left May 1998. Scotland v. Colombia. Paul Lambert has the more sensible hairstyle!

the conviction that Brown did not like McCoist, and further weakened the links between some Rangers supporters and the national team.

*   *   *

The World Cup draw had seen Scotland attached to Brazil yet again (for the fourth time in World Cup finals), Norway and Morocco. As Brazil were the defending champions, tradition and protocol demanded that they played the first game to open the tournament. This was against Scotland, who thus had the honour of playing the first game in Paris on 10 June 1998 in front of a huge world audience.

Scotland had tried hard to gain the neutral support by appearing before the start in kilts, something that certainly seemed to impress the lady supporters. The game itself was actually one of Scotland's best performances against Brazil and it was really cruel luck that gave the South Americans the victory. Having gone behind after only five minutes, Scotland then were awarded a penalty, and when John Collins scored impressively from the spot, Scotland went in level at half-time.

In the second half, Scotland played well and bravely against a team who were clearly technically superior, and looked as if they might earn a draw. Indeed they would have done just that had the ill-starred Tom Boyd not had the bad luck to get in the way of an attempted clearance and score one of the most unlucky own goals of all time.

June 1998. Scotland and Norway fans show the acceptable side of football fanaticism.

1998. Not all the members of the Tartan Army can travel to France, so a large-screen TV on Glasgow Green has to suffice. Given Scotland's weather, the event was arranged indors!

Thus the first match at Saint-Denis, near Paris, was an unfortunate defeat for Scotland, but they were not disheartened. The action now switched south-west to Bordeaux where their next opponents, Norway, had drawn their first game with Morocco. This game was also a draw, Craig Burley levelling matters for Scotland. Thus Scotland only had one point from two games, but so too did Morocco who had similarly drawn with Norway and lost to Brazil, in their case an emphatic 3-0 drubbing.

St Etienne on 23 June was to be the showdown. A win was not enough for Scotland. They had to hope that Brazil also beat Norway, although such a course of events did not look improbable. The nation once again sat down and expected. They were in for one of the biggest disappointments of the lot. The phrase 'they were never in it' is often overused in football as people will exaggerate, but in this case Scotland really were never in it and after Morocco scored their second goal soon after half-time, Scotland looked a beaten side, unable to stir themselves or fight back. Misery was compounded when Craig Burley was sent off. Long before full time, television viewers had gone to sit in their gardens to enjoy the beautiful summer night instead of the depressing football. It was a dreadful anticlimax about which little can be said other than to hold up one's hands and say that we weren't good enough.

Ironically, even if Scotland had won that game, they would not have gone any further, for Brazil, already beginning the process of self-destruction that culminated in their poor showing the final, went down to Norway. The cynics might say that the Brazilians were seeing too much of Scotland and learning their habits! But it mattered little. Scotland came home in a low-key manner. Another World Cup dream had ended. Would there ever be another opportunity?

TWELVE

Turn of the Century
1998-2004

The last few years of the twentieth century saw a major change on Scotland's political scene with the establishment of a Scottish Parliament. Tony Blair's Labour Party had won the General Election of 1997, and his Government, instead of talking about devolution as previous ones had done, thereby boring the whole nation, actually went ahead and did it. The Scottish Parliament, with a Liberal-Labour Coalition Executive under Donald Dewar opened in summer 1999, the nation being particularly impressed by Sheila Wellington's impassioned rendition of Robbie Burns's *A Man's A Man For A That*. One wonders however what HM The Queen thought of it all as she sat listening impassively. Some of the lyrics smack of radicalism and even socialism, after all.

This was the political state of Scotland at the turn of the century, and Craig Brown continued as manager of the national team. The European Championships would be held in the Low Countries in 2000, and Scotland were treated fairly leniently in the draw in that they were given the Czech Republic, Estonia, Bosnia, Lithuania and the Faroe Islands. One team would qualify directly for the finals, and the other would be in the play-offs. It was generally accepted that although Scotland would struggle against the Czech Republic, they should be good enough to deal with the rest.

So, effectively, it proved, but there were many tough problems en route. A goalless draw in Lithuania to begin the campaign in September 1998 was as dull as it sounded, but then Scotland had a really tough tie in October at Tynecastle Park, Edinburgh against Estonia. (Scotland continued their policy of playing games at different venues while Hampden was being refurbished, and Celtic Park, Tynecastle, Pittodrie and Ibrox were all pressed into service before the eventual return to Hampden). The Tynecastle game attracted a crowd of 16,000, and Scotland were twice behind. Indeed it was the substitution of the ineffective McCoist by Billy

Dodds of Dundee United that was required to galvanise the Scottish attack into something like its proper function. At that point Scotland were a goal down and not really looking likely to score. Dodds, however, immediately got one, but then the hardworking Estonians took the lead again. Scotland needed an own goal to draw level before Dodds scored the winner with time fast running out.

It was generally agreed that this was a disgraceful performance, even though three points were registered, and the mood of the fans and the media was hardly improved by the next game against the Faroes at Pittodrie four days later. This time it was a 2-1 victory over part timers. Scotland had been two-up at half-time, but then frittered away such chances as came from a dysfunctional midfield, before the Faroes were awarded a penalty. When the kick was put away, the Aberdeen crowd were condemned to four minutes of the sort of agony that only Scotland can inflict on their supporters.

By any standards this was bad, and criticism rained down on Craig Brown – and yet an objective analysis would have had to point out the sheer dearth of Scottish talent available to the manager. No longer did talented Scotsmen regularly shine in the English Leagues; worse still was the obvious lack of talent in the Scottish game when Celtic and Rangers contained very few Scotsmen, and other teams, notably Aberdeen and the two Dundee teams, always capable of supplying some Scottish talent in the past, had collapsed more or less completely – and apparently irreversibly. Scotland should, however, still be able to beat the Faroe Islands.

*　　　*　　　*

There was also an increasing isolation of the Scottish team, particularly from the vast Celtic and Rangers supports. It had always been very easy to be cynical about Scotland and jeer when they were doing badly. In some cases of course this is a defence mechanism in that if you are sneering, you think you are showing the world that you are not hurting. Anyone can do that, but it now appeared to be almost a national sport to laugh at Scotland's latest attempts to beat lowly opposition.

The Czech Republic were certainly not lowly opposition. They came to Celtic Park at the end of March 1999 to beat Scotland 2-1, a defeat more emphatic than the score suggested, even though Scotland had fought well in the last quarter of the game after Eoin Jess had pulled a goal back. Yet the frustrations of the Scottish crowd (at 44,000 still a respectable attendance) were apparent at the booing of Gary McAllister as he was being substituted.

This was a strange phenomenon. McAllister admittedly was not having a particularly good game in the Scottish midfield, but he was the captain and no more committed character had ever donned the Scottish jersey. It was hard to believe that he was still being blamed for his unfortunate penalty miss at Wembley three years previously. Perhaps it was the Celtic faction in the Parkhead crowd who resented McAllister's widely believed Rangers sympathies. More likely it was just sheer frustration. When a proud nation is losing, it has to find a scapegoat. McAllister just happened to be in the wrong place at the wrong time. He was shaken nevertheless at this treatment.

But then Scotland suddenly gave their fans a pleasant surprise. In April (in what was admittedly a meaningless friendly in which Scotland made no fewer than six substitutions), Scotland beat Germany 1-0 in Bremen. As someone said in a rather unfortunate turn of phrase, it was 'One of the few times that Scotland had beaten Germany since the war', but Don Hutchison's goal did at least give Scottish fans something to cheer about.

Normal depressing service was restored in summer 1999. In June, Scotland went on tour to the Faroes and to the Czech Republic. In Toftir in the Faroe Islands they drew. It was what was fast becoming a normal Scottish performance against poor opposition, it would have to be said. Allan Johnston of Sunderland scored in the first half, Scottish players then played as if they had never met each other, failing to finish the game off, then conceding a late sucker punch.

This was bad enough but Matt Elliott, who had impressed in the defence, was red carded for a really foolish piece of mini-fisticuffs and therefore missed the game against the Czech Republic in Prague. Craig Brown was angry at Matt, for Scotland needed his aerial power, and the Prague game turned out to be a collectors' item of Scottish self-destruction. Two-up after an hour's play and looking as if they were saying 'sorry' for the Faroes fiasco, they then managed to lose one goal, then another and we could have written the script that they would lose another just at the end.

It was now becoming more and more difficult to disagree with the strident voices that were calling for Brown's head, but Brown was saved by two things. One was that it was summer and the apathy about Scotland was even more pronounced than normal, and the other was that in fact Scotland (unbelievably and undeservedly) still had an excellent chance of making the play-offs. The Czech Republic were indeed beating everyone else, as had been predicted, and the other teams were beating each other. Scotland were still second.

Two results against Bosnia ensured Scottish entrance into the play-offs. The first was on 4 September 1999 in Sarajevo. Historians would tell us that that was where the First World War originated, but more to the point, just recently a bloody and, to Western eyes, pointless, civil war had come to an end. Foreign Office advice was sought, and Scotland went, returning safely with a competent 2-1 win. They didn't return home directly, for they flew to Estonia for a game four days later. This game was absolutely dire, with little to commend it other than that Scotland earned a 0-0 draw that they would have settled for. Sometimes, it is necessary to bore the public if you want to qualify for tournaments. It was nice to notice to that the Estonian floodlights were functioning well, following the sad events of 1996!

There now remained, at the beginning of October, two home games – at Ibrox against Bosnia and at Hampden against Lithuania. In fact the 1-0 win over Bosnia (a John Collins penalty doing the trick) was sufficient to see Scotland into the play-offs, but it was nice in any case to be back at Hampden to see Scotland beating Lithuania 3-0, Hutchison, McSwegan and Cameron securing the comfortable win.

Any apathy and cynicism over Scotland was immediately dispelled after the draw was made for the play-offs in November. It paired Scotland against England. Now was the time to close ranks, and dig out once again the tartan tammies. For a spell, international football took centre stage once again, and it begged the question why did the authorities ever give away the Scotland *v*. England game in the first place? It was to be a two-legged game with the first game at Hampden on Saturday 13 November, followed by a trip to Wembley the following midweek.

At long last we saw the return of the fortunes of the Scottish international team to prominence in Scottish social life. At long last too we saw players determined to play for the country. There was a distinct absence this time of 'injuries' and 'knocks' in players who had looked very fit the previous game. Craig Brown was by no means the first manager to notice the beneficial effect that a big game had on 'niggling injuries'. Even the cynics who rather hoped that Scotland would lose to inferior opposition so that they could have a laugh, now closed ranks and backed the team. Tickets for both games were difficult to get hold of, and all in all, it was a welcome return to the days of the 1950s and '60s, when beating England took precedence over narrow factional interests.

The Hampden game was definitely England's, with two goals scored by Paul Scholes. He did not endear himself by running towards the Scottish crowd with cupped ear, sarcastically asking where the Hampden Roar was, and he was justly booked by the referee for provocative over-celebration. Indeed, it said a great deal for the Scottish fans' self-restraint.

The 2-0 scoreline was a blow, but it did at least remove whatever doubt there might have been in Craig Brown's head about tactics at Wembley. Scotland had to attack. Neil McCann of Rangers was brought in to supplement Don Hutchison and Billy Dodds up front, and the TV audience which watched the Wembley game in huge numbers that night was treated to the rare sight of a Scottish team playing with skill and passion, and, significantly, giving the impression that they were wanting to play for Scotland and enjoying doing so. In the thirty-seventh-minute Hutchison scored and thus Scotland went in at half-time only one goal down on aggregate.

The second half saw more Scottish aggression and commitment in a way that made the commentators and fans wonder why they had to play such rubbish against the Faroes and Estonia. Football like this would have guaranteed Scotland qualification for any tournament they wanted to, but sadly, no further goals came, even though there were a few narrow escapes for the English defence.

It was of course a moral victory for Scotland, a point conceded by the English media themselves, but it would be England at Euro 2000, not Scotland. Scottish history, as we have seen, is full of 'moral' victories, but enough had been shown in the Wembley game to prove that 'it disnae need tae be like this'. The Faroes, Costa Rica, Iran and other disasters could have been avoided. All that is needed are the twin qualities of professionalism and passion – and each is as important as the other.

Scotland thus watched from the sidelines in 2000. In the run-up to the tournament, they had lost (while playing creditably) to France, the World Champions and eventual winners of Euro 2000, drawn with Holland (who would reach the semi-finals before losing on penalties) and then, most encouragingly of all, beaten the Republic of Ireland in Dublin. The Euro 2000 tournament was exciting, with the final being a monumental heartbreak for the Italians. It would have been nice for Scotland to have been there.

*　　　*　　　*

The 2002 World Cup was destined for the exotic venues of Japan and Korea. Craig Brown, who had now been Scotland's manager since 1993, must have been aware of the pressure he was under. Since the early 1970s, Scotland had never failed to qualify for two tournaments in a row. Only once since 1974 had Scotland not been in the World Cup finals. The year of Scotland's absence had been 1994, but Scotland had qualified for the European Championships on both sides of this failure. Now, having failed to be at Euro 2000, absence from the Far East in 2002 would be intolerable for what was still a proud and obsessive football nation.

The draw gave Scotland a chance, although it was by no means an easy group. Croatia had impressed everyone by some fine performances in the late 1990s, and Belgium, as always, would be doughty opponents. The other two would be San Marino and Latvia, and it would have been a brave man, given Scotland's record, who would have guaranteed twelve points from the rabbits. Being second, however, would possibly be enough to guarantee qualification, although it depended on other groups.

Scotland began solidly and respectably, at least in terms of results. The first game in Riga, Latvia did not show Scotland at their best, to put it tactfully, but the goal did finally come late in the game from Neil McCann. It was a similar toil against San Marino a month later in Serraville before 4,377 Tartan Army folk and a few locals, but goals did come during the second half and Scotland, winning 2-0, had completed the task of beating the rabbits away from home.

Four days later, Scotland went to Croatia and there fought hard to earn a 1-1 draw, which we would have settled for before the start. Kevin Gallacher equalized Boksic's strike, and Scotland had arguably completed their most difficult fixture of the group. Uncharacteristically, Craig Brown, normally the mildest mannered of men, was sent to the stand by an overzealous French referee, after getting too excited for the liking of the Gallic gentleman. However, Belgium had also drawn with Croatia in the opening game of the group and it was obvious that the section was going to be tight; it was also disturbing to note that Belgium and Croatia had put the minnows to the sword to a greater extent than Scotland had.

Scotland then embarrassed themselves in a feckless friendly by losing 2-0 to Australia at Hampden Park in November 2000. There did not seem to be any great point in playing this fixture, but somehow or other 30,000 were enticed along to Hampden, there to see Scotland without many first-choice players who had called off with 'injuries', lose 0-2 to an Australian side. Amid all the black humour of 'bowled out', 'caught off the pads', 'we should have appealed against the light', 'we are as bad as England', there was the serious point that this sort of thing did not do anything for morale. If you are going to arrange such meaningless fixtures, you really must make sure you win them!

The spring of 2001 saw more serious opposition in the shape of Belgium. It was the Hampden fixture on 24 March rather than any other which sealed the fate of Craig Brown and meant that there would be no Tartan Army in Japan. It was once again another example of Scotland taking their foot off the pedal and squandering a comfortable position. Scotland led 2-0 at half-time, one goal well taken by Billy Dodds, the other a penalty. Not only that, Belgium were reduced to ten men and Scotland looked comfortable.

Then Belgium pulled one back on the hour mark, but even then, Scotland looked in command. The minutes ticked away without any great alarms. Brown made no substitutions until the late and questionable one of replacing Dodds by Gallacher. Dodds ran off to a deserved ovation, but one wondered whether this might just have distracted the players when concentration was still required. In any event, with the ninety minutes up and injury time being played, Belgium grabbed a late equalizer through central defender Van Buyten, who had replaced Celtic's Joos Valgaeren, and scored from a set piece.

It was a serious blow to Scotland, who knew that in a tight three-headed group like this (if one discounted the minnows for a while), it is crucial to win home games. The celebrations by the Belgians bore ample testimony to that. San Marino were dispatched 4-0 at Hampden four days later, but there was a feeling now that more than a little damage had been done to Scotland's World Cup bid, and renewed questions were now beginning to be asked about Craig Brown.

Over the summer of 2001, Croatia and Belgium kept winning against the poorer opposition, and it was obvious that Scotland really had to beat Croatia at Hampden on 1 September and get at least a draw against Belgium in Belgium the following midweek. In the event they got neither. A goalless draw, bereft of any good constructive play from Scotland, was what happened against the Croats, even though 47,384 turned up at Hampden to give them every encouragement.

The roof finally fell in on Brown and his makeshift team in Belgium when they went down 0-2 and indeed were lucky to get off with only two goals scored against them. Belgium's second goal came almost on the final whistle and it was difficult not to hear the bells of hell ringing loudly for the unfortunate Craig Brown. Yet three days later, a possible reason for it all appeared when Glasgow Celtic took the field to play against Dunfermline Athletic without a single Scotsman on board. Rangers had done this sort of thing before as well, but now Celtic, who would win the Premier League that season, could also play a game without any Scots. It was sad.

Scotland were now out of the 2002 World Cup, and it was no secret that Craig Brown was on his way as well. He did see them through the last meaningless game against Latvia a month later before his departure was official. He was happy to stay as a technical director and promised to work for and with his successor, but he was soon off to sample English football, having managed the Scottish team for a record amount of games. He could not in all honesty be blamed for all that was wrong with the Scottish team. The problems were far deeper and more complex than that.

*   *   *

The winter of 2001/02 was thus spent in the deepest form of navel gazing, as the search went on for a new manager. Thousands were not killed in the rush, it must be said, and there was a general perception among the managerial profession that looking after Scotland was not a plum job. The usual suspects were trotted out on quiet days in newspapers and confidently predicted as being the new manager: Tommy Burns, George Graham, Frank McLintock and others all

Scotland's management team of Berti Vogts and Tommy Burns at Glasgow Airport in 2002.

had their brief but insubstantial moments in this respect, but hardly anyone was totally discounted.

Soon after the New Year of 2002, informed speculation began to centre on Berti Vogts. The purists began to object that he was not Scottish. So what, we asked, was Jack Charlton an Irishman? Look what he achieved with Ireland. Sven-Goran Eriksson was not exactly an Englishman either, was he? Yet Scotland did have those who argued that a German was not a good idea. A valid historical parallel might have been George I, the Hannoverian, the 'German lairdie' that caused so much trouble in the eighteenth century with Jacobite rebellions and so on. Mind you, the Jacobites' leader, one Charles Edward Stuart, aka Bonnie Prince Charlie, was Italian, was he not?

Enough of this nonsense was talked about in Scottish pubs and workplaces to make one despair. Berti Vogts it was to be as from 1 March 2002. Vogts was a proven winner on the field with Germany, both as a player and as a manager, his most recent triumph being Euro 1996. He therefore knew how to win, but was winning with Germany (who won things regularly anyway) liable to be carried on to winning with Scotland, now possibly at the lowest ebb of their history – yet still a country with a great interest in football and which nursed (sometimes unrealistic) expectations?

Berti's start could not have been worse. A friendly had been arranged against World and European Cup holders, France in Paris on 27 March 2002. It was highly embarrassing as Trezeguet, Henry and Zidane ran Scotland ragged and won 5-0. They were four up at half-time and visibly eased in the second half when they brought on substitutes to give more of their players a game, otherwise the score might well have been double figures. Berti took this one on the chin and said that it was a learning experience.

Then the colourful Nigerians came to Pittodrie. Nigeria were drawn against England in Japan and clearly wanted to find out more about British football. In fact, it was they who taught a dismal Scottish side quite a bit. Scotland scored first through Christian Dailly, but then collapsed to a side who cheered up the douce Aberdeen public with players wearing bandanas and indulging in elaborate celebrations when they scored. It said quite a great deal about the current and future

Scotland's management team in the early twenty-first
century. Berti Vogts and Tommy Burns.

strength of football in the African nations, but it also told Berti, if he hadn't already begun to suspect it, that the Scotland management job was not a cushy number!

After the domestic season was over, Scotland went on a tour of the Far East to play in Busan and Hong Kong. It became distinctly embarrassing to put on the tele-texts in the mornings and discover that Scotland had gone down 1-4 to South Korea and then 0-2 to South Africa before eventually registering Berti Vogts' first win against a Hong Kong team of dubious status and not officially recognised by FIFA. It was just as well that Scotland were not at the World Cup, we reckoned. It would have been even more humiliating than previous ones.

As Scotland embarked on their quest to reach Portugal for Euro 2004, an attempt was being made to stage Euro 2008 in Scotland. This bid, a joint venture involving Scotland and Republic of Ireland, ultimately failed because the political support was distinctly lukewarm in Scotland and something approaching non-existent in Ireland, but it did show a welcome sense of ambition. It was, however, a sideshow to the struggle to reach Portugal in 2004.

Lithuania, Iceland, Faroe Islands and Germany were the opponents. The top team would qualify automatically and the second team would go into play-offs. Scotland's first assignment was in Toftir, the scene of a disastrous draw three years previously. Scotland had already lost a friendly to Denmark at Hampden in August 2002, but no-one could have expected the cataclysm that was to affect Scotland in the North Atlantic. Within quarter of an hour, the Faroes were two goals up, one of them a ludicrous rat-a-tat goal that would not have looked out of place in a pinball game in an amusement arcade. Even worse than that was the apparent lack of commitment by certain Scots who didn't seem to care that Scotland were now approaching the status of being the laughing stocks of world football.

At half-time, the two elder statesmen, a Ranger and a Celt, Barry Ferguson and Paul Lambert, lost their tempers in the dressing room and berated everyone for a performance that even the hard-bitten seasoned commentators of Radio Scotland were describing as 'public park stuff'. Indeed, Ferguson and Lambert then set an example. Both those gentlemen scored the goals in the second half which salvaged something out of this game, but the damage had been done.

It was not so much the loss of two points, but the now apparently permanent loss of credibility. The whole population of the Faroe Islands was about the size of Kirkcaldy or Perth! Had Vogts not been in the job for only a matter of months, his head would have been called for. As it was, the anger, depression and frustration that settled on the nation was intense and all-pervasive, unless of course one supported Rangers or Celtic, who continued their merry ways with foreign mercenaries. This was not possible for Vogts. There is no transfer market in international football.

The next game was in Iceland. We were afraid to watch our television screens on 12 October, but Vogts had made a few changes, notably the re-introduction of the business-like Jackie McNamara of Celtic. He had also clearly laid a few things on the line to others. There would be no excuse for another lapse. In fact there wasn't. Scotland played in a professional and worthy fashion. Without exactly convincing the fans that a new millennium was dawning, Scotland nevertheless took a couple of goals well and won 2-0.

There then followed a series of friendlies. Scotland played six in all that season, and turned on some highly embarrassing performances. They had already lost to Denmark before the Faroes game and then they were well beaten by Portugal, Ireland and Austria (2-0 in each case), but beat Canada before, most embarrassingly of all, drawing with New Zealand. It was difficult, from a spectator's point of view, to get excited about the team. Only 12,000 appeared at Hampden to see Austria and 10,000 at Tynecastle to see New Zealand, although Berti Vogts would always insist that he was learning from these games. The days of the Scottish public being inter-ested in friendlies was, however, long gone.

Interest remained high for the European Championship games. Iceland came to Hampden on 29 March 2003 and 37,938 saw a competent Scottish win, even though there was a slight wobble just after half-time. This meant that Scotland had done a double over Iceland, but then four days later in Kaunas, Lithuania, all the good work was undone as Scotland went down 0-1. It was a game that Scotland might have won if chances had been taken, but as it was, the longer the game went on, the more the Lithuanians took charge. With only fifteen minutes remaining, the home side got a penalty (although a dubious one it must be said), converted it and hung on. Scotland were now struggling once again.

7 June at Hampden Park saw Scotland once again winning back the support of the nation as they drew 1-1 with Germany. This is another factor, incidentally, of the Scottish support. They will come back, like an ill-treated dog, no matter how shod-dily they have been dealt with in the past, because the love is still there. Hampden Park was full, the atmosphere was terrific and Scotland, having gone a goal down, fought back in workmanlike fashion, spurred on by the home crowd, to earn an equalizer through Kenny Miller. A winner would not have looked entirely out of place for the Scots, but a draw it was. It meant that Scotland, in spite of their lapses, were now in with a chance of making at least the play-offs for Euro 2004. More importantly, national self-respect was being restored.

Following yet another meaningless friendly, this time a goalless draw in Norway, Scotland now had three games in which to qualify. The Faroe Islands came to

Hampden exactly fifty-two weeks after the Scottish disaster in Toftir, but this time Scotland were up to the task. The 40,109 crowd created a tremendous atmosphere which visibly affected the Faroese, and Scotland won 3-1 with crisp goals coming from McCann, Dickov and McFadden.

It was perhaps an indication that Scotland were on the way back, and this game certainly proved that there was no lack of support for Scotland. The half-time rendition by everyone of the *Bonnie Bonnie Banks of Loch Lomond* was particularly moving and reminiscent of the earlier days of following Scotland. The nation was given a further boost when Iceland and Germany drew that same night, but the big trial of the new Scotland was to be when Scotland played Germany in Dortmund the following Wednesday.

It was another Scottish hard-luck story. Lambert was taken off injured at half-time to be replaced by Maurice Ross, who managed to get two yellow cards in his first twenty minutes, his cause not helped by a diving German and a 'homer' of a referee. Christian Dailly was heard on TV to use foul language to express his opinion that the Germans had been prone to cheat. Berti Vogts had little sympathy, however: 'That is international football', he said.

The first goal came from bad defending, then Steven Pressley took hold of a German player's jersey to concede a penalty before a good move involving Thomson and McCann got one back for Scotland. But one was all that they got, and Scotland were now dependent on other results as well as their own final game against Lithuania to reach a play-off.

Fortunately, on 11 October 2003 Scotland did make it. The Lithuanian game was played in front of Hampden's first sell-out international crowd for many years and saw Scotland scrape through 1-0, thanks to a brilliant goal from young substitute Darren Fletcher at the same time as Germany were beating Iceland. This meant that Scotland were through to the play-offs.

Not many people fancied Scotland's chances against Holland. Far from being the Holland of old, this team were nevertheless a strong outfit, managed by Dick Advocaat, who had recently been manager of Rangers. Yet the tickets sold quickly for the Hampden game on 15 November, and the Scottish crowd were delighted with their 1-0 victory. Not only was there a brilliant goal involving Scotland's young lions Darren Fletcher and Jamie McFadden, but there was also some sound defensive play when the Dutch turned on the pressure.

Just for a few days, Scotland's pride returned. Wednesday night in Amsterdam became a nightmare, however, as Scotland went down 0-6, their heaviest defeat for over four decades. Holland were good, but the Scottish defence were far from blameless in that three of the goals came from set pieces, and the other ones might well have been prevented. Scotland were out, and the vast and impeccably behaved Tartan Army, over 25,000 strong, went home from Amsterdam 'to think again'.

2004 would bring more horrors for Scotland. The European Championships in Portugal took place without Scotland but Scotland's form in friendlies continued to be poor. Yet Greece won the Europen Championship. Why couldn't Scotland do such things?

THIRTEEN

The Uncertain Future
2004 onwards

Still thou art blest, compared wi' me
The present only touches thee
But, och, I backward cast my e'e
On prospects drear,
An' forrit, tho I cannae see,
I guess and fear

So says Robbie Burns to the mouse, as if these words would be a consolation to the poor beast that has lost house and home. One likes the use of the word 'prospects' – normally looking forward, here obviously looking back, but in some way capturing the totality of time. Maybe a more valid Burns quote to symbolise the Scottish football team might come from his dirge *Man Was Made To Mourn:*

The sun that overhangs yon moor
Outspreading far and wide
Where hundreds labour to support
A haughty lordling's pride.
I've seen you weary winter sun
Twice forty times return
And every time has added proof
That Man Was Made To Mourn

But the first thing that a Scottish football fan must retain is a sense of perspective. Bill Shankly's much quoted remark about football being more important than life or death is, of course, pure rubbish. Thank heaven that football still remains a game.

There are admittedly times when one wonders about that – when the stomach churns before a game, when the heart aches afterwards – but the Scottish race have always been able to be resilient and to fight back.

Two men looked through prison bars
One saw mud and the other saw stars

The scene was Wembley in 1969, when Scotland had just been tanked 4-1. Two tearful tartan-clad Scottish lads came out. One was utterly forlorn, a pathetic figure, swollen eyed and what is known in football parlance as 'gutted'. His friend was equally woebegone, but then suddenly, as if someone had pressed a button, said 'C'mon, Jimmy, this is London. Let's see what we can pick up in Soho!'

The thing that perpetually mystifies about Scotland and Scotland's supporters is that they are always disappointed when Scotland do not win the World Cup. Yet Scotland is a small nation of about five million people, such numbers paling into insignificance in comparison with the likes of Germany, Brazil, Argentina and even England. The idea that Scotland produces the best football players in the world (an idea not entirely without foundation historically, and certainly true of the early years of the twentieth century) dies hard in the twenty-first century.

The problem often is with Scotsmen that their success is achieved furth of Hadrian's Wall, and that their achievements are massive, but in a non-Scottish context. Two cases in point are Denis Law and Kenny Dalglish. Both of them were tremendous players who did great things for Manchester United and Liverpool respectively. But Scotland? How often was the tramp of feet away from Hampden or the switching off of a television set after a defeat on foreign soil accompanied by moans that our superstars had not performed adequately *for Scotland*? One has to recall yet again the painful sight – the sight that haunts all Scotland fans – of Kenny Dalglish jumping over advertising hoardings in ecstatic glee at Wembley because he had scored and had landed the European Cup *for Liverpool*. This was a matter of weeks before the 1978 World Cup in Argentina. Could he do that *for Scotland*? Sadly the answer would have to be no.

Kenny and Denis are, of course, little more than metaphors for Scotland. Scotland will indeed continue to churn out its geniuses, but the genius will probably have to flourish in another environment. Scotland will probably never win the World Cup – unless and until we happen to have eleven geniuses at the same time. But even that will not be enough. We will need another few geniuses on the bench, we will need a good, firm, visionary manager, we will need proper commitment and attitude – and we will also need luck… and we will absolutely have to avoid that self-destruct button.

Two things that are certainly there are fan support and, curiously, perhaps, media support. Fan support is self-evident. One simply has to look out of one's window on a night when Scotland are playing in a World Cup game on the telly and notice the lack of traffic. Media support has also been, to a large extent, loyal. One has often suspected that there are journalists in countries like England, Italy and Spain who enjoy the downfall of their national team. Not so in Scotland. There is, of course, criticism when appropriate, but never the slightest hint of disloyalty.

'Fifth column' activity is rare. There are sections of the Rangers support who prefer England or Holland, and some Celtic fans who prefer the land of their ancestors, Ireland, but they are, one hopes, the minority. Other 'fifth columnists' include the defeatists who seem to enjoy a moan about Scotland's latest underperformance. They have had much scope for their activities of late, but one suspects that it is a desire not to appear to be backing a losing cause too zealously and that a winning Scotland team would make them change their mind.

There have been times when it would have been difficult to argue against the contention that Scotland were the best football team in the world. The mid-1880s were a clear case in point, as were the 1920s. Both these eras were vastly different socially. The 1880s players were the Glasgow bourgeoisie who played for Queen's Park and Dumbarton; the 1920s men hailed from the teeming tenements of Glasgow and the industrial horrors of Scotland's central belt. Yet both could beat anyone else. Although Scotland's teams in those eras unfortunately only played the other British teams, they were usually able to beat England, a country with tenfold the population of Scotland.

And what about the 1960s? Had Scotland managed to beat Czechoslovakia in that play-off in late 1961, had Scotland managed to keep their discipline and performed to their potential to reach Chile in 1962, had they enjoyed a little luck, they might have done very well indeed. Similarly in 1966, the players that Scotland had were potentially the best in the world. We all know who actually did win the World Cup in 1966... but who were the first to beat them some nine months later? Scotland playing in England in 1966 would have been formidable opposition for anyone.

Argentina in 1978 certainly saw Scotland with loads of talented players, not least Mr Dalglish, but sadly collectively unable to cope with the emotional pressures of playing in the World Cup. Possibly too, they had all reached their peak in 1977 rather than in 1978. Never again since 1978 could it honestly be said that Scotland had the players to do the job of capturing that trophy. An isolated brilliant performance perhaps, one or two genuine 'world-class' players (but literally only one or two) and some stalwart honest performances is all that one could justifiably say in defence of the Scottish national team.

If asked to name the best Scottish football side of all time, one would get all sorts of answers. It is indeed an impossible task, for Scotland have played football for 130 years and more, and no-one has seen them all. In addition, there are one's own preferences, prejudices and indeed vendettas to allow for. Having said that this eleven in the 2-3-5 formation of most of the twentieth century might be a good one. The author allows for ability, talent and – as important as anything – attitude towards playing for Scotland. He makes no allowance for the amount of caps won, for some of these players listed below were scandalously underused. The team might be: Bill Brown (Dundee and Spurs); Danny McGrain (Celtic), Eric Caldow (Rangers); Bobby Murdoch (Celtic), David Morris (Raith Rovers), Jim Baxter (Rangers); Jimmy Johnstone (Celtic), Hughie Gallacher (Airdrie and Newcastle

United), Jimmy McGrory (Celtic), Alec James (Preston North End and Arsenal) and Alan Morton (Rangers). Perhaps one day a game can be arranged against a team from Heaven, Mars or (more probably) a computer to play against them.

It is possibly a good thing that Scotland expects to win every game. Life is often about living up to expectations. An expectation and a self-fulfilling prophecy are by no means totally different from each other. The only thing that we lack is the wherewithal in terms of players to back it all up… but it is important that we keep hoping and expecting.

Scotland's Results
1872-2003

YEAR	DATE	OPPOSITION	SCORE	VENUE
1872	30 November	England	0-0	Hamilton Crescent
1873	8 March	England	2-4	Oval
1874	7 March	England	2-1	Hamilton Crescent
1875	6 March	England	2-2	Oval
1876	4 March	England	3-0	Hamilton Crescent
	25 March	Wales	4-0	Hamilton Crescent
1877	3 March	England	3-1	Oval
	5 March	Wales	2-0	Wrexham
1878	2 March	England	7-2	Hampden (First)
	23 March	Wales	9-0	Hampden (First)
1879	5 April	England	4-5	Oval
	7 April	Wales	3-0	Wrexham
1880	13 March	England	5-4	Hampden (First)
	27 March	Wales	5-1	Hampden (First)
1881	12 March	England	6-1	Oval
	14 March	Wales	5-1	Wrexham
1882	11 March	England	5-1	Hampden (First)
	25 March	Wales	5-0	Hampden (First)
1883	10 March	England	3-2	Bramall Lane
	12 March	Wales	3-0	Wrexham
1884	26 January	Ireland	5-0	Ballynafeigh
	15 March	England	1-0	Cathkin
	29 March	Wales	4-1	Cathkin
1885	14 March	Ireland	8-2	Hampden (First)
	21 March	England	1-1	Oval
	23 March	Wales	8-1	Wrexham

YEAR	DATE	OPPOSITION	SCORE	VENUE
1886	20 March	Ireland	7-2	Ballynafeigh
	27 March	England	1-1	Hampden (First)
	10 April	Wales	4-1	Hampden (First)
1887	19 February	Ireland	4-1	Hampden (First)
	19 March	England	3-2	Blackburn
	21 March	Wales	2-0	Wrexham
1888	10 March	Wales	5-1	Easter Road
	17 March	England	0-5	Hampden (First)
	24 March	Ireland	10-2	Solitude
1889	9 March	Ireland	7-0	Ibrox
	13 April	England	3-2	Oval
	15 April	Wales	0-0	Wrexham
1890	22 March	Wales	5-0	Uederwood, Paisley
	29 March	Ireland	4-1	Ballynafeigh
	5 April	England	1-1	Hampden (Second)
1891	21 March	Wales	4-3	Wrexham
	28 March	Ireland	2-1	Old Celtic Park
	4 April	England	1-2	Blackburn
1892	19 March	Ireland	3-2	Solitude
	26 March	Wales	6-1	Tynecastle
	2 April	England	1-4	Ibrox
1893	18 March	Wales	8-0	Wrexham
	25 March	Ireland	6-1	Celtic Park
	1 April	England	2-5	Richmond
1894	24 March	Wales	5-2	Kilmarnock
	31 March	Ireland	2-1	Solitude
	7 April	England	2-2	Celtic Park
1895	23 March	Wales	2-2	Wrexham
	30 March	Ireland	3-1	Celtic Park
	6 April	England	0-3	Goodison
1896	21 March	Wales	4-0	Carolina Port, Dundee
	28 March	Ireland	3-3	Solitude
	4 April	England	2-1	Celtic Park
1897	20 March	Wales	2-2	Wrexham
	27 March	Ireland	5-1	Ibrox
	3 April	England	2-1	Crystal Palace
1898	19 March	Wales	5-2	Motherwell
	26 March	Ireland	3-0	Solitude
	2 April	England	1-3	Celtic Park
1899	18 March	Wales	6-0	Wrexham
	25 March	Ireland	9-1	Celtic Park
	8 April	England	1-2	Villa Park
1900	3 February	Wales	5-2	Pittodrie
	3 March	Ireland	3-0	Solitude
	7 April	England	4-1	Celtic Park
1901	23 February	Ireland	11-0	Celtic Park
	2 March	Wales	1-1	Wrexham

YEAR	DATE	OPPOSITION	SCORE	VENUE
	30 March	England	2-2	Crystal Palace
1902	1 March	Ireland	5-1	Grosvenor Park
	15 March	Wales	5-1	Cappielow
	5 April	England	1-1	Ibrox
GAME DECLARED NULL AND VOID BECAUSE OF IBROX DISASTER				
	3 May	England	2-2	Villa Park
1903	9 March	Wales	1-0	Cardiff Arms
	21 March	Ireland	0-2	Celtic Park
	4 April	England	2-1	Bramall Lane
1904	12 March	Wales	1-1	Dens Park
	26 March	Ireland	1-1	Dublin
	9 April	England	0-1	Celtic Park
1905	6 March	Wales	1-3	Wrexham
	18 March	Ireland	4-0	Celtic Park
	1 April	England	0-1	Crystal Palace
1906	3 March	Wales	0-2	Tynecastle
	17 March	Ireland	1-0	Dublin
	7 April	England	2-1	Hampden
1907	4 March	Wales	0-1	Wrexham
	16 March	Ireland	3-0	Celtic Park
	6 April	England	1-1	Newcastle
1908	7 March	Wales	2-1	Dens Park
	14 March	Ireland	5-0	Dublin
	4 April	England	1-1	Hampden
1909	1 March	Wales	2-3	Wrexham
	15 March	Ireland	5-0	Ibrox
	3 April	England	0-2	Crystal Palace
1910	5 March	Wales	1-0	Kilmarnock
	19 March	Ireland	0-1	Windsor Park
	2 April	England	2-0	Hampden
1911	6 March	Wales	2-2	Ninian Park
	18 March	Ireland	2-0	Celtic Park
	1 April	England	1-1	Goodison
1912	2 March	Wales	1-0	Tynecastle
	16 March	Ireland	4-1	Windsor Park
	23 March	England	1-1	Hampden
1913	3 March	Wales	0-0	Wrexham
	15 March	Ireland	2-1	Dublin
	5 April	England	0-1	Stamford Bridge
1914	28 February	Wales	0-0	Celtic Park
	14 March	Ireland	1-1	Windsor Park
	4 April	England	3-1	Hampden
1920	26 February	Wales	1-1	Ninian Park
	13 March	Ireland	3-0	Celtic Park
	10 April	England	4-5	Hillsborough
1921	12 February	Wales	2-1	Pittodrie
	26 February	Ireland	2-0	Windsor Park

YEAR	DATE	OPPOSITION	SCORE	VENUE
	9 April	England	3-0	Hampden
1922	4 February	Wales	1-2	Wrexham
	4 March	Ireland	2-1	Celtic Park
	8 April	England	1-0	Villa Park
1923	3 March	Ireland	1-0	Windsor Park
	17 March	Wales	2-0	Love Street
	14 April	England	2-2	Hampden
1924	16 February	Wales	0-2	Ninian Park
	1 March	Ireland	2-0	Celtic Park
	12 April	England	1-1	Wembley
1925	14 February	Wales	3-1	Tynecastle
	28 February	Ireland	3-0	Windsor Park
	4 April	England	2-0	Hampden
	31 October	Wales	3-0	Ninian Park
1926	27 February	Ireland	4-0	Ibrox
	17 April	England	1-0	Old Trafford
	30 October	Wales	3-0	Ibrox
1927	26 February	Ireland	2-0	Windsor Park
	2 April	England	1-2	Hampden
	29 October	Wales	2-2	Wrexham
1928	25 February	Ireland	0-1	Firhill
	31 March	England	5-1	Wembley
	27 October	Wales	4-2	Ibrox
1929	23 February	Ireland	7-3	Windsor Park
	13 April	England	1-0	Hampden
	26 May	Norway	7-3	Bergen
	1 June	Germany	1-1	Berlin
	4 June	Holland	2-0	Amsterdam
	26 October	Wales	4-2	Ninian Park
1930	22 February	Ireland	3-1	Celtic Park
	5 April	England	2-5	Wembley
	18 May	France	2-0	Paris
	25 October	Wales	1-1	Ibrox
1931	21 February	Ireland	0-0	Windsor Park
	28 March	England	2-0	Hampden
	16 May	Austria	0-5	Vienna
	20 May	Italy	0-3	Rome
	24 May	Switzerland	3-2	Geneva
	19 September	Ireland	3-1	Ibrox
	31 October	Wales	3-2	Wrexham
1932	9 April	England	0-3	Wembley
	8 May	France	3-1	Paris
	17 September	Ireland	4-0	Windsor Park
	26 October	Wales	2-5	Tynecastle
1933	1 April	England	2-1	Hampden
	16 September	Ireland	1-2	Celtic Park
	4 October	Wales	2-3	Ninian Park
	29 November	Austria	2-2	Hampden

YEAR	DATE	OPPOSITION	SCORE	VENUE
1934	14 April	England	0-3	Wembley
	20 October	Ireland	1-2	Windsor Park
	21 November	Wales	3-2	Pittodrie
1935	6 April	England	2-0	Hampden
	5 October	Wales	1-1	Ninian Park
	13 November	Ireland	2-1	Tynecastle
1936	4 April	England	1-1	Wembley
	14 October	Germany	2-0	Ibrox
	31 October	Ireland	3-1	Windsor Park
	2 December	Wales	1-2	Dens Park
1937	17 April	England	3-1	Hampden
	9 May	Austria	1-1	Vienna
	15 May	Czechoslovakia	3-1	Prague
	30 October	Wales	1-2	Ninian Park
	10 November	Ireland	1-1	Pittodrie
	8 December	Czechoslovakia	5-0	Hampden
1938	9 April	England	1-0	Wembley
	21 May	Holland	3-1	Amsterdam
	8 October	Ireland	2-0	Windsor Park
	9 November	Wales	3-2	Tynecastle
	7 December	Hungary	3-1	Ibrox
1939	15 April	England	1-2	Hampden
1946	19 October	Wales	1-3	Wrexham
	27 November	Northern Ireland	0-0	Hampden
1947	12 April	England	1-1	Wembley
	18 May	Belgium	1-2	Brussels
	24 May	Luxembourg	6-0	Luxembourg-Ville
	4 October	Northern Ireland	0-2	Windsor Park
	12 November	Wales	1-2	Hampden
1948	10 April	England	0-2	Hampden
	28 April	Belgium	2-0	Hampden
	17 May	Switzerland	1-2	Berne
	23 May	France	0-3	Paris
	23 October	Wales	3-1	Ninian Park
	17 November	Northern Ireland	3-2	Hampden
1949	9 April	England	3-1	Wembley
	27 April	France	2-0	Hampden
	1 October	Northern Ireland	8-2	Windsor Park
	9 November	Wales	2-0	Hampden
1950	15 April	England	0-1	Hampden
	26 April	Switzerland	3-1	Hampden
	21 May	Portugal	2-2	Lisbon
	27 May	France	1-0	Paris
	21 October	Wales	3-1	Ninian Park
	1 November	Northern Ireland	6-1	Hampden
	13 December	Austria	0-1	Hampden
1951	14 April	England	3-2	Wembley

YEAR	DATE	OPPOSITION	SCORE	VENUE
	12 May	Denmark	3-1	Hampden
	16 May	France	1-0	Hampden
	20 May	Belgium	5-0	Brussels
	27 May	Austria	0-4	Vienna
	6 October	Northern Ireland	3-0	Windsor Park
	14 November	Wales	0-1	Hampden
1952	5 April	England	1-2	Hampden
	30 April	USA	6-0	Hampden
	25 May	Denmark	2-1	Copenhagen
	30 May	Sweden	1-3	Stockholm
	18 October	Wales	2-1	Ninian Park
	5 November	Northern Ireland	1-1	Hampden
1953	18 April	England	2-2	Wembley
	6 May	Sweden	1-2	Hampden
	3 October	Northern Ireland	3-1	Windsor Park
	4 November	Wales	3-3	Hampden
1954	3 April	England	2-4	Hampden
	5 May	Norway	1-0	Hampden
	19 May	Norway	1-1	Oslo
	25 May	Finland	2-1	Helsinki
	16 June	Austria	0-1	Zurich
	19 June	Uruguay	0-7	Basle
	16 October	Wales	1-0	Ninian Park
	3 November	Northern Ireland	2-2	Hampden
	8 December	Hungary	2-4	Hampden
1955	2 April	England	2-7	Wembley
	4 May	Portugal	3-0	Hampden
	15 May	Yugoslavia	2-2	Belgrade
	19 May	Austria	4-1	Vienna
	29 May	Hungary	1-3	Budapest
	8 October	Northern Ireland	1-2	Belfast
	9 November	Wales	2-0	Hampden
1956	14 April	England	1-1	Hampden
	2 May	Austria	1-1	Hampden
	20 October	Wales	2-2	Ninian Park
	7 November	Northern Ireland	1-0	Hampden
	21 November	Yugoslavia	2-0	Hampden
1957	6 April	England	1-2	Wembley
	8 May	Spain	4-2	Hampden
	19 May	Switzerland	2-1	Basle
	22 May	West Germany	3-1	Stuttgart
	26 May	Spain	1-4	Madrid
	5 October	Northern Ireland	1-1	Windsor Park
	6 November	Switzerland	3-2	Hampden
	13 November	Wales	1-1	Hampden
1958	19 April	England	0-4	Hampden
	7 May	Hungary	1-1	Hampden
	1 June	Poland	2-1	Warsaw
	8 June	Yugoslavia	1-1	Vasteras

YEAR	DATE	OPPOSITION	SCORE	VENUE
	11 June	Paraguay	2-3	Norrkoping
	15 June	France	1-2	Orebro
	18 October	Wales	3-0	Ninian Park
	5 November	Northern Ireland	2-2	Hampden
1959	11 April	England	0-1	Wembley
	6 May	West Germany	3-2	Hampden
	27 May	Holland	2-1	Amsterdam
	3 June	Portugal	0-1	Lisbon
	3 October	Northern Ireland	4-0	Windsor Park
	4 November	Wales	1-1	Hampden
1960	9 April	England	1-1	Hampden
	4 May	Poland	2-3	Hampden
	29 May	Austria	1-4	Vienna
	5 June	Hungary	3-3	Budapest
	8 June	Turkey	2-4	Ankara
	22 October	Wales	0-2	Ninian Park
	9 November	Northern Ireland	5-2	Hampden
1961	15 April	England	3-9	Wembley
	3 May	Eire	4-1	Hampden
	7 May	Eire	3-0	Dublin
	14 May	Czechoslovakia	0-4	Bratislava
	26 September	Czechoslovakia	3-2	Hampden
	7 October	Northern Ireland	6-1	Windsor Park
	8 November	Wales	2-0	Hampden
	29 November	Czechoslovakia	2-4aet	Brussels
1962	14 April	England	2-0	Hampden
	2 May	Uruguay	2-3	Hampden
	20 October	Wales	3-2	Ninian Park
	7 November	Northern Ireland	5-1	Hampden
1963	6 April	England	2-1	Wembley
	8 May	Austria	4-1Ab.	Hampden
	4 June	Norway	3-4	Bergen
	9 June	Eire	0-1	Dublin
	13 June	Spain	6-2	Madrid
	12 October	Northern Ireland	1-2	Windsor Park
	7 November	Norway	6-1	Hampden
	20 November	Wales	2-1	Hampden
1964	11 April	England	1-0	Hampden
	12 May	West Germany	2-2	Hanover
	3 October	Wales	2-3	Ninian Park
	21 October	Finland	3-1	Hampden
	25 November	Northern Ireland	3-2	Hampden
1965	10 April	England	2-2	Wembley
	8 May	Spain	0-0	Hampden
	23 May	Poland	1-1	Chorzow
	27 May	Finland	2-1	Helsinki
	2 October	Northern Ireland	2-3	Windsor Park
	13 October	Poland	1-2	Hampden

YEAR	DATE	OPPOSITION	SCORE	VENUE
	9 November	Italy	1-0	Hampden
	24 November	Wales	4-1	Hampden
	7 December	Italy	0-3	Naples
1966	2 April	England	3-4	Hampden
	11 May	Holland	0-3	Hampden
	18 June	Portugal	0-1	Hampden
	25 June	Brazil	1-1	Hampden
	22 October	Wales	1-1	Ninian Park
	16 November	Northern Ireland	2-1	Hampden
1967	15 April	England	3-2	Wembley
	10 May	U.S.S.R.	0-2	Hampden
	21 October	Northern Ireland	0-1	Windsor Park
	22 November	Wales	3-2	Hampden
1968	24 February	England	1-1	Hampden
	30 May	Holland	0-0	Amsterdam
	16 October	Denmark	1-0	Copenhagen
	6 November	Austria	2-1	Hampden
	11 December	Cyprus	5-0	Nicosia
1969	16 April	West Germany	1-1	Hampden
	3 May	Wales	5-3	Wrexham
	6 May	Northern Ireland	1-1	Hampden
	10 May	England	1-4	Wembley
	17 May	Cyprus	8-0	Hampden
	21 September	Eire	1-1	Dublin
	22 October	West Germany	2-3	Hamburg
	5 November	Austria	0-2	Vienna
1970	18 April	Northern Ireland	1-0	Windsor Park
	22 April	Wales	0-0	Hampden
	25 April	England	0-0	Hampden
	11 November	Denmark	1-0	Hampden
1971	3 February	Belgium	0-3	Liege
	21 April	Portugal	0-2	Lisbon
	15 May	Wales	0-0	Ninian Park
	18 May	Northern Ireland	0-1	Hampden
	22 May	England	1-3	Wembley
	9 June	Denmark	0-1	Copenhagen
	14 June	U.S.S.R	0-1	Moscow
	13 October	Portugal	2-1	Hampden
	10 November	Belgium	1-0	Pittodrie
	1 December	Holland	1-2	Amsterdam
1972	26 April	Peru	2-0	Hampden
	20 May	Northern Ireland	2-0	Hampden
	24 May	Wales	1-0	Hampden
	27 May	England	0-1	Hampden
	29 June	Yugoslavia	2-2	Belo Horizonte
	2 July	Czechoslovakia	0-0	Porto Alegre
	5 July	Brazil	0-1	Rio de Janeiro
	18 October	Denmark	4-1	Copenhagen

YEAR	DATE	OPPOSITION	SCORE	VENUE
	15 November	Denmark	2-0	Hampden
1973	14 February	England	0-5	Hampden
	12 May	Wales	2-0	Wrexham
	16 May	Northern Ireland	1-2	Hampden
	19 May	England	0-1	Wembley
	22 June	Switzerland	0-1	Berne
	30 June	Brazil	0-1	Hampden
	26 September	Czechoslovakia	2-1	Hampden
	17 October	Czechoslovakia	0-1	Bratislava
	14 November	West Germany	1-1	Hampden
1974	27 March	West Germany	1-2	Frankfurt
	11 May	Northern Ireland	0-1	Hampden
	14 May	Wales	2-0	Hampden
	18 May	England	2-0	Hampden
	1 June	Belgium	1-2	Bruges
	6 June	Norway	2-1	Oslo
	14 June	Zaire	2-0	Dortmund
	18 June	Brazil	0-0	Frankfurt
	22 June	Yugoslavia	1-1	Frankfurt
	30 October	East Germany	3-0	Hampden
	20 November	Spain	1-2	Hampden
1975	5 February	Spain	1-1	Valencia
	16 April	Sweden	1-1	Gothenburg
	13 May	Portugal	1-0	Hampden
	17 May	Wales	2-2	Ninian Park
	20 May	Northern Ireland	3-0	Hampden
	24 May	England	1-5	Wembley
	1 June	Romania	1-1	Bucharest
	3 September	Denmark	1-0	Copenhagen
	29 October	Denmark	3-1	Hampden
	17 December	Romania	1-1	Hampden
1976	7 April	Switzerland	1-0	Hampden
	6 May	Wales	3-1	Hampden
	8 May	Northern Ireland	3-0	Hampden
	15 May	England	2-1	Hampden
	8 September	Finland	6-0	Hampden
	13 October	Czechoslovakia	0-2	Prague
	17 November	Wales	1-0	Hampden
1977	27 April	Sweden	3-1	Hampden
	28 May	Wales	0-0	Wrexham
	1 June	Northern Ireland	3-0	Hampden
	4 June	England	2-1	Wembley
	15 June	Chile	4-2	Santiago
	18 June	Argentina	1-1	Buenos Aires
	23 June	Brazil	0-2	Rio de Janeiro
	7 September	East Germany	0-1	Berlin
	21 September	Czechoslovakia	3-1	Hampden
	12 October	Wales	2-0	Anfield
1978	22 February	Bulgaria	2-1	Hampden

YEAR	DATE	OPPOSITION	SCORE	VENUE
	13 May	Northern Ireland	1-1	Hampden
	17 May	Wales	1-1	Hampden
	20 May	England	0-1	Hampden
	3 June	Peru	1-3	Cordoba
	7 June	Iran	1-1	Cordoba
	11 June	Holland	3-2	Mendoza
	20 September	Austria	2-3	Vienna
	25 October	Norway	3-2	Hampden
	29 November	Portugal	0-1	Lisbon
1979	19 May	Wales	0-3	Ninian Park
	22 May	Northern Ireland	1-0	Hampden
	26 May	England	1-3	Wembley
	2 June	Argentina	1-3	Hampden
	7 June	Norway	4-0	Oslo
	12 September	Peru	1-1	Hampden
	17 October	Austria	1-1	Hampden
	21 November	Belgium	0-2	Brussels
	19 December	Belgium	1-3	Hampden
1980	26 March	Portugal	4-1	Hampden
	16 May	Northern Ireland	0-1	Windsor Park
	21 May	Wales	1-0	Hampden
	24 May	England	0-2	Hampden
	28 May	Poland	0-1	Poznan
	31 May	Hungary	1-3	Budapest
	10 September	Sweden	1-0	Stockholm
	15 October	Portugal	0-0	Hampden
1981	25 February	Israel	1-0	Tel Aviv
	25 March	Northern Ireland	1-1	Hampden
	28 April	Israel	3-1	Hampden
	16 May	Wales	0-2	Swansea
	19 May	Northern Ireland	2-0	Hampden
	23 May	England	1-0	Wembley
	9 September	Sweden	2-0	Hampden
	14 October	Northern Ireland	0-0	Windsor Park
	18 November	Portugal	1-2	Lisbon
1982	24 February	Spain	0-3	Valencia
	23 March	Holland	2-1	Hampden
	28 April	Northern Ireland	1-1	Windsor Park
	24 May	Wales	1-0	Hampden
	29 May	England	0-1	Hampden
	15 June	New Zealand	5-2	Malaga
	18 June	Brazil	1-4	Seville
	22 June	USSR	2-2	Malaga
	13 October	East Germany	2-0	Hampden
	17 November	Switzerland	0-2	Berne
	15 December	Belgium	2-3	Brussels
1983	30 March	Switzerland	2-2	Hampden
	24 May	Northern Ireland	0-0	Hampden

YEAR	DATE	OPPOSITION	SCORE	VENUE
	28 May	Wales	2-0	Ninian Park
	1 June	England	0-2	Wembley
	12 June	Canada	2-0	Vancouver
	16 June	Canada	3-0	Edmonton
	19 June	Canada	2-0	Toronto
	21 September	Uruguay	2-0	Hampden
	12 October	Belgium	1-1	Hampden
	16 November	East Germany	1-2	Halle
	13 December	Northern Ireland	0-2	Windsor Park
1984	28 February	Wales	2-1	Hampden
	26 May	England	1-1	Hampden
	1 June	France	0-2	Marseille
	12 September	Yugoslavia	6-1	Hampden
	17 October	Iceland	3-0	Hampden
	14 November	Spain	3-1	Hampden
1985	27 February	Spain	0-1	Seville
	27 March	Wales	0-1	Hampden
	25 May	England	1-0	Hampden
	28 May	Iceland	1-0	Reykjavik
	10 September	Wales	1-1	Cardiff
	16 October	East Germany	0-0	Hampden
	20 November	Australia	2-0	Hampden
	4 December	Australia	0-0	Melbourne
1986	28 January	Israel	1-0	Tel Aviv
	26 March	Romania	3-0	Hampden
	23 April	England	1-2	Wembley
	29 April	Holland	0-0	Eindhoven
	4 June	Denmark	0-1	Nezahualcoyotl
	8 June	West Germany	1-2	Queretaro
	13 June	Uruguay	0-0	Nezahualcoyotl
	10 September	Bulgaria	0-0	Hampden
	15 October	Eire	0-0	Dublin
	12 November	Luxembourg	3-0	Hampden
1987	18 February	Eire	0-1	Hampden
	1 April	Belgium	1-4	Brussels
	23 May	England	0-0	Hampden
	26 May	Brazil	0-2	Hampden
	9 September	Hungary	2-0	Hampden
	14 October	Belgium	2-0	Hampden
	11 November	Bulgaria	1-0	Sofia
	2 December	Luxembourg	0-0	Esch
1988	17 February	Saudi Arabia	2-2	Riyadh
	22 March	Malta	1-1	Valletta
	27 April	Spain	0-0	Madrid
	17 May	Colombia	0-0	Hampden
	21 May	England	0-1	Wembley
	14 September	Norway	2-1	Oslo
	19 October	Yugoslavia	1-1	Hampden
	22 December	Italy	0-2	Perugia

YEAR	DATE	OPPOSITION	SCORE	VENUE
1989	8 February	Cyprus	3-2	Limassol
	8 March	France	2-0	Hampden
	26 April	Cyprus	2-1	Hampden
	27 May	England	0-2	Hampden
	30 May	Chile	2-0	Hampden
	6 September	Yugoslavia	3-1	Zagreb
	11 October	France	0-3	Paris
	15 November	Norway	1-1	Hampden
1990	28 March	Argentina	1-0	Hampden
	25 April	East Germany	0-1	Hampden
	16 May	Egypt	1-3	Pittodrie
	19 May	Poland	1-1	Hampden
	28 May	Malta	2-1	Valletta
	11 June	Costa Rica	0-1	Genoa
	16 June	Sweden	2-1	Genoa
	20 June	Brazil	0-1	Turin
	12 September	Romania	2-1	Hampden
	17 October	Switzerland	2-1	Hampden
	14 November	Bulgaria	1-1	Sofia
1991	6 February	USSR	0-1	Ibrox
	27 March	Bulgaria	1-1	Hampden
	1 May	San Marino	2-0	Serraville
	11 September	Switzerland	2-2	Berne
	16 October	Romania	0-1	Bucharest
	13 November	San Marino	4-0	Hampden
1992	19 February	Northern Ireland	1-0	Hampden
	25 March	Finland	1-1	Hampden
	17 May	USA	1-0	Denver
	20 May	Canada	3-1	Toronto
	3 June	Norway	0-0	Oslo
	12 June	Holland	0-1	Gothenburg
	15 June	Germany	0-2	Norrkoping
	18 June	CIS	3-0	Norrkoping
	9 September	Switzerland	1-3	Berne
	14 October	Portugal	0-0	Ibrox
	18 November	Italy	0-0	Ibrox
1993	17 February	Malta	3-0	Ibrox
	24 March	Germany	0-1	Ibrox
	28 April	Portugal	0-5	Lisbon
	19 May	Estonia	3-0	Tallinn
	2 June	Estonia	3-1	Pittodrie
	8 September	Switzerland	1-1	Pittodrie
	13 October	Italy	1-3	Rome
	17 November	Malta	2-0	Valletta
1994	23 March	Holland	0-1	Hampden
	20 April	Austria	2-1	Vienna
	27 May	Holland	1-3	Utrecht
	7 September	Finland	2-0	Helsinki

YEAR	DATE	OPPOSITION	SCORE	VENUE
	12 October	Faroe Islands	5-1	Hampden
	16 November	Russia	1-1	Hampden
	18 December	Greece	0-1	Athens
1995	29 March	Russia	0-0	Moscow
	26 April	San Marino	2-0	Serraville
	21 May	Japan	0-0	Hiroshima
	24 May	Ecuador	2-1	Toyama
	7 June	Faroe Islands	2-0	Toftir
	16 August	Greece	1-0	Hampden
	6 September	Finland	1-0	Hampden
	11 October	Sweden	0-2	Stockholm
	15 November	San Marino	5-0	Hampden
1996	27 March	Australia	1-0	Hampden
	24 April	Denmark	0-2	Copenhagen
	26 May	USA	1-2	New Britain
	30 May	Colombia	0-1	Miami
	10 June	Holland	0-0	Villa Park
	15 June	England	0-2	Wembley
	18 June	Switzerland	1-0	Villa Park
	31 August	Austria	0-0	Vienna
	5 October	Latvia	2-0	Riga
	10 November	Sweden	1-0	Ibrox
1997	11 February	Estonia	0-0	Monaco
	29 March	Estonia	2-0	Rugby Park
	2 April	Austria	2-0	Celtic Park
	30 April	Sweden	1-2	Gothenburg
	27 May	Wales	0-1	Rugby Park
	1 June	Malta	3-2	Valletta
	8 June	Belarus	1-0	Minsk
	7 September	Belarus	4-1	Pittodrie
	11 October	Latvia	2-0	Celtic Park
	12 November	France	1-2	St Etienne
1998	25 March	Denmark	0-1	Ibrox
	22 April	Finland	1-1	Easter Road
	23 May	Colombia	2-2	New York
	30 May	USA	0-0	Washington
	10 June	Brazil	1-2	St Denis
	16 June	Norway	1-1	Bordeaux
	23 June	Morocco	0-3	St Etienne
	5 September	Lithuania	0-0	Vilnius
	10 October	Estonia	3-2	Tynecastle
	14 October	Faroe Islands	2-1	Pittodrie
1999	31 March	Czech Republic	1-2	Celtic Park
	28 April	Germany	1-0	Bremen
	5 June	Faroe Islands	1-1	Toftir
	9 June	Czech Republic	2-3	Prague
	4 September	Bosnia	2-1	Sarajevo
	8 September	Estonia	0-0	Tallinn
	5 October	Bosnia	1-0	Ibrox

YEAR	DATE	OPPOSITION	SCORE	VENUE
	9 October	Lithuania	3-0	Hampden
	13 November	England	0-2	Hampden
	17 November	England	1-0	Wembley
2000	29 March	France	0-2	Hampden
	26 April	Holland	0-0	Arnhem
	30 May	Eire	2-1	Dublin
	2 September	Latvia	1-0	Riga
	7 October	San Marino	2-0	Serraville
	11 October	Croatia	1-1	Zagreb
	15 November	Australia	0-2	Hampden
2001	24 March	Belgium	2-2	Hampden
	28 March	San Marino	4-0	Hampden
	25 April	Poland	1-1	Bydgoszcz
	1 September	Croatia	0-0	Hampden
	5 September	Belgium	0-2	Brussels
	6 October	Latvia	2-1	Hampden
2002	27 March	France	0-5	Paris
	17 April	Nigeria	1-2	Pittodrie
	16 May	South Korea	1-4	Busan
	20 May	South Africa	0-2	Hong Kong
	21 August	Denmark	0-1	Hampden
	7 September	Faroe Islands	2-2	Toftir
	12 October	Iceland	2-0	Reykjavik
	15 October	Canada	3-1	Easter Road
	20 November	Portugal	0-2	Braga
2003	12 February	Eire	0-2	Hampden
	29 March	Iceland	2-1	Hampden
	2 April	Lithuania	0-1	Kaunas
	30 April	Austria	0-2	Hampden
	27 May	New Zealand	1-1	Tynecastle
	7 June	Germany	1-1	Hampden
	20 August	Norway	0-0	Oslo
	6 September	Faroe Islands	3-1	Hampden
	10 September	Germany	1-2	Dortmund
	11 October	Lithuania	1-0	Hampden
	15 November	Holland	1-0	Hampden
	19 November	Holland	0-6	Amsterdam
2004	18 February	Wales	0-4	Cardiff
	31 March	Romania	1-2	Hampden
	28 April	Denmark	0-1	Copenhagen
	27 May	Estonai	1-0	Tallin
	30 May	Trinidad & Tobago	4-1	Easter Road

If you are interested in purchasing other books published by Tempus,
or in case you have difficulty finding any Tempus books in your local bookshop,
you can also place orders directly through our website

www.tempus-publishing.com